# Teaching Word Recognition Skills

## Sixth Edition

Lee Ann Rinsky
*De Anza College*

GSP

**GORSUCH SCARISBRICK, PUBLISHERS**
An imprint of PRENTICE HALL
Upper Saddle River, New Jersey 07458

**Library of Congress Cataloging-in-Publication Data**
**Rinsky, Lee Ann.**
      Teaching word recognition skills / by Lee Ann Rinsky. — 6th ed.
        p.  cm.
      Includes bibliographical references (p.   ) and index.
      ISBN 0-13-776865-6 (alk. paper)
      1. Word recognition.  2. Reading (Elementary)  I. Title
LB1573.6.R56   1997
372.4'144—DC20                                 96-41592
                                            CIP

| | |
|---|---|
| *Publisher:* | Gay L. Pauley |
| *Editor:* | A. Colette Kelly |
| *Developmental Editor:* | Katie E. Bradford |
| *Production Editor:* | Eric Kingsbury |
| *Cover Design:* | Don Giannatti |
| *Typesetting:* | Aerocraft/John & Rhonda Wincek |

Printed in the United States of America.

10 9 8 7 6

ISBN 0-13-776865-6

Prentice-Hall International (UK) Limited, *London*
Prentice-Hall of Australia Pty. Limited, *Sydney*
Prentice-Hall of Canada, Inc., *Toronto*
Prentice-Hall Hispanoamericana, S. A., *Mexico*
Prentice-Hall of India Private Limited, *New Delhi*
Prentice-Hall of Japan, Inc., *Tokyo*
Pearson Education Asia Pte. Ltd., *Singapore*
Editora Prentice-Hall do Brasil, Ltda., *Rio de Janeiro*

# Brief Contents

*For a full table of contents, see page iv.*

# Contents

## 2  THE ROLE OF PHONICS IN WORD RECOGNITION     37

# Preface

This new edition of *Teaching Word Recognition Skills* includes revisions and updates in all areas. It has benefited greatly from the suggestions offered by users and elementary teachers-in-service and has been strengthened by findings from current reading research.

## Balance in the Reading Program

This text was written in response to the pre-service and in-service teachers' need for a self-instructional manual in word recognition skills. The organization, presentation of information, and suggested learning methods presented here facilitate acquisition of the needed background. In addition, the linguistic and historical insights provided clarify some of the more complicated sound–symbol relationships.

The introduction to the text discusses the controversy concerning early phonics (direct) instruction versus use of the whole language approach. For too long, extreme views on this topic have dominated debates among reading scholars, precluding a middle position such as the one I have tried to take in this textbook. Reading programs should, of course, be balanced in their application of these approaches, depending upon the student, the situation, and other variables. After all, the goal is to best prepare students to deal with reading challenges.

As in previous editions, this new edition teaches the benefit of systematic instruction in decoding strategies, of which phonics is a key element. It stresses reading instruction in an environment that has comprehension as its goal, with quality reading materials constituting the core of the early reading program. Phonics does not have to be taught through endless handouts and worksheets, although these materials do have a place in practice and review for some students. Phonics does not always have to be taught separately from actual reading, although sometimes the need does arise, depending on individual or group needs. Phonics does not have to preclude a strong, energetic reading/writing program that incorporates quality literature and creative language investigations and pursuits.

Good phonics instruction enables students to move from a decoding strategy in which individual letters and sounds are initially used to one in which words can be identified as subunits of language through patterns. As children move into content areas such as social studies and science, they do not always naturally become successful decoders of the more demanding vocabulary essential to comprehension. Lacking the tools to unlock these words can make reading in these areas distasteful. Knowing the building blocks of the English language, students can read and learn independently without frustration. Thus, the solution to the dilemma concerning phonics and the whole language approach is balance in the reading program!

## New in This Edition

1. additional review questions added to many quick self-checks
2. further suggestions for beginning to read
3. handwriting modeling and classroom suggestions
4. additional activities in readiness, blending, and context clues, as well as activity guides for parents

5. model lessons in teaching phonics in a basal, in a program with a strong phonics component, and in the whole language approach

6. a section on additional oral/writing activities

7. a section on spelling and its relationship to decoding, with traditional and creative activities

8. a revised section on using computers to teach word recognition skills

All resources, materials, and references have been checked for accuracy and timeliness.

## The Text

As in previous editions, the section on phonics systematizes the needed background so that teachers-in-training and teachers-in-service learn or review the variant consonants, blends, consonant digraphs, single vowel sounds, vowel digraphs, and diphthongs; the variety of ways the letter *y* is used; the controlling effect of the letter *r;* and the special combinations *ci, ti,* and *si.* Following a discussion of reading readiness, procedures for introducing a beginning sound–symbol relationship are detailed, and the controversy surrounding blending techniques is outlined. The differences between analytic, synthetic, and "linguistic" phonics are explained, and sample lessons of each type are provided. The importance of sight words is detailed, and a basic sight word list is included, with suggestions for teaching these critical words. Structural analysis focuses on compound words, affixed words, and syllabication. Difficulties encountered by students with these words are explained with suggested procedures for teaching. The text discusses the importance of context as an aid in decoding and enumerates types of clues.

As a further aid to learning these word recognition skills and their interrelatedness, this manual includes periodic generalizations set off in boldface type, as well as on-going "self-checks" for readers. Most sections, whether relating to a particular phonics relationship or a feature of structural analysis, have a short built-in review and a self-check. In addition, there is an final review for each chapter. Guidelines for teaching the skills and answers to questions that teachers frequently ask also are included. A section on spelling shows the relationship between learning sound/symbol patterns, learning to spell, and learning to read.

Two final chapters focus on the use of the computer to teach word recognition skills and the importance of parental involvement in children's success.

Because of special considerations with speakers of non-mainstream English, a separate section deals with dialect differences. These include the African-American dialect and the language of Spanish-speaking and Vietnamese children for whom English is a second language.

The research done during the revision of this textbook reemphasizes that success in reading is based not only on the methods and materials used, but also on teacher competency and the amount of time students actually spend reading.

As teachers engage students in reading meaningful selections, they must be concerned with developing both the skills of reading and the love of reading.

## Acknowledgments

As always, I am indebted to the many teachers and students who have offered ideas for continued improvement of the text over its several editions. For this edition, I would like to thank the following individuals for reviewing the manuscript at various stages and offering constructive suggestions; the book is greatly improved as a result of their help: Nancy Alexander, Louisiana Tech University; Nancy A. Burris, Texas Lutheran College; and A. Phillip Butler, Grambling State University. Thanks, also, to Doris Walker-Dalhouse, Moorhead State University; LaVerne Raine, East Texas State University; Elizabeth Webre, University of Southwestern Louisiana; Robert E. Leibert, University of Missouri, Kansas City; Kathleen L. Daly, University of Wisconsin, River Falls; Shirley A. Reed, University of Montevallo; and Lio Garzone, Oswego, State University of New York.

I also wish to thank the members of the editorial and production departments of Gorsuch Scarisbrick, Publishers, for their help during the publication process.

# Introduction

## The Great Debate Revisited

The theory and practice of teaching word recognition skills and strategies to beginning and advancing readers has engendered considerable controversy for years. As long ago as 1844, Horace Mann, considered the father of public education, wrote a report critical of schools that stressed only a decoding process as reading. For years afterward, the pendulum swung back and forth between a skills approach and a model that stressed reading-for-meaning. In the 1950s, a strong pro-decoding, or phonics, movement regained momentum. This was due in some measure to Rudolph Flesch's book, Why Johnny Can't Read, in which he berated school administrators for abandoning phonics for a "look–see" model. In the 1960s, however, a movement de-emphasizing decoding and the basal text called the whole language (WL) approach was endorsed by The National Council of Teachers of English. The movement stressed a pedagogy that moved from the focus on subskills in teaching reading to one that emphasized holistic concerns for language development. (Clark, 1995; Beck & Juel, 1995).1

In response to the controversy involving phonics/decoding skills versus the whole language approach, Jeanne Chall, a Harvard professor of education, spent two years researching the issue. The 1967 publication of her now classic book, *Learning to Read: The Great Debate,* concluded that learning to decode *in beginning reading* by direct teacher instruction using phonics showed superior results. Chall revised her book in 1983 and confirmed the earlier findings as did continuing research: Johnson and Bauman (1984); Williams (1985); Samuels (1988); Jacobs, Baldwin, and Chall (1990); Samuels and Farstrup (1990); Stahl (1990); and Adams and Bruck (1995).

During the 1980s and 1990s, however, whole language advocates again gained greater momentum despite the many published reports supporting the findings of Chall. Even the federal government became involved in the continuing controversy. It commissioned a widely respected independent reading researcher, Marilyn Adams, to restudy and report again on *The Great Debate.* Her published report, *Beginning to Read: Thinking and Learning About Print* (1990), again supported Chall, but even her subsequent critique, published a year later defending her original findings, did little to settle the ongoing controversy.[2] The result today is that the issue is still politicized, as the following examples illustrate:

In 1987, California—often touted as the bellwether state—adopted for its schools a whole language philosophy, and in so doing, changed their curriculum. Professor Siegfried Engelman at the University of Oregon, whose phonics program had been used in California, saw his program eliminated as a result of the new philosophy. He successfully sued California, which had failed to cite the reasons for its action in violation of federal regulation (Clark, 1995). The results of this changeover are still debated today.

Publications such as *Science News* (1993), the *National Review* (1993), the *Atlantic Monthly* (1994), and the *Congressional Quarterly* (1995) continue to present articles highlighting the differences that separate the two philosophies. News-

(1) See Clark for a comprehensive overview of a history of the pro- and anti-phonics movements.
(2) See *Beginning to Read: A Critique by Literary Professionals: A Response by Adams,* 1991.

papers consistently report on local, state, and national reading scores with articles such as "Why Juan and Jenny can't R-E-A-D" (Jacobs 1995; Dole, 1995). Moreover, two groups, The National Right to Read Foundation and the Reading Reform Foundation,[3] began to attract many members, promising to keep the phonics issue alive until changes in reading programs take place.[4]

For the beginning and in-service teacher who encounters conflicting statements concerning direct instruction (DI) with phonics versus whole language, the sometimes intense debate does not offer much insight. But it is important to remember that both sides are genuinely interested in what is best for children, each side sees reading from different perspectives, each side is biased by what has worked best for them, and therefore, the passion and continuing rhetoric is understandable.

## Reading Scores Today

According to the 1994 NAEP (National Assessment of Educational Progress) little change occurred in reading scores during 1992–1993, but the statistics leave cause for concern At the national level, only about one-fourth of fourth- and eighth-graders reach the proficient level, and only one-third of the twelfth-graders. *Proficiency* is defined as solid academic performance. Only 5 percent across the three grades reach advanced levels. Thirty percent at each grade level fail to reach even the basic level.[5] (*Reading Teacher,* June/July 1995).

Many reasons—social, economic, and educational—can be cited as the culprits in the analysis of such reading scores. But germane to our interests in this text, it is important to detail the similarities and differences in the two reading approaches, direct instruction with phonics versus whole language, remembering that a "pure" form of either is unlikely to be found.

## Similarities Between Direct Instruction and Whole Language

Chall (Dec./Jan. 1993), who continues in her support for a DI code-emphasis approach with phonics in beginning reading, points out the commonalities in the two approaches. Both approaches

- are concerned with enhancing student achievement in reading.
- want children to develop a love of reading and become lifelong readers.
- believe children should read good literature and expository texts.
- support methods where reading and writing are combined.
- want to increase potential in reading and decrease the number of failures.
- wish to free teachers from mindless uncritical use of materials.

But, along with supporters such as Goff (1993), McKenna, Robinson, and Miller (1994), Spiegel (1995), and Kameenui (1995), she outlines major differences, some in theory and some in practice.

(3) The Reading Reform Foundation is run by educators whose major focus is teaching disadvantaged children and who aim to restore intensive phonics to the teaching of reading throughout the nation. (See Clarke, 1995.)

(4) The National Right to Read Foundation is headed by a former Reagan administration education official. The foundation monitors educational issues and promotes the use of phonics through proposed national and state legislation.

(5) Partial mastery of the prerequisite knowledge and skills fundamental for proficient work at that level.

## Differences in Theory and Practice Between Direct Instruction and Whole Language

1. DI disagrees with whole language that views reading as essentially the same from emerging literacy to advanced reading.

2. DI disagrees with WL that views learning to read as a natural process, developing in ways similar to language.

3. DI views reading as needing to be taught and taught systematically, instilling the relationships of sound and symbols.

4. DI sees reading in developmental terms, where the critical task in beginning reading is to identify and decode words. Progressing to more advanced stages of reading, the critical tasks are word meanings, comprehension, and critical reaction.

5. DI has always been supported by research.

## Whole Language Theory and Practice

The theory and practice of whole language that follows has often been articulated by Goodman (1972, 1992, 1993), and whole language continues to have many supporters: Mills, O'Keefe, and Stephens (1992), Atwell (Nov./Dec. 1992), Maryann and Gary Manning (1993, 1995). The following are its important tenets:

1. Whole language is holistic reading and writing, using literature and real books.

2. The learner is in control of what he or she reads and writes; the teacher's role changes to observer and facilitator. The classroom is child-centered.

3. The curriculum is integrated around problem solving in science and social studies.

4. The schools are nongraded; assessment is through anecdotal records, observation, and students' work.

5. The relationship of sound to symbol, or phonics, is taught as an integral part of the reading process, not as an isolated skill, and is considered only one of many clues readers use to understand print.

An examination of both the DI and WL approaches shows that while there is disagreement, there is still a common core of objectives. What is fundamentally different between the two is the role of the teacher in the presentation of word recognition, in the way recognition, and therefore decoding, is taught, and in the methods of evaluating reading growth. Practices that include literature as the core reading material, a curriculum centered around interest and problem solving, integrated with science and social studies, as well as recommendations that children should use a number of strategies when decoding, are simply good teaching. Teachers who believe that *some teaching must be direct and sequential* can also use these practices in the classroom. They are not necessarily exclusive to a whole language philosophy.

Chall (1993) states

> . . .with regard to both direct instruction and whole language models, it is possible to overdo a good thing. Thus, if students get only direct instruction they will not grow as they should because they will not read and write enough. And if whole language students do only whole language, they will miss out on learning the skills and strategies that will help them grow in reading. It would seem that balance and moderation are as important in reading instruction as in life.

## Support for a Balanced Approach

In an extensive interview with whole language teachers from New York, Walmsley and Adams (1993) found that most were not purists. They did not always eschew the basal; they did some direct instruction of skills, used workbooks, and some formal standardized testing. To one degree or another, most teachers compromised, either adding on whole language activities to a traditional program or supplementing a whole language program with traditional materials. Kasner (1994) and Eller (1995) identify a new interest group as part of the International Reading Association (IRA), the Balanced Reading Group, which advocates an approach that incorporates the best of the two philosophies. Former president of the IRA, Susan Glazer (Feb/Mar. 1995), points out that phonics is an important part of the whole language system, and that reading has three parts: meaning (semantics); rules of grammar (syntax); and phonology (the sounds). These parts should be taught in an integrated way in order for students to read successfully. At a basic level, Glazer ties the two models together.

As part of their recommendations at their annual meeting, the American Psychological Association suggested that educators should avoid relying exclusively on whole language techniques, especially for children who start out with meager reading skills. Rather, they suggest, teachers must tailor lessons to each student's needs by weaving together appropriate strands of phonics, whole language, and mental strategies. (*Science News,* 1993). Dixie Lee Spiegel (1995) recommends that advocates on both sides of the issue need "to question their beliefs . . . and that neither side can assume to have all the answers." While criticizing some claims of the whole language advocates, Spiegel states that her teaching has been enriched by considering and adopting many whole language practices. In agreement with her, Levine (1994) cites evidence from critics of whole language who concede that traditional phonics instruction could benefit from several of the innovative whole language practices. Certainly many ideas from the whole language approach have paved the way for the better use of literature and a greater appreciation for authors and writing style.

The most recent report in support of a balanced program comes from former Superintendent Bill Honig of California, who introduced whole language into the curriculum in 1987. He regrets how it was interpreted in the development of the California curriculum. The original intent was that literature would be used as the core reading material, and it was assumed that skills would still be taught, but this was not so. (Honig, 1996). The result is that more than two-thirds of the fourth-graders are reading below basic levels on state and federal tests, and at present, California's reading scores are next to last in all the states.

The new superintendent of schools, Delanie Eastin, appointed a task force whose published reports in 1995 concluded that the instruction of reading should follow a more balanced approach. The report was emphatic: "The 1987 English-Language Arts Framework did not present a comprehensive and balanced reading program and gave insufficient attention to a systematic skills instruction program."

The task force recommended revising the framework to acknowledge the need for an "organized explicit skills program that includes phonemic awareness, phonics, and decoding skills" as part of "a strong literature, language and comprehension program. Basic skills have to be part of the program."*

With these recommendations, I am in complete agreement!

## Conclusion

The strong evidence in favor of a code-emphasis approach in beginning reading cannot be discounted. In *American Education* (Summer 1995), an entire issue devoted to learning to read, writer and researcher Keith Stanovich is quoted:

> That direct instruction in alphabetic coding facilitates early reading instruction is one of the most well-established conclusions in all of behavioral science. Conversely, the idea that learning to read is just like learning to speak is accepted by no responsible linguist, psychologist, or cognitive scientist in the research community. (p. 4.)

Furthermore, the evidence for a strong program with phonics seems to work especially well for children whose background experiences have *not* prepared them for beginning to read. While it is true that some students will learn to read without being directly taught, it can be attributed to their predisposition to learn to read and their experiences before attending school.

What is not always considered, however, is teacher style (Walmsley & Adams, 1993). Some teachers operate better in a more tightly controlled classroom while others work best in a less structured environment, which bring us to the central issue. In the final analysis, a successful classroom *depends on the teacher.* It has always been so and will continue to be so. To paraphrase an old cliche: For forms of teaching, let fools contest, that which is best taught, is best. With either approach, knowledgeable and competent teachers are the key. Such teachers understand the English sound–symbol system so they know *how* to teach phonics, *when* to teach it, and *how much* of it to teach (Moats, 1995). Accordingly, we will examine the five areas of word recognition so that you develop the necessary background for supporting student learning, no matter which program or program combination your school system adopts.

* The report may be obtained from the Bureau of Publications, California Department of Education, P.O. Box 271, Sacramento, CA 95812-0071 or by calling 1-800-995-4098.

# The English Sound System

## and Its Relationship to Word Recognition

**1**

## FACTORS IN WORD RECOGNITION

The word *reading* derives from a word that means *having the power of magic.* In a way, the process of turning the symbols we call letters into meaningful words that become ideas, concepts, and stories is a magic of its own. Children who have achieved decoding competency have one of the keys to that magic.

Decoding competency of the written language may be defined as the ability to recognize letters and their related sounds as *meaningful words.* Children who do this automatically and with little apparent effort get the meaning from the pages they are reading. Lacking the ability to decode words not only limits a child's understanding of what is being read but may also lead to frustration and a distaste for reading.

Generally, five areas are considered when evaluating the decoding competency of students:

1. ability to use phonics clues.
2. knowledge of basic sight words.
3. ability to use context clues.
4. ability to use structural clues.
5. ability to use the dictionary.

The separation of these areas is an arbitrary one. By focusing on one strategy at a time, it is easier for teachers to develop a thorough understanding of each one. As students learn to read, however, teachers should encourage them to be flexible and use a variety of word recognition skills. Students should know that sometimes a single clue works best to decode words, while at other times a combination of clues is necessary. Often, the effectiveness of any one word recognition skill is enhanced when used in combination with others.

See Appendix D for a Teacher's Test of Decoding Skills to evaluate your own knowledge in these areas. After you have completed Chapter 1 of this book, you should be able to achieve a perfect score on this test. (Answers to the questions follow the test.) You can then feel confident in your ability to understand the English sound system and its relationship to the writing system and can impart that understanding to students when appropriate and needed.

## VARIATIONS IN PROGRAMS

Many phonics programs are available, each providing similar information with slight variation. (Phonics is simply defined as the way that specific sounds, phonemes, are related to specific letters, graphemes, or combinations of letters.) The variations in programs arise because some strive to cover all the possible letter combinations while others classify only the most regular writing features of English. Additionally, certain programs organize and group their sound-symbol relationships differently. Most programs, however, place the basic division between the consonants and vowels, and these two basic groups may be further divided. In the consonant group are:

1. single consonant letters with a single sound.
2. single consonant letters with dual sounds.
3. blends—two or three consonant letters with the sounds blended rapidly together.
4. digraphs—two consonant letters with only a single sound/sounds.
5. special consonant combinations.

In the vowel group are:

1. single vowels (long, short, and special vowel sounds).
2. schwa—a "reduced" vowel sound, neither short nor long.
3. vowel digraphs—two vowels together with only a single vowel sound/sounds.
4. vowel diphthongs—two vowels with a "gliding" sound between them.

The letter *y* has a unique position, sometimes operating as a consonant, vowel, digraph, or diphthong. In addition, there is a special group of *r-controlled* vowels. See Table 1.1 for a model overview.[1]

Writers of phonics programs often find themselves in a dilemma. If they try to give attention to all letter combinations, their classifications become too cumbersome. If they strive for simplicity, they often omit combinations that deserve explanation. *Since teachers need far more background in sound-symbol relationships than their students do,* a rather extensive phonics program will be presented for the teacher. This does not mean, however, that all students will need this kind of background to master reading. When the occasion arises, however, for letter-sound relationships to be discussed, it is important that teachers possess the knowledge to explain why a word decodes or encodes[2] as it does.

Such explanations show word groups and patterns and not only satisfy the curiosity of students but also help to reinforce learning. When explanations begin by

**TABLE 1.1**  Basic division of a phonics program.*

| CONSONANT GROUP WITH EXAMPLES | VOWEL GROUP WITH EXAMPLES | *y* | The Letter *r* |
|---|---|---|---|
| Single: b, m, p | Single: a, e, i, o, u | May be a | Conditions |
| Variant Consonants: c, g | (long, short, special sound) | consonant | the preceding |
| Blends: cr, gl, st | Schwa: ə | and vowel: | vowel sound: |
|  |  | yes, cry | ar, ur |
| Digraphs: ch, th, ng | Digraphs: ai, oa, ee |  |  |
| Special Combination: dge, tch | Diphthongs: ou, ow, oo |  |  |

*Detailed overview of an entire phonics program is provided in Table 1.2.

(1) Such terms as *blends, digraphs, diphthongs, the schwa,* and *r-controlled vowels* will each be discussed in detail.
(2) *Encode* means to write the word or sound. *Decode* means to recognize letters and their related sounds as meaningful words.

showing a generalization for one example, such as the *dge* in the word *bridge,* and then include other words that "behave" in a similar fashion, such as *dodge, edge,* and *fudge,* difficult reading-writing combinations are clarified.

Most single consonant letters and their related sounds are introduced early in reading. To indicate that we are discussing a letter, we will italicize it as follows: *b, d, f.* To indicate that we are discussing a sound, we will enclose it in slash lines as follows: /b/, /d/, /f/.

## SECTION 1

## CONSONANTS

## Single Consonant Letters

The single consonant letters *b, d, f, h, j, k, m, n, p, qu,*[3] *r, t, v, w, x, y,* and *z* are generally decoded as the following sounds:

| | | | | | | | | | | | |
|---|---|---|---|---|---|---|---|---|---|---|---|
| *b* | /b/ | bat | *l* | /l/ | land | *t* | /t/ | top |
| *d* | /d/ | dent | *m* | /m/ | mat | *v* | /v/ | vane |
| *f* | /f/ | fall | *n* | /n/ | name | *w* | /w/ | well |
| *h* | /h/ | hit | *p* | /p/ | pan | *x* | /ks/ | box[4] |
| *j* | /j/ | jam | *qu* | /kw/ | quite[3] | *y* | /y/ | yellow |
| *k* | /k/ | kite | *r* | /r/ | road | *z* | /z/ | zebra |

Notice that we have excluded mention of the consonants *c, g,* and *s* at this point because they will be discussed thoroughly in the following sections.

## Consonants with More Than One Sound

The letters *c, g,* and *s* are sometimes called "variant" consonants.

### The letter *c*

Examine the words in lists *A* and *B.*

| A | | | B | | |
|---|---|---|---|---|---|
| **c as /k/** | | | **c as /s/** | | |
| *cat* | *cot* | *cut* | *cell* | *city* | *cycle* |
| *came* | *cold* | *cub* | *cent* | *circus* | *cyclone* |
| *cab* | *cone* | *curl* | *cement* | *citrus* | *cypress* |

Notice that when the vowel following *c* is an *a, o,* or *u,* the letter c decodes (reads as) the sound of the letter *k.* As mentioned, sounds are written like this with slash lines, /k/. The /k/ sound is called the hard sound of the letter *c.* See the examples of *cat, cot,* and *cut* in list *A.* Repeat these words to yourself and listen to the sound.

When the vowel following the letter *c* is *e, i,* or *y,* the letter *c* decodes as the sound of the letter *s* (the sound for s is written /s/). This is called the soft *c* sound. See the examples of *cell, city,* and *cycle* in list *B.* Repeat these words to yourself and listen to the sound.

(3) Since *q* is always written with *u,* both letters are included with the single consonants.
(4) The letter *x* decodes as /z/ in the beginning of words, such as in *xylophone.* Because there are few words beginning with this letter, one sound, as in the word *box,* is usually taught.

### The letter *g*

|  | *A* |  |  | *B* |  |
|---|---|---|---|---|---|
|  | **g as /g/** |  |  | **g as /j/** |  |
| *g*ang | *g*ot | *g*um | *g*em | *g*iant | *g*ym |
| *g*as | *g*oat | *g*ull | *g*entle | *g*inger | *g*ypsy |
| *g*ame | *g*old | *g*uppy | *g*enius | *g*iraffe | *g*yrate |

Notice in list *A* that the words begin with the most frequent sound that single *g* encodes. As with the letter *c*, when the vowel following *g* is an *a, o,* or *u,* the letter *g* decodes as the hard sound, and this hard sound is written as /g/. Examples from the list are *gang, got,* and *gum.* Repeat these words to yourself in order to hear the sound.

In list *B,* the words begin with a second sound that the letter *g* may encode. When the vowel following the letter *g* is an *e, i,* or *y,* the letter *g* may decode as the sound of the letter *j* and this sound is written as /j/. Examples from the list are *gem, giant,* and *gym.* Repeat these words to yourself to hear the sound. This sound is called the soft *g.*

There is, however, a difference between the two generalizations for *c* and *g.* Some simple but often used words such as *girl, get,* and *give* have the hard *g* sound. There are a few other exceptions to the *g* generalization, but it "works" a substantial number of times, so it is worth learning. In contrast, the *c* generalization "works" almost all the time.

Stated simply, then, in regard to the two letters *c* and *g:*

1. **When *a, o,* and *u* follow *c* or *g,* these letters (*c* and *g*) encode the hard sound.**
2. **When *e, i,* and *y* follow *c* or *g,* these letters (*c* and *g*) encode the soft sound. *G* has several exceptions, such as *girl, get,* and *give.***

### The letter *s*

The letter *s* encodes three sounds. Pronounce the following words and notice the sound of *s* in each one.

| *A* | *B* | *C* |
|---|---|---|
| **s as /s/** | **s as /z/** | **s as /sh/** |
| *s*ale | hi*s* | as*s*ure |
| *s*end | name*s* | *s*ugar |
| *s*it | rea*s*on | *s*ure |
| *s*ob | ro*s*e |  |
| u*s* | u*s*e |  |

Notice the difference between the words in lists *A* and *B.* In list *A* the letter *s* encodes its most common sound written as /s/. As shown, examples are *sale, send,* and *sit.* Say the words to hear the sound. In list *B, s* encodes a second sound called the /z/ sound. Unlike *c* and *g,* the vowels following the *s* consonant do not always affect whether the sound is /s/ as in *set* or /z/ as in *use.* (Often, when the *s* is followed at the end of the word by an *e* it may encode the sound /z/, as in the word *rose.*)

Some intensive phonics programs teach a third sound /sh/, such as in the words *sugar, sure,* and *assure,* shown in list *C.* There are, however, only a few such words.

Stated simply, we may generalize about the single letter *s*.

**Single letter *s* can decode as three sounds:**

1. /s/  as in *s*at.
2. /z/  as in hi*s*.
3. /sh/ as in *s*ugar.

Before proceeding further, you may want to make cards as shown here to assist you as you study.[5] Note again the various sounds encoded by each letter.

| **c** | **g** | **s** |
|---|---|---|
| 2 sounds | 2 sounds | 3 sounds |
| hard *c* /k/ before *a, o, u,* as in *c*at, *c*ot, *c*ut | hard *g* /g/ before *a, o, u,* as in *g*ate, *g*ot, *g*um | /s/ as in *s*un |
| | | /z/ as in hi*s* |
| soft *c* /s/ before *e, i, y,* as in *c*ent, *c*ity, *c*yclone | soft *g* /j/ before *e, i, y,* as in *g*em, *g*iant, *g*ym | /sh/ as in *s*ugar |

**Quick Self-Check 1**

1. The letters *c* and *g* are conditioned by the vowels that follow them.
   a. What vowel letters cause *c* and *g* to decode as hard sounds?
   b. What vowel letters cause *c* and *g* to decode as soft sounds?
   c. What is the difference between the two generalizations?
2. The letter *s* can vary in the sounds it encodes. Explain.
   See Appendix A for answers to this and the following Quick Self-Checks.
   See Appendix C for example words to use in teaching the variant consonants *c, g,* and *se,* and all the subsequent letter and letter combinations.

## Consonant Blends

### Beginning blends

English does not permit the blending of two or more consonant *sounds* at the beginning of words unless they are one of the four combinations listed below. These four blend groups combine at the beginning of words (and sometimes in the middle, or medially) to give us hundreds of words in English. They are of four major types: the *r* blends, the *l* blends, the *s* blends, and the *tw* blend. By definition, a consonant blend occurs when two or three consonant sounds (with their related letters) cluster together and are pronounced rapidly. As you study the following lists of words, you will notice several things.

When *r* or *l* is part of a blend, such as *cr* or *cl,* the *r* and *l* are second. With the *s* blends, the letter *s* comes first in the consonant cluster, as in *s*can, *s*lip, and *s*mall. Also the *s* blends may combine three consonant letter/sounds, as in the words *s*crub, *s*plash, and *s*treak.

(5) This is the first set of cards. If you make each succeeding set in a different color, it will be easier for you to study. Explanations may be written on the front or back of the cards with a black felt pen.

With the letter *t*, the *tw* consonant blend is the only beginning *t* blend permitted in English.[6]

| A | B | C₁ | C₂ | D |
|---|---|---|---|---|
| *r* blends | *l* blends | *s* blends | *s* blends | *tw* blends |
| *br*eak | *bl*onde | *sc*an | *scr*ap | *tw*eak |
| *cr*ate | *cl*ean | *sk*ate | *scr*ub | *tw*eed |
| *dr*eam | *fl*y | *sl*eet | *spl*ash | *tw*in |
| *fr*ight | *gl*eam | *sm*all | *spl*it | *tw*inkle |
| *gr*im | *pl*ease | *sn*atch | *str*aw | *tw*irl |
| *pr*unes | *pl*ate | *sp*urt | *str*eak | *tw*ist |
| *tr*ain | | *squ*eak | | |
| | | *sw*im | | |

We might generalize about consonant blends as follows:

**There are four consonant blend groups found at the beginning (and sometimes in the middle) of words. These are the *r*, *l*, *s*, and *tw* blends.**

**1. The *r* and *l* blends consist of two letters with the *r* and *l* coming second.**

**2. The *s* blend comes first and may consist of three beginning consonants.**

**3. There is also a *tw* blend.**

Before proceeding further, you may want to make cards as shown here and study the various sounds encoded by each.

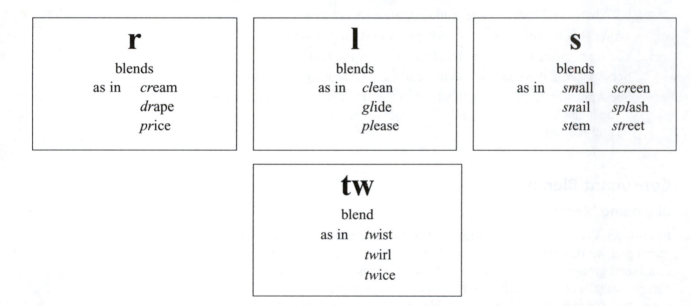

See Appendix C for example words to use in teaching the consonant blends *r, l, s,* and *tw.*

### Ending blends

In addition to the beginning consonant blends, many English words also have ending consonant blends. Examples of these combinations are *ld* as in bo*ld, nd* as in ba*nd, nt* as in se*nt, nk* as in tha*nk*,[7] and *lk* as in sta*lk*. Some phonics programs also

---

(6) There are three words beginning with *dw: dwarf, dwell,* and *dwindle.* Some phonics programs also include these.

(7) Some phonics programs classify this as a consonant digraph.

include these blends. Others do not, because certain program writers believe that in decoding strategies the beginning letter/sounds are more important than the ending letter/sounds.

***Phonograms.***    Another way of teaching ending blends is by combining a blend with a vowel. This cluster of vowel and blend is frequently referred to as a phonogram.[8] Some examples of these combinations are:

| Phonogram | Word |
|-----------|------|
| *old*     | sold |
| *ind*     | find |
| *ent*     | sent |
| *ank*     | rank |
| *alk*[9]  | walk |

Of the 286 phonograms[9] that appear in primary grade texts, 95 percent are pronounced the same in every word in which they appear (Adams, 1990). These 37 phonograms alone can derive 500 words (Stahl, 1992).

| -ack | -ain | -ake | -ale | -all | -ame |      |
|------|------|------|------|------|------|------|
| -an  | -ank | -ap  | -ash | -at  | -ate |      |
| -aw  | -ay  | -eat | -ell | -est | -ice |      |
| -ick | -ide | -ight| -ill | -in  | -ine |      |
| -ing | -ink | -ip  | -ir  | -ock | -oke |      |
| -op  | -or  | -ore | -uck | -ug  | -ump | -unk |

We might generalize about ending blends as follows:

**Certain consonants combine at the ends of words. Some of the more common of these are *ld, nd, nt, nk,* and *lk.* To teach these ending blends, they are sometimes combined with a vowel.**

You may want to make the following cards with final consonant blends to study and include with the *r, l, s,* and *tw* blends.

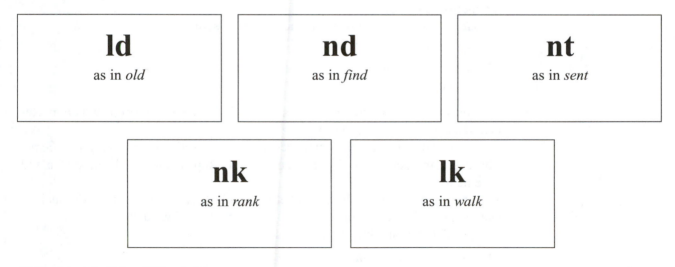

| **ld** | **nd** | **nt** |
|:------:|:------:|:------:|
| as in *old* | as in *find* | as in *sent* |

| **nk** | **lk** |
|:------:|:------:|
| as in *rank* | as in *walk* |

(8) See Appendix B for additional phonograms.
(9) Phonograms are sometimes referred to as *rimes* and the letter or syllable before them as an *onset.* See Gunning, Thomas, "Word building: A strategic approach to the teaching of phonics." *The Reading Teacher* 48, no. 6 (March 1995): 48–85, for a more comprehensive list.

**Quick Self-Check 2**

1. English contains four types of beginning consonant blends.
   a. Name the beginning blends.
   b. How are they similar?
   c. How are they different?
2. Some phonics programs include ending blends.
   a. Name some of the ending blends.
   b. How are they sometimes taught?

## Consonant Digraphs

Two consonant letters together encoding only a single sound are called consonant digraphs. In the word *digraph,* the syllable *di* stands for "two" and the syllable *graph* stands for "any written symbol (letter)." Digraph then means "two written symbols or letters that encode a single sound." As you will see below, some digraphs encode more than one single sound.

### The unique *h* digraphs

Look at the following list of words and note the sound/sounds encoded by each digraph.

| Words | Digraphs and Sounds | | |
|-------|------|------|------|
| *ch*air, s*ch*ool, *ch*ef | ch | /ch/ /k/ | /sh/ |
| *gh*ost, lau*gh,* thou*gh** | gh | /g/ /f/ | /-/ |
| *ph*oto | ph | /f/ | |
| *sh*ip | sh | /sh/ | |
| *th*at, *th*in | th / ~~th~~/ | /th/ | |
| *wh*at, *wh*o | wh | /w/ | /h/ |

You will notice that each digraph includes the letter *h.* Each digraph also has distinctive features:

*ch*   This consonant digraph encodes three sounds:

1. /ch/ as in *ch*air.
2. /k/  as in s*ch*ool.
3. sh/ as in *ch*ef.

The most common sound *ch* encodes is the /ch/ as in *ch*air, *ch*amp, and *ch*op. Repeat these words to hear the sound.

A second sound, the /k/ sound, occurs in words such as *ch*aracter and s*ch*eme. These are frequently words of Greek origin. Repeat the words *ch*aracter and s*ch*eme to hear the /k/ sound.

The third sound of /sh/ as in *ch*ef is usually found in French words, such as *ch*ampagne, *ch*andelier, and *ch*aise. (There are only a few such words.)

*gh*   This digraph has three sounds:

1. /g/          as in *gh*ost.
2. /f/          as in enou*gh*.
3. /silent/ or /-/ as in thorou*gh*.

*Usually learned as sight words.

The *gh* digraph causes a lot of problems because it derives from the former gutteral *gh,* a part of Old English. Through the years this gutteral sound has been replaced or modified so that today it appears as any of the three sounds in *ghost,* *enough,* and *thorough.* Say these words with *gh* to remember the sounds. Actually, there are few words with the latter two sounds. These words are usually learned as sight words.

**ph**   This digraph does not include the sound of /p/ but encodes the sound of /f/ as in *phar*macy. It often appears at the beginning of words but may also appear in the middle as in *phosphorus,* or at the end as in gra*ph.* Repeat these words to hear the sound.

**sh**   This digraph encodes only one sound as /sh/ in *ship* and da*sh.* Say the words to hear the sound.

**th**   This digraph has two sounds called voiced *th* and unvoiced *th.* Say the words *there* and *think,* while at the same time placing your hands on your throat. Notice that when you say the word *there* you feel the vibrations of your vocal cords on the /th/ sound. This sound is written /th/. The /th/ sound that vibrates is called the voiced sound. When you say the word *think,* you do not feel these vibrations. Repeat several times. The /th/ sound that does not vibrate is called the voiceless sound.

Study the following additional examples. Say these words to yourself and again note the difference between the beginning sounds:

|                *A*                 |                  *B*                  |
|------------------------------------|---------------------------------------|
| **Voiced *th* as /th/**            | **Voiceless *th* as /th/**            |
| *th*an                             | *th*ank                               |
| *th*at                             | *th*atch                              |
| *th*em                             | *th*eater                             |
| *th*en                             | *th*ick                               |
| *th*ere                            | *th*ink                               |

**wh**   This digraph has two sounds: the sound of /w/ in *wh*at and the sound of /h/ in *wh*o. In Old English a word such as *wh*at was written as *hw*at and pronounced with the *h* initially. Later the letters *hw* were reversed to become *wh.* In pronunciation, however, we differentiated between *wh*ich and *w*itch by pronouncing the /h/ of *wh*ich first. Today with language still changing, most people pronounce such words as *wh*at, *wh*en, and *wh*ere with only the /w/ sound.

Notice the words below beginning with the digraph *wh* and followed by the letter *o:*

*wh*o

*wh*ole

*wh*olly

When *o* follows the *wh* digraph, this digraph decodes as /h/. (These words are generally taught as sight words.)

Insofar as the consonant digraphs with *h,* we might generalize as follows:

**Digraphs are two consonant letters placed together that encode a single sound or several single sounds. The letter *h* combines to form six digraphs as follows: *ch, gh, ph, sh, th,* and *wh.* The digraph**

  1. ***ch* encodes three sounds as the /ch/ in *ch*air, /k/ in s*ch*eme, and /sh/ in *ch*andelier.**

2. *gh* encodes three sounds as the /g/ in *ghost*, /f/ in *rough*, and /-/ in *thorough*.

3. *ph* encodes the /f/ sound as in *photo*.

4. *sh* encodes the /sh/ sound as in *ship*.

5. *th* encodes two sounds as the /t̶h̶/ in *there* and /th/ in *thick*.

6. *wh* encodes two sounds as the /w/ in *what* and /h/ in *who*.

Before proceeding further, you may want to make cards with the unique *h* digraph and study the various sounds encoded by each.

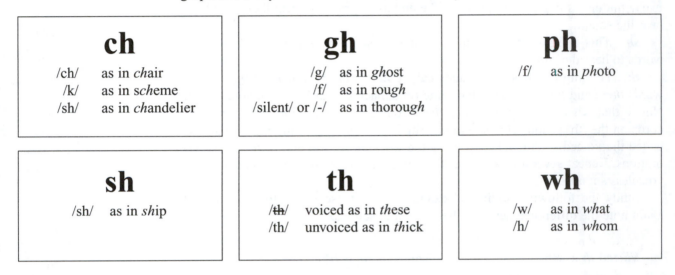

See Appendix C for example words to use in teaching consonant digraphs with *h*.

**Quick Self-Check 3**

1. The letter *h* combines with other consonants to encode unique sounds.
   a. Which combinations encode three sounds? List these with their respective sounds?
   b. Which combinations encode two sounds? List these with their respective sounds.
   c. Which combinations encode one sound? List these with their respective sounds.

**Review**

A. What vowel letters cause *c* and *g* to decode as soft sounds?
B. Four consonant letters form beginning blends. What are these four consonants?

**Digraphs with a first silent letter**

There is a second group of consonant digraphs, all of which have a silent letter. These digraphs are *gn, kn, wr,* and *ck.* Note the following:

| A | B | C | D |
|---|---|---|---|
| *gn* **as** /n/ | *kn* **as** /n/ | *wr* **as** /r/ | *ck* **as** /k/ |
| *gn*arl | *kn*ack | *wr*ap | ta*ck* |
| *gn*at | *kn*ee | *wr*eck | che*ck* |
| rei*gn* | *kn*ife | *wr*inkle | sti*ck* |
| *gn*ome | *kn*ow | *wr*ist | tru*ck* |

*gn* and *kn*    Notice that when the letters *gn* or *kn* are used together, only the sound of /n/ is heard. The *g* is silent in the *gn* digraph as in *gn*arl, and the *k* is silent in the *kn* digraph as in *kn*ack.

*wr*    In the *wr* digraph the *w* is silent. Interestingly enough, most words beginning with *wr*, such as *wr*ap and *wr*inkle, denote a twisting motion in their meanings.

*ck*    The digraph *ck* also has a first silent letter when it appears at the end of a syllable or word (often with one syllable) and *follows a short vowel*. Notice the following two groups of words. In list *A* all the vowels are short and the ending /k/ sound is written as *ck*. In list *B* all the vowels are long and the ending /k/ sound is written as *ke*.

| A | B |
|---|---|
| ***ck* as /k/** | ***ke* as /k/** |
| sa*ck* | ma*ke* |
| de*ck* | e*ke*[10] |
| ti*ck* | ti*ke* |
| do*ck* | po*ke* |
| lu*ck* | du*ke* |

We might generalize about these four digraphs, *gn, kn, wr,* and *ck* as follows:

1. **In the consonant digraphs, *gn, kn, wr,* and *ck*, the first letter is always silent.**

2. **The digraph *ck* follows a short vowel.**

## Special combinations

*dge* and *tch*    There is a third group of three-letter consonant combinations that behaves similarly to *ck*. Even though these combinations include three letters and not two, they are still often referred to as digraphs, principally because they encode a single sound. These two combinations are *dge* and *tch*. Note the following:

| A | B |
|---|---|
| ***dge* as /j/** | ***tch* as /ch/** |
| ba*dge* | la*tch* |
| le*dge* | stre*tch* |
| ri*dge* | sti*tch* |
| do*dge* | blo*tch* |
| smu*dge* | clu*tch* |

In every instance, the vowels preceding these combinations are short, just as with the *ck* digraph. Also, as with the *ck* digraph, these combinations are often found at the end of one syllable words. The reason for the combination *dge* goes back several hundred years when printers attempted to show whether vowel sounds were long or short. Often, an extra consonant letter was added to indicate that the previous vowel sound was short. The words in column *A* were written as *bagge, legge,* etc. The first *g* was eventually turned around and became the letter *d*.

We still see evidence of this printing device—doubling a consonant letter to keep the prior vowel short—in such words as la*dd*er, le*tt*er, li*tt*er, o*tt*er, and ru*dd*er.

(10) Very few words end in *eke*.

This is also the reason we usually only pronounce a single consonant letter in English even when it is doubled. (Other reasons for doubling consonant letters will be discussed later.)

We might generalize as follows for the special combinations *dge* and *tch:*

1. **The combination *dge* decodes as the sound of /j/, as in do*dge*.**

2. **The combination *tch* decodes as the sound of /ch/, as in sti*tch*.**

3. **These combinations follow a short vowel, often at the end of a one-syllable word.**

*ng*   The two letters *n* and *g* blur to become one distinctive sound, or digraph. You can hear this unique nasal sound if you pronounce the following words: si*ng,* ra*ng,* lo*ng.*

You may want to make and study the following cards with these special digraphs and special combinations before proceeding further.

|  |  |  |
|---|---|---|
| **gn** | **kn** | **wr** |
| /n/ as in *gn*ome | /n/ as in *kn*ee | /r/ as in *wr*ite |

|  |  |  |
|---|---|---|
| **ck** | **dge** | **tch** |
| /k/ as in che*ck* | /j/ as in ri*dge* | /ch/ as in ba*tch* |
| used after a short vowel | used after a short vowel | used after a short vowel |

**ng**

/ng/ as in ri*ng*

See Appendix C for example words to use in teaching the consonant digraphs with a first silent letter, and the special combinations *dge* and *tch*.

**Quick Self-Check 4**

1. What do the digraphs *gn, kn, wr,* and *ck* have in common?
2. Why are the special combinations of *dge* and *tch* referred to as digraphs?
3. What do the digraphs *ck, dge,* and *tch* have in common?

You have now completed what you should know about consonant letters and sounds. Before proceeding further, you may want to study your cards again. Group them into categories, such as consonants with more than one sound, blends, unique *h* digraphs, and digraphs with a silent first letter. Doing this will facilitate learning them. If you can answer the following questions, you are probably ready to proceed with the vowel sequence:

1. List the consonant letters that encode more than one sound. Two of these consonants are conditioned by the vowels following them. Explain, using word examples. Determine whether these generalizations work all the time.

2. Underline the unique *h* digraphs in the following words:

   graph            think

   chaise           airship

   ghastly          while

   Give word examples of the sounds that each of these respective digraphs encode.

3. Four consonant digraphs contain a silent first letter. List these digraphs and indicate the sound encoded by each. Give word examples.

4. Name the sounds decoded by the digraphs *ck* and the clusters *dge* and *tch*. Give word examples. Explain what these three combinations have in common.

   Answers to the Section Reviews and Self-Checks may be found in Appendix A.

**Chapter 1, Section 1:**

**Review and Self-Check**

The second major division in phonics analysis, and also the more difficult, includes the vowels.

**SECTION 2**

**VOWELS**

## The Single Vowels, *a, e, i, o, u,* and the Schwa

Each vowel encodes a short and long sound, and also a schwa sound. While this latter sound has many regional variations, it is usually similar to short *u* as in *up* and is shown in texts as an upside down *e*, as ə. The vowels *a, o,* and *u* also encode an additional sound, sometimes called a special or third sound, to be discussed later.

| Short Vowel Sound | Long Vowel Sound | Schwa Sound |
|---|---|---|
| *a*ct | *a*ble | b*a* na na /ə/ |
| *e*lephant | *e*ven | tick *e*t /ə/ |
| *i*t | *i*vy | pen c*i*l /ə/ |
| *o*live | *o*men | a pr*o*n /ə/ |
| *u*ntil | *u*nit, r*u*de | |

### The short vowel sound

The short vowel sound is the most prominent in English. The breve mark (˘) is used in writing to indicate the short vowel. Examples: *ăct, ĕlephant.*

To aid in recalling vowel sounds, teachers with the help of their students often compose fun sentences beginning with these sounds as in the example below:

*A*n *e*lephant *is o*ddly *u*npredictable.

Another way to remember the short vowel sound is by thinking of key words that are similar:

bă̆t    bŏp
bĕt    bŭt
bĭt

## The long vowel sound

The macron (ˉ) is positioned above the vowel to indicate that it is long. Examples: *āble, ēven.* The long vowel sound is identical to the name of the vowel as *ā, ē, ī, ō, ū.* In addition, sometimes the letter *u* has the "long" vowel sound /ō͞o/ as in the word *rūde.* The reason there are two long vowel sounds for *u* is the result of a change in language that has taken place during the last 50 years. An examination of the two word lists below will indicate the two long *ū* sounds.

| A | B |
|---|---|
| ***u* as /yū/** | ***u* as /ō͞o/** |
| cūte | brūte |
| fūture | dūke |
| hūman | Jūne |
| mūle | lūte |
| pūny | nūmeral |
| ūse | tūbe |

Repeat these words to hear the difference between the two sounds. The words in list *A* have the traditional long /yū/ sound, while in list *B*, the long *ū* has the sound of /ō͞o/, not /yū/. As indicated, this sound change began to take place in the 1930s. Prior to that time, the long *ū* appearing in words was generally pronounced as /yū/. (The sound /yū/ or /ō͞o/ is dependent on the preceding consonant sound.)

In sum, while the vowel letters *ā, ē, ī,* and *ō* may each decode as one long vowel sound the letter *ū* may decode as two, /yū/ and /ō͞o/.

## Special vowel sounds

Repeat the following words to hear the special or third vowel sounds of *a, o,* and *u.*

| ***a* as /ä/** | ***o* as /ō͞o/** | ***u* as /o̽o/** |
|---|---|---|
| call | lose | push |
| wand | whom | bullet |
| father | prove | bushel |

***Many reading programs only teach short and long vowel sounds.*** Words such as those listed previously, representative of special vowel sounds, are sometimes treated as sight words and considered unphonetic.

***A word of caution about these sounds.*** Except for the long vowels, it is extremely difficult to pronounce the vowel sounds in isolation. When learning or teaching the short vowels, place a consonant sound such as /t/ after each of them to make pronunciation easier. These combinations are often referred to as phonograms.[11] (Refer to Appendix B.) The short vowels would then be pronounced in a phonogram or word as follows:

/at/ as in săt

/et/ as in sĕt

/it/ as in sĭt

/ot/ as in tŏt

/ut/ as in hŭt

Key words are very important for remembering sounds, as we do not speak in sounds but in words! Capitalize on what is familiar.

## The schwa

One of the changes occurring in the English language at the present time is the reduction of the short vowel to the schwa sound. What this means is that in *unaccented* syllables many of the short vowels have an /uh/ kind of sound, similar to short *u* as in *up.*[12]

Consider the following words as spoken in context:

*a*cróss       He walked *a*cross the street.

tíck*e*t       She waited for a tick*e*t.

pénc*i*l      The penc*i*l needed sharpening.

séc*o*nd      Just one sec*o*nd, please.

In each instance the vowel in the unaccented syllable has a schwa sound, written like an upside down e, /ə/. To indicate the sound, you will often find words such as the above written in dictionaries, glossaries, and textbooks as follows:

ə cross       tick ət

pen səl       sec nəd

In view of what we have just mentioned in regard to short vowels, long vowels, third sound, and schwa, we might make the following generalizations about single vowels:

1. **Single vowel letters have a short and long sound.**

2. **The short vowel sounds are ă (ăct); ĕ (ĕlephant); ĭ (ĭt); ŏ (ŏlive); and ŭ (ŭntil).**

3. **The long vowel sounds are the same as the names of the vowel letters, /a/, /ē/, /ī/, /ō/, /ū/. The letter u has a second additional long vowel sound of /o͞o/ (brute).**

4. **The letters *a* as /ä/ (call); *o* as /o͞o/ (prove); and *u* as /o͝o/ (push) have a special, or third sound. Sometimes words with these sounds are taught as sight words.**

5. **Unaccented syllables with a single vowel letter may have a schwa sound. The sound is written as /ə/ (tickət).**

You may want to make and study the following cards showing the single vowel letter/sounds before proceeding further.

_____

(11) Sometimes phonograms are referred to as a base.

(12) Regional variations must be considered when discussing the schwa.

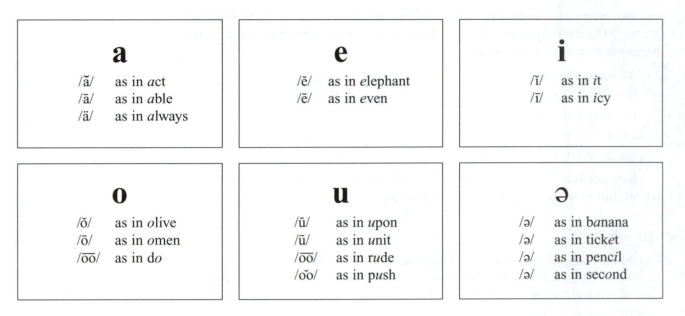

| **a** | **e** | **i** |
|---|---|---|
| /ă/    as in *a*ct | /ĕ/    as in *e*lephant | /ĭ/    as in *i*t |
| /ā/    as in *a*ble | /ē/    as in *e*ven | /ī/    as in *i*cy |
| /ä/    as in *a*lways | | |

| **o** | **u** | **ə** |
|---|---|---|
| /ŏ/    as in *o*live | /ŭ/    as in *u*pon | /ə/    as in b*a*nana |
| /ō/    as in *o*men | /ū/    as in *u*nit | /ə/    as in tick*e*t |
| /o͞o/    as in d*o* | /o͞o/    as in r*u*de | /ə/    as in penc*i*l |
| | /o͝o/    as in p*u*sh | /ə/    as in sec*o*nd |

See Appendix C for example words to use in teaching vowel sounds.

**Quick Self-Check 5**

1. The vowel letters, *a, e, i, o,* and *u* may encode a long or short sound.
   a. In addition, what vowel letter has a second long sound? What is it?
   b. Which vowel letters may encode a third sound? Are words with these sounds taught phonetically or by sight?
   c. What is the schwa sound? In what part of a word is it usually heard?

**Review**

A. What are the four consonant digraphs whose first letter is silent?
B. What three sounds can the consonant digraph *ch* encode?

## Final Unpronounced Letter *e*

We sometimes use the single letter vowel and a final *e* to encode the long vowel sound. We do this to differentiate between words such as the following:

| *A* | *B* |
|---|---|
| măd | māde |
| mĕt | mēte |
| rĭd | rīde |
| nŏt | nōte |
| cŭt | cūte |

Therefore, we might generalize about final *e* changing the preceding vowel sound as follows:

**The letter *e* at the end of a word may sometimes indicate that the preceding vowel is long. (Remember, too, that a final *e* may also indicate that the preceding *c* or *g* has a soft sound as in stan*ce* and bar*ge*.)**[13]

(13) Refer to page 3, "Consonants With More Than One Sound," if you do not remember this generalization.

The final *e* generalization needs a further word of explanation, and we will have to digress for a moment to do so. You should now understand two reasons for the final unpronounced *e* at the end of certain words. Stated simply:

1. **Final *e* may indicate that the preceding vowel is long as shown by the contrasting words *mat* and *mate*.**

2. **Final *e* may indicate that the preceding *c* or *g* has a soft sound as in stan*c*e and bar*g*e.**

There are other reasons for the unpronounced final *e*. Language is often arbitrary in decisions it makes about spelling. In English we have a particular rule to the effect that English words will not end in the letter *v*. With words such as *have, prove,* and *love,* the *e* does not make the preceding vowel long. It is simply there because English words do not end in *v*. Sometimes, however, the final *e* after *v* does make the preceding vowel long in such words as *shave* and *stove*. In these and other similar words, the *e* plays a dual role.

We now have three reasons for words ending in unpronounced final *e*. We might generalize as follows:

1. **Final *e* may indicate that the vowel before it is long, as in *mate*.**

2. **Final *e* may indicate that the preceding *c* or *g* is soft, as in *stance* and *barge*.**

3. **Final *e* is used after the letter *v,* as in *have,* because English words do not end in *v*.**

Another reason an unpronounced final *e* appears after certain words, such as *house* and *awe,* is simply due to historical circumstance and the whims of early printers. When several words began to change during the Middle English period, the final *e,* formerly pronounced as an /ĕ/, became silent, but printers nonetheless retained the written letter. Second, during the earlier printing periods the letter *e* was added to fill up the line when words did not complete the required number of spaces. We still have to struggle with words such as these. Therefore, in addition to the preceding three reasons, we can generalize a fourth reason for the final unpronounced *e*.

4. **Final *e* may appear at the end of some words for historical reasons.**

The last reason for unpronounced final *e* can be found in such words as *table, maple,* and *noble*. The *e* follows an *l* and is needed to complete the second syllable; otherwise, the first vowel would be short, and the word would be unpronounceable. (For example, try pronouncing *tabl, mapl,* and *nobl*.)

We now have five reasons why English words have a final unpronounced letter *e*.

You may want to make and study the following card:

---

**Final Unpronounced *e***

   1. Final *e* may indicate that the vowel before it is long.

   2. Final *e* may indicate that the preceding *c* or *g* has a soft sound.

   3. Final *e* is used after *v* because English words do not end in *v*.

   4. Final *e* may be a historical leftover.

   5. Final *e* follows *l* in a two-syllable word to complete the syllable.

A further note on final *e*. While this rule has about 93 percent predictability, most exceptions occur with words that end in *ile* as *facile, ine* as *machine,* both derived from French spellings, and words ending in *Vre* as *mare.* See Louis and Heath, "A Face Lift for the Silent *e*" (1983).

See Appendix C for example words to use in teaching long vowels with final silent *e*.

## Quick Self-Check 6

Next to each word indicate the final *e* generalization.

1. prove
2. stable
3. fence
4. stake
5. else

## Vowel Digraphs and Diphthongs

Recall that a consonant *digraph* means two letters encoding only a single sound or several single sounds. In addition to consonant digraphs, there are vowel digraphs. Recall that some digraphs encode more than one single sound. There is also within the vowels a second category called diphthongs. The dictionary defines a diphthong[14] as "a gliding sound from one vowel to another."

### Vowel digraphs and diphthongs that begin with *a*

| Vowel Pair | Word |
|---|---|
| *ai* | m*ai*d  /ā/ |
| *ay* | st*ay*  /ā/ |
| *au* | v*au*lt  /ä/ |
| *aw* | dr*aw*  /ä/ |

***ai*** and ***ay***   As you can see, we have, in addition to the silent *e* pattern, ways of writing the long *a* sound using two letters. Examples: m*ai*d and st*ay.* This is one of the difficulties in understanding the English writing-decoding system. We have too many different ways of representing the same sound!

The vowel digraph *ai* may decode as long *a* in the middle of a word while *ay* decodes as long *a* at the end.[15] The reason for this is that English words do not end in *i* except for the foreign words we have borrowed, such as *spaghetti* and *macaroni.*

***au*** and ***aw***   In some phonics systems the combinations *au* and *aw* are considered digraphs and in others diphthongs. Both *au* and *aw* decode as the sound /ä/. Since English words do not usually end in *u* (as in the case of *v*), *au* is used at the beginning and middle of a word, as in *au*thor and f*au*lt, and *aw* is used at the end, as in l*aw.*

These four pairs, *ai, ay, au,* and *aw,* are considered stable in that they almost always decode as these sounds.

We might generalize about these digraphs/diphthongs beginning with the letter *a* as follows:

(14) Diphthongs will be discussed in more detail later.
(15) When a suffix has been added to the word, *ay* may be in the middle. Example: *playing.*

1. There are four vowel pairs beginning with *a*: *ai, ay, au,* and *aw.*
2. The digraphs *ai* and *ay* decode as the long /ā/ sound. *Ai* may be used at the beginning or in the middle of a word. *Ay* may be used at the end.
3. *Au* and *aw* decode as the /ä/ sound. *Au* may be used at the beginning or in the middle of a word. *Aw* may be used at the end.

You may want to make and study the following cards before proceeding further.

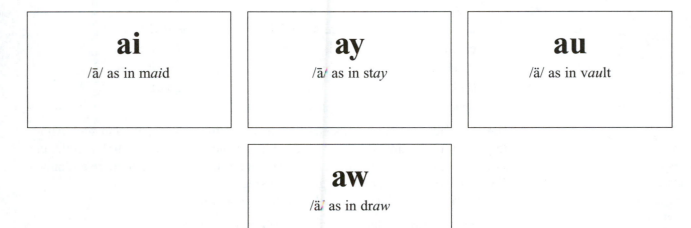

| | | |
|---|---|---|
| **ai** | **ay** | **au** |
| /ā/ as in m*ai*d | /ā/ as in st*ay* | /ä/ as in v*au*lt |

| |
|---|
| **aw** |
| /ä/ as in dr*aw* |

See Appendix C for example words to use in teaching vowel digraphs and diphthongs beginning with *a.*

**Quick Self-Check 7**

1. Why do we have the two digraphs *ai* and *ay*? What sound do they encode?
2. Why do we have the two digraphs *au* and *aw*? What sound do they encode?
3. Why are these combinations considered stable?

**Review**

A. What are combinations such as *ack, ide,* and *unk* called?
B. What sound does the consonant digraph *ph* encode?

## Vowel digraphs with *e*

Vowel digraphs that contain the letter *e* are as follows:

| Digraph | Word | | |
|---|---|---|---|
| *ee* | sl*ee*p /ē/ | | |
| *ea* | h*ea*t /ē/ | spr*ea*d /ĕ/ | st*ea*k /ā/ |
| *ie* | bel*ie*f /ē/ | t*ie* /ī/ | |
| *ei* | rec*ei*ve /ē/ | v*ei*n /ā/ | |
| | (very irregular digraph) | | |
| *ey* | donk*ey* /ē/ | pr*ey* /ā/ | |

Since the *e* digraphs are more complicated than the *a* digraphs, we will generalize about each one individually.

*ee*    The vowel digraph *ee* is usually the first vowel digraph introduced in reading because of its stability. Since it usually decodes as long /ē/ (sl*ee*p, j*ee*p, st*ee*p), we may generalize as follows:

**The vowel digraph *ee* decodes as /ē/.**

*ea*    The vowel digraph *ea* is more complicated because it decodes as three sounds. Look at the following lists of words:

| *A* | *B* | *C* |
|---|---|---|
| *ea* as /ē/ | *ea* as /ĕ/ | *ea* as /ā/ |
| cl*ea*n | l*ea*ther | st*ea*k |
| r*ea*ch | br*ea*th | br*ea*k |
| s*ea*l | r*ea*dy | gr*ea*t |
| p*ea*ch | pl*ea*sant | |

The first and most common sound is long /ē/ as in cl*ea*n, r*ea*ch, and s*ea*l. About 25 percent of the time this digraph decodes as short /ĕ/, as in l*ea*ther, br*ea*th, and r*ea*dy. A third sound this digraph decodes as is long /ā/, although there are only a few such words. Examples are gr*ea*t and st*ea*k.

We might generalize about the *ea* digraph as follows:

1. **The *ea* digraph decodes as three sounds.**
2. **It most commonly decodes as long /ē/ as in h*ea*t.**
3. **It also decodes as short /ĕ/ as in br*ea*d.**
4. **In a few words *ea* decodes as /ā/ as in st*ea*k.**

*ie*    The *ie* digraph decodes as two sounds, long /ē/ and long /ī/. Excluding suffixed words, the most common sound is long /ē/. Only a few base words with *ie* decode as long /ī/. These are words such as p*ie*, t*ie*, l*ie*, and d*ie*. Words with suffix endings, however, often do decode as /ī/ as in tr*ie*d (try + ed), dr*ie*d (dry + ed), and suppl*ie*s (supply + s). This is because the *y* is dropped and changed to *i*. There are, as stated, many examples of base words with *ie* decoding as long /ē/ such as the following:

| *ie* as /ē/ | |
|---|---|
| bel*ie*ve | p*ie*ce |
| br*ie*f | sh*ie*ld |
| gr*ie*f | th*ie*f |
| n*ie*ce | y*ie*ld |

We might generalize about the *ie* digraph as follows:

**The *ie* vowel digraph decodes as two sounds, long /ē/ as in br*ie*f and long /ī/ as in p*ie*. Excluding suffixed words, the most common sound is long /ē/.**

*ei*    The *ei* digraph is highly irregular and difficult to classify except for its relationship to *c*. When *ei* follows a *c,* it always decodes as long /ē/. This digraph may also decode as long /ā/ in a few words. See the following:

| *A* | *B* |
|---|---|
| *ei* as /ē/ after *c* | *ei* as /ā/ |
| rec*ei*ve | v*ei*n |
| conc*ei*ve | r*ei*gn |
| rec*ei*pt | v*ei*l |

However, in addition to long /ē/ after *c* and the long /ā/ sound, this digraph shows considerable variability, as evidenced in the following words:

| | | | |
|---|---|---|---|
| counterf*ei*t | /ĭ/ | l*ei*sure | /ē/ |
| *ei*ther | /ē/ | s*ei*zed | /ē/ |
| forf*ei*ted | /ĭ/ | sover*ei*gn | /ī/ |
| h*ei*fer | /ĕ/ | prot*ei*n | /ē/ |

Teachers sometimes use nonsense sentences to help students recall these words: "N*ei*ther counterf*ei*ter s*ei*zed the sover*ei*gn. They wanted the h*ei*fer, prot*ei*n, and l*ei*sure."

We might generalize about the vowel digraph *ei* as follows:

**The vowel digraph *ei* decodes as the sound of long /ē/ after *c*. It also decodes as the sound of /ā/ as in v*ei*n. Its vowel sound also varies in other words.**

*ey*　The vowel digraph *ey* usually decodes as the sound of long /ē/. In a few words it decodes as the sound of /ā/. See the following lists of words:

| A | B |
|---|---|
| ***ey* as /ē/** | ***ey* as /ā/** |
| vall*ey* | th*ey* |
| k*ey* | pr*ey* |
| pull*ey* | conv*ey* |
| attorn*ey* | ob*ey* |

We might generalize about the *ey* digraph as follows:

**The *ey* digraph generally decodes as the long sound of /ē/. In a few words it decodes as /ā/.**

We can now summarize all the generalizations of the *e* vowel digraphs as follows:

**The digraph**

1. *ee* decodes as /ē/, as in sl*ee*p.
2. *ea* decodes most often as long /ē/, as in h*ea*t; also as short /ĕ/, as in br*ea*d; and in a few words as long /ā/, as in st*ea*k.
3. *ie* usually decodes as /ē/, as in bel*ie*ve; also as /ī/, as in t*ie*.
4. *ei* decodes as /ē/ after *c,* as in rec*ei*ve; as /ā/, as in v*ei*n; and varies in its sound.
5. *ey* decodes as /ē/, as in donk*ey*; as /ā/, as in ob*ey*.

You may want to make and study these cards before proceeding further.

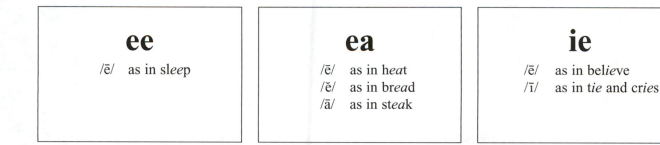

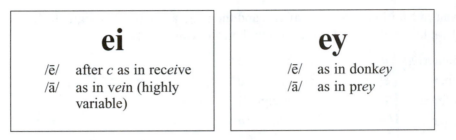

| **ei** | **ey** |
|---|---|
| /ē/   after *c* as in rec*ei*ve | /ē/   as in donk*ey* |
| /ā/   as in v*ei*n (highly variable) | /ā/   as in pr*ey* |

See Appendix C for example words to use in teaching digraphs with *e*.

To simplify all these generalizations, we may conclude that the *e* digraphs decode mainly as long /ē/ and sometimes as long /ā/.

**Quick Self-Check 8**

*ee   ea   ie   ei   ey*

1. Which digraph is fairly stable and encodes one sound?
2. Which digraph has the greatest variability?
3. Which digraph usually encodes /ē/ and /ĕ/ and /ā/ ?
4. Which digraph usually encodes /ē/ and /ā/ ?
5. Which digraph usually encodes /ē/ and /ī/ ?
6. What would be a simplified generalization for the digraphs with *e?*

**Vowel digraph with *i***

The letter *i,* as mentioned on page 18, combines with *a* to form the vowel digraph *ai* that decodes as long /ā/. The letter *i* also combines with e in the vowel digraphs *ie* and *ei* (see page 19).

The letter *i* will also combine with the consonant digraph *gh* mentioned under the unique *h* digraph on page 8. This three-letter combination *igh,* called a digraph by some, decodes as long /ī/ after a beginning sound. (It is often referred to as "the three-letter i.") See the following word group for examples:

> ***igh* as /ī/**
> bl*igh*t      r*igh*t
> fl*igh*t      s*igh*

We might generalize about the letter *i* as follows:

**The letter *i* combines with *gh* in the middle or end of some words and decodes as long /ī/.**

Make and study this card before proceeding further.

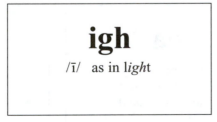

| **igh** |
|---|
| /ī/   as in l*igh*t |

See Appendix C for example words to use when teaching the three-letter *i*.

## Vowel digraphs and diphthongs with *o*

As previously mentioned, there is not always agreement as to what is a digraph and what is a diphthong. By definition, a diphthong is a "gliding sound from one vowel to another." If you say the long *o* sound and watch your lips in a mirror, you will see that your mouth formation remains stationary. However, if you pronounce the diphthong /oy/ as in *oil,* your mouth moves or glides as it goes from one sound to the other.

This lack of agreement as to what is a digraph and what is a diphthong comes about because linguists and reading specialists, who define these terms, have different points of reference. Linguists are usually concerned with the nature of the sounds, and those who teach reading are concerned with decoding the letters that encode those sounds.

Learning such terminology as *digraph* and *diphthong* is not that important for children who are learning decoding strategies. What is important is that they see such vowel combinations as *oa* or *au* as units and do not try to read them as individual vowel sounds.

The following digraph/diphthong classification beginning with *o* is based on the examination of current basals.

*oa*    The letter *o* combines with the letter *a* to form the *oa* vowel digraph and decodes as the long /o/ sound rather consistently. See the following examples:

> **oa as /ō/**
>
> | | |
> |---|---|
> | c*oa*ch | fl*oa*t |
> | c*oa*st | gl*oa*t |

We might generalize about the *oa* digraph as follows:

**The *oa* digraph decodes as the sound of long /ō/.**

*oo*    The letter *o* combines with a second letter *o* to form the combination *oo,* and this combination, together with *ou, ow, oi,* and *oy,* is usually considered a diphthong. Examine the following two lists containing words with the *oo* diphthong.

| *A* | | *B* |
|---|---|---|
| ***oo* as /o͞o/** | | ***oo* as /o͝o/** |
| bl*oo*m | s*oo*the | br*oo*k |
| br*oo*m | sp*oo*l | cr*oo*k |
| cr*oo*n | t*oo*th | sh*oo*k |
| sh*oo*t | tr*oo*p | st*oo*d |

There are many more words with the long /o͞o/ sound as in list *A.* Say the words in these two lists to yourself very slowly and hear the difference between the two sounds. Put a consonant such as *m* after the long /o͞o/ (o͞om) as in the word br*oo*m to hear the isolated long /o͞o/ sound. Put a consonant *k* after the /o͝o/ (o͝ok) as in the word cr*oo*k to hear the isolated short /o͝o/ sound.

We might generalize about the *oo* diphthong as follows:

**The *oo* diphthong decodes as two sounds: long /o͞o/ as in br*oo*m and short /o͝o/ as in l*oo*k. The long /o͞o/ sound is the more common of the two.**

*ou*    The letter *o* also combines with the letter *u* and encodes several sounds. It is a very complex combination. Its two most common sounds are /ow/ as in cl*ou*d and /ŭ/ as in t*ou*ch. See the following lists for additional words:

|        *A*         |        *B*        |
| ----------------- | ----------------- |
| *ou* as /ow/      | *ou* as /ŭ/       |
| ab*ou*t           | c*ou*sin          |
| cr*ou*ch          | d*ou*ble          |
| h*ou*nd           | t*ou*ch           |
| pr*ou*d           | tr*ou*ble         |
| th*ou*sand        | y*ou*ng           |

Say these words to hear the sounds.

Two additional sounds encoded by *ou* are /ō/ as in s*ou*l, and /o͞o/ as in gr*ou*p. Note these two lists:

|        *A*        |        *B*         |
| ----------------- | ------------------ |
| *ou* as /ō/       | *ou* as /o͞o/       |
| s*ou*l            | gr*ou*p            |
| p*ou*ltry         | r*ou*te            |
| sh*ou*lder        | w*ou*nd            |

Say these words to hear the sounds.

These last two sounds are not too common and are not always taught because together they represent only about 10 percent of the words containing *ou*.

We might generalize about the *ou* combination as follows:

1. **When *ou* is a diphthong, it most commonly decodes as /ow/ as in s*ou*nd.**

2. **Its second most common sound is /ŭ/ as in c*ou*sin.**

3. **In only a few words does it decode as /ō/ as in sh*ou*lder and /o͞o/ as in gr*ou*p.**

Now you can understand why it is so difficult to classify diphthongs and digraphs. Some vowel pairs as *ou* are diphthongs in one context, as in ab*ou*t, and digraphs in another, as in t*ou*ch.

*ow*    The letter *o* combines with *w* to form both the /ow/ diphthong and the long /ō/ vowel sound.[16] Examine the following two lists.

|        *A*        |        *B*        |
| ----------------- | ----------------- |
| *ow* as /ow/      | *ow* as /ō/       |
| cl*ow*n           | fl*ow*            |
| dr*ow*n           | gr*ow*            |
| fr*ow*n           | gr*ow*th          |
| n*ow*             | kn*ow*            |
| pr*ow*l           | sn*ow*            |
| t*ow*el           |                   |

Repeat the words to hear these sounds.

In the first list *ow* decodes as the sound of /ow/ as in t*ow*el. In the second list *ow* decodes as the sound of long /ō/ in kn*ow*. Notice that most of the *B* list words are ending sounds.

We might generalize about the combination *ow* as follows:

**The combination *ow* decodes as two sounds: /ow/ as in t*ow*el and long /ō/ as in gl*ow*.**

(16) Many linguists consider all long vowels diphthongs.

*oi* and *oy*   The letter *o* combines with *i* and also with *y* to form the two diphthongs *oi* and *oy*. Both encode the same sound of /oy/. Note the following lists:

| *A* | *B* |
|---|---|
| *oi* **as /oy/** | *oy* **as /oy/** |
| *oi*l | t*oy* |
| so*i*l | empl*oy* |
| m*oi*st | destr*oy* |

The *oi* is used at the beginning and in the middle of base words, and *oy* is used at the end. (This is similar to *ai* and *ay*.) English words, as mentioned, do not end with the letter *i* except for borrowed foreign words.

We might generalize about these two diphthongs as follows:

**The two diphthongs *oi* and *oy* both decode as the /oy/ sound. *Oi* is used at the beginning and in the middle of base words, while *oy* is used at the end.**

You may want to make these cards with the *o* digraphs and diphthongs and study them before proceeding further.

**The letter *o* combines with other vowels to form digraphs and diphthongs. The combination(s):**

1. *oa* decodes as /ō/ in c*oa*t.

2. *oo* decodes as /o͞o/ in m*oo*n and as /o͝o/ in b*oo*k.

3. *ou* usually decodes as /ow/ in cl*ou*d and as /ŭ/ in t*ou*ch; it also decodes in a few words as /ō/ in sh*ou*lder and as /o͞o/ in gr*ou*p.

4. *ow* decodes as /ow/ in c*ow*, and as /ō/ in l*ow*.

5. *oi* and *oy* decode as /oy/. The *oi* diphthong comes at the beginning and middle of words while *oy* is used at the end.

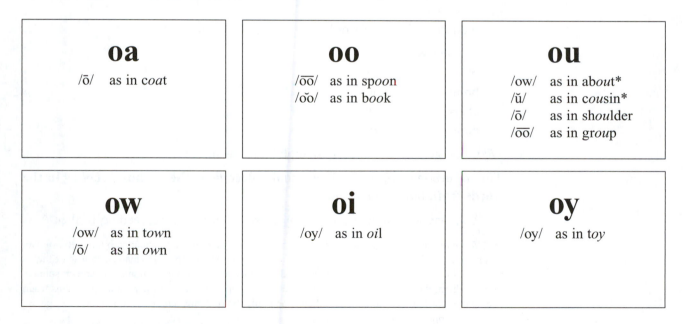

See Appendix C for example words to use in teaching the *o* combinations.

*These are the most common sounds for ou.

**Quick Self-Check 9**

oa   oo   ou   ow   oi   oy

1. Which combination may encode four different sounds? Identify the sounds and give key words. What are its two most common sounds?
2. Why do we have two diphthongs, *oi* and *oy*, encoding the same sound?
3. Which digraph encodes one sound? What is it?
4. List the two sounds encoded by *ow*. Write key words.
5. List the two sounds encoded by *oo*. Write key words.

**Review**

A. What are the two most common sounds of the *e* digraphs?
B. Which consonant letter cannot end an English word?

### Vowel diphthongs encoding /o͞o/

***ui*** and ***ue***   The letter *u* combines with the letter *i* and also with the letter *e* to form diphthongs that decode as /o͞o/. Note the following two lists:

| A | B |
|---|---|
| *ui* as /o͞o/ | *ue* as /o͞o/ |
| j*ui*ce | bl*ue* |
| j*ui*cy | d*ue* |
| sl*ui*ce | fl*ue* |
| s*ui*t | tr*ue* |

Say the words to hear the sounds.

***ew***   There is also another two-letter diphthong that begins with the letter *e* and decodes as /o͞o/. This combination *ew* could have been included with the vowel *e* combinations, but since it decodes as /o͞o/, it seemed more advantageous to place it here.

Examine this list of words:

| | |
|---|---|
| *ew* as /o͞o/ | |
| bl*ew* | dr*ew* |
| br*ew* | fl*ew* |
| ch*ew* | st*ew* |
| cr*ew* | str*ew*n |

We might generalize about these diphthongs as follows:[17]

**The diphthongs *ui*, *ue*, and *ew* usually decode as the sound of /o͞o/ as in the words fr*ui*t, bl*ue*, and str*ew*.**

You may want to make and study these cards before proceeding further.[18]

(17) You will recall that during our discussion of the long vowel sound encoded by the letter u, we mentioned that there were actually two long vowel sounds: /yo͞o/ and /o͞o/. This is also true of the vowel diphthongs *ew* and *ui*. While they usually decode as /o͞o/, when particular consonant sounds precede them, the sound will be /yo͞o/. Examples: *few, hue, cue, mew*. Some phonics programs teach two sounds for these combinations; others teach only the one most common sound /o͞o/. See page 179 for example words.

(18) Note again one of the difficulties encountered by children who are learning decoding strategies—too many ways of writing the same sound. For example, in addition to these three diphthongs that decode as /o͞o/, we also have *ou* as /o͞o/ in *group*; *oo* as /o͞o/ in *moon*; *o* as /o͞o/ in *prove*; *u* as /o͞o/ in *rude*.

| **ue** | **ui** | **ew** |
|--------|--------|--------|
| /o͞o/   as in bl*ue* | /o͞o/   as in s*ui*t | /o͞o/   as in st*ew* |

See Appendix C for example words to use in teaching these special diphthongs.

**Quick Self-Check 10**

1. The special diphthongs *ui, ue,* and *ew* encode what sound?
2. Recall other grapheme possibilities for encoding this sound. What are they?

**Chapter 1, Section 2:**

**Review and Self-Check**

Review the cards and questions for Section 1. Study your cards for Section 2 again. If you can answer the following questions you should be able to proceed to Section 3.

1. What are the single vowels? Give a key word for the short sound of each.
2. What is the schwa sound? Why do we have it? Give word examples.
3. In addition to short and long vowels, *a, o,* and *u* encode a third sound. Give word examples for the third sound of *a, o,* and *u*.
4. What single vowel letter has two long vowel sounds? Why? What are these sounds? List some key words.
5. Two vowel digraphs beginning with *a* decode as long /ā/. What are they? Why are there two? List key words.
6. What vowel digraphs (some call them diphthongs) decode as the sound of broad /ä/? Why are there two? List key words.
7. The vowel digraph *ee* decodes as what sound? Give key words.
8. The vowel digraph *ea* decodes as three sounds. What are they? Which is most common? Least? Give key words.
9. What are the two most common sounds encoded by *ie?* Give word examples.
10. Why is the digraph *ei* so variable? What different sounds does *ei* encode?
11. The digraph *ey* generally decodes as what two sounds? Give word examples.
12. What three-letter combination decodes as long /ī/? Give word examples.
13. What is the difference between a diphthong and a digraph? Write the digraph and diphthong combinations with the letter *o* and give a word example of each.
14. The combined letters *ui, ue,* and *ew* decode as what sound? Give key words.
15. How many ways may the sound of /o͞o/ be encoded in English?

## SECTION 3

## THE LETTER *y*

The letter *y* has a unique position in our language and may function as either a consonant or a vowel. Also, *y* combines with other vowels to form digraphs as *ay* in pl*ay*, *ey* in vall*ey*, and additionally forms a diphthong as *oy* in empl*oy*.

### *y* as a Consonant and Vowel

At the beginning of words, *y* is always a consonant letter as in the words *yacht, yard,* and *yellow.* However, *y* in the middle and at the end of words has a variety of vowel sounds.[19]

| *A* | *B* | *C* | *D* |
|---|---|---|---|
| **y as /ĭ/** | **y as /ī/** | **y as final /ī/** | **y as final /ē/** |
| cr*y*stal | c*y*cle | appl*y* | cand*y* |
| g*y*m | tr*y*ing | fl*y* | hill*y* |
| m*y*sterious | | m*y* | penn*y* |

Say these words to hear these sounds.

*A word of caution.*   There are regional differences to be aware of with ending *y* words. Some people in various parts of the United States would pronounce the words in column *D* with a short /ĭ/ sound instead of the long /ē/ sound.

We might generalize about single letter *y* as follows:

1. **When single letter *y* is first in a word it decodes as the consonant sound /y/ in words like *y*ard and *y*ellow.**

2. **When single letter *y* is in the middle or at the end of words it decodes as a vowel. The vowel can be short /ĭ/ as in g*y*m, long /ī/ as in c*y*cle or repl*y*, or long /ē/ as in prett*y*.**

### Other Considerations with *y*

As mentioned during our discussion of the vowels, the letter *y* also combines with vowel letters. Recall *ay* as in pl*ay*, *ey* as in vall*ey*, and *oy* as in empl*oy*. Putting all this together, we see a variety of possibilities with the letter *y*.

| | | | |
|---|---|---|---|
| *y* as a consonant at the beginning: | /y/ | *y*ard | |
| *y* as a vowel in the middle of words: | /ĭ/ | g*y*m, | /ī/   c*y*cle |
| *y* as a vowel at the end of words: | /ē/ | prett*y*, | /ī/   appl*y* |
| *y* as part of the vowel digraph *ay:* | /ā/ | m*ay* | |
| *y* as part of the vowel digraph *ey:* | /e/ | vall*ey* | |
| *y* as part of the diphthong *oy:* | /oy/ | destr*oy* | |

You may want to make and study the card on the following page showing *y* in its entirety before proceeding further.

See Appendix C for example *y* words to use in teaching.

(19) One reason for this is that the letters *i* and *y* were used interchangeably during the Middle Ages, and even later. Note this sentence from an early New England account. "The pylgrims were pyoneers in the land."

| | |
|---|---|
| *y* as a consonant at the beginning of a word | *y*ellow |
| *y* as the vowel /ĭ/ /ī/ in the middle of words | g*y*m |
| or | c*y*cle |
| *y* as the vowel /ē/ /ī/ at the end of words | prett*y* |
| or | appl*y* |
| *y* as a digraph /ā/ | ma*y* |
| *y* as a digraph /ē/ | vall*ey* |
| *y* as a diphthong /oy/ | bo*y* |

1. When does the letter *y* function as a consonant?
2. How does *y* function in the following words: *yes, cry, play, royal?*

A. Why does a word such as *table* have a final *e?*
B. What sound do these three digraphs—*ue, ui,* and *ew*—decode as?

**Quick Self-Check 11**

**Review**

## *r* with Single Vowel Letters

**SECTION 4**

***r*-CONTROLLED VOWELS**

***er, ir, ur,* and *wor***   The letter *r,* often referred to as "bossy *r,*" combines with certain single vowels and may condition the *preceding* vowel sound. Look at the following four columns of words:

| *A* | *B* | *C* | *D* |
|---|---|---|---|
| ***er* as /er/** | ***ir* as /er/** | ***ur* as /er/** | ***wor* as /wer/** |
| p*er*t | s*ir* | h*ur*t | *wor*se |
| f*er*n | f*ir*st | ch*ur*n | *wor*thy |
| h*er*d | squ*ir*m | c*ur*l | *wor*ld |
| | ch*ir*p | | |

Pronounce all of these words and note that in each instance the vowel letter and following letter combine to encode the same sound of /er/.

In list *D* you will note that the sound of /w/ precedes the sound of /er/ as in *wor*se, *wor*thy, and *wor*ld. The letters *or* decode as /er/ when the letter *w* precedes them.

Several questions might arise in teaching these sounds. A student might ask, "How about words like *here, fire,* and *pure?*" In these words *er, ir,* and *ur* do not decode as /er/. Notice what these three words have in common:

here    fire    pure

All of them end in a final *e!* Remember that we discussed several reasons for final *e,* one of which was to change the preceding vowel sound. In words that end in *re,* the final *e* also conditions the preceding vowel sound; therefore it will not have the /er/ sound.

We might make the following generalization about the above *r* combinations.

1. **The combinations *er, ir,* and *ur* decode as /er/ when not followed by final *e.***
2. **When the letter *w* precedes *or,* it decodes as /wer/.**

A word of caution about the letter *r* and the /r/ sound. *No other sound in the English language is pronounced in such a variety of ways.* For example: Easterners tend to omit a final /r/ altogether and then add an /r/ where none exists! Midwesterners tend to give *r* its full pronunciation regardless of placement in a word. African-American dialect speakers sometimes omit final /r/ unless the following sound is a vowel. In certain areas, many unaccented syllables that end with an r have a preceding schwa sound instead of a full vowel sound. Therefore, as a teacher you must *take into consideration the regional pronunciation of your area.*

   *ar*    The letter *r* with the single vowel *a*. See the following combinations:

| A | B |
|---|---|
| **ar** as /är/ | **are** as /âr/ |
| f*ar* | f*are* |
| st*ar* | st*are* |
| m*ar* | m*are* |

You will notice two different letter-sound combinations. In column *A,* the words, f*ar,* st*ar,* and m*ar* have the sound of /är/. In column *B* the words f*are,* st*are,* and m*are* have a different sound because of the final *e*. The sound is written /âr/. Say the words to hear the sounds.

We might make a second generalization.

**The combination *ar* decodes as /är/ as in f*ar*. When *ar* is followed by an *e*, the sound changes to /âr/ as in f*are*.**

   *or*    The letter *r* combines with the letter *o* to encode the sound /or/ as in f*or*. Sometimes *or* encodes the schwa vowel sound /ər/ in final unaccented syllables. Again, this has to do with regional variation. Examine the following groups of words and note the difference:

| A | B |
|---|---|
| *or* as /ôr/ | *or* as ər |
| c*or*k | fác*tor* |
| f*or*th | dóc*tor* |
| p*or*ch | flá*vor* |
| st*or*k | saí*lor* |
| th*or*n | vísi*tor* |

We might therefore make a third generalization about the letter *r:*

1. **The letter *r* combines with *o* to decode as the sound of /or/ as in st*or*k.**

2. **Sometimes it decodes as /ər/ in final unaccented syllables as in words like flav*or*.**

## *r* with Vowel Digraphs

The letter *r* combines with the digraphs *ea, ai,* and *ee*. We will consider the *ea* digraph initially.

   *ea*    Note the following three columns:

| *A* | *B* | *C* |
|---|---|---|
| *ear* as /ē-r/ | *ear* as /er/[20] | *ear* as /âr/ |
| clear | earn | bear |
| dear | heard | pear |
| fear | learn | tear |
| <u>hear</u> | <u>search</u> | <u>wear</u> |
| 9% | 6% | 2% |

In list *A* the *ear* combination decodes as /ē-r/, its most common sound. In *B*, however, the *ear* combination decodes as /er/ while in *C*, *ear* decodes as /âr/. You will note from the percentages that only a few *ear* words (2%) have the /âr/ sound; therefore, words such as these are often taught as sight words. These percentages indicate the number of times such words are usually found in relation to the total number of words with the *ea* combination. About 83 percent of the time *ea* is followed by other consonants as in *mean, dread,* and *break.* See page 20 if you need to review the *ea* digraph.

**ai**   When *r* combines with the digraph *ai*, there is also a controlling of the vowel sound to /âr/ as in st*ai*r. Note the following group of words:

**ai*r* as /âr/**
> f*ai*r
>
> p*ai*r
>
> st*ai*r
>
> pr*ai*rie

About 15 percent of all *ai* words have a following *r* and therefore have this sound.

**ee**   The digraph *ee* is also controlled by a following *r.* The sound becomes /ē-r/. See examples below:

**ee*r* as /ē-r/**
> p*ee*r
>
> st*ee*r
>
> qu*ee*r
>
> ch*ee*r

Taking into consideration that there are regional differences, we might generalize about the letter *r* with vowel digraphs *ea, ai,* and *ee* as follows:

1. **When the letter *r* follows the vowel digraph *ea,* it usually decodes as /ē-r/ as in cl*ear*. It may also decode as /ēr/ as in l*ear*n. In only a few words does it decode as /âr/ as in b*ear*.**
2. **The vowel digraph *ai* when followed by *r* decodes as /âr/ as in ch*ai*r.**
3. **The vowel digraph *ee* when followed by *r* decodes as /ē-r/ as in ch*ee*r.**

Examination of the following lists will show more clearly the relationship of *r* with single vowels and with vowel digraphs.[21]

(20) Sometimes the *ear* combination decoding as /er/ is included with *er, ir, ur,* and *wor.* See page 29.
(21) The letter *r* controls the vowel when it appears *in the same syllable* and *follows that vowel.* In a word such as *arise* the *r* does not change the *a* to /ă/ because it is not in the same syllable. It does not affect the sound of /ī/ in any way since it *precedes i* in the syllable.

| /er/ | /âr/ | /ôr/ | /ē-r/ | /är/ |
|------|------|------|-------|------|
| p*er*t | c*are* | f*or*k | h*ear* | f*ar* |
| f*ir*st | b*ear* | st*or*k | ch*eer* | p*ar*k |
| p*ur*se | ch*air* | m*ore* | r*ear* | b*ar*gain |
| w*or*se | | | | |
| *ear*n | | | | |

We can now put together all of the generalizations for *r*.

**The letter *r* controls the *preceding* vowel sound in the same syllable.**

1. Combinations of *er* (p*er*t), *ir* (f*ir*st), and *ur* (h*ur*t) decode as /er/. When *w* precedes *or,* the cluster decodes as /wer/ as in *worth*.
2. The combination *ar* decodes as /är/ as in f*ar*. When followed by an *e,* it decodes as /âr/ as in f*are*.
3. The combination *or* decodes as /ôr/ as in st*or*k. Sometimes it decodes as /ər/ as in visit*or*.
4. The combination *ear* decodes as /ē-r/ as in h*ear*; as /er/ as in l*ear*n; and as /âr/ as in b*ear*.
5. The combination *air* decodes as /âr/ as in p*air*.
6. The combination *eer* decodes as /ē-r/ as in ch*eer*.
7. Regional differences must be considered with the highly variable sound of /r/.

You may want to make and study the following cards before proceeding further.

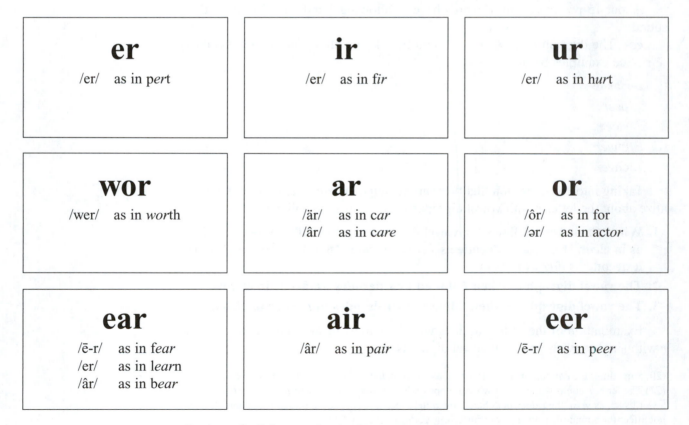

| | | |
|---|---|---|
| **er**<br>/er/   as in p*er*t | **ir**<br>/er/   as in f*ir* | **ur**<br>/er/   as in h*ur*t |
| **wor**<br>/wer/   as in w*or*th | **ar**<br>/är/   as in c*ar*<br>/âr/   as in c*are* | **or**<br>/ôr/   as in for<br>/ər/   as in act*or* |
| **ear**<br>/ē-r/   as in f*ear*<br>/er/   as in l*ear*n<br>/âr/   as in b*ear* | **air**<br>/âr/   as in p*air* | **eer**<br>/ē-r/   as in p*eer* |

See Appendix C for example *r* words to use in teaching.

1. What do these *r*-combinations have in common?
   her      fur      stir
2. How is *wor* like the above three words?
3. Examine the following words:
   fear      search      pear
   What conclusion can be drawn about the *ear* combination?
4. What other vowel digraphs combine with the letter *r?* What sounds do they encode?

## SECTION 5

## SPECIAL COMBINATIONS THAT DECODE AS /sh/

Certain combinations in addition to *sh* as in ship decode as /sh/. In Section 1, page 8, recall that the vowel consonant *ch* was shown to have three sounds, one of which was the /sh/ sound as in *ch*ampagne. There are three other common combinations that decode as /sh/ in addition to the two mentioned above.

Note the following words:

| A | B | C |
|---|---|---|
| *ci* as /sh/ | *ti* as /sh/ | *si* as /sh/ |
| so*ci*al | cau*ti*ous | man*si*on |
| deli*ci*ous | men*ti*on | mi*ssi*on |
| spe*ci*al | sta*ti*on | ten*si*on |
| gra*ci*ous | fi*cti*on | permi*ssi*on |

In each instance the *ci, ti,* and *si* all decode as the /sh/ sound. There was a period when these words were pronounced exactly as they are spelled, but this sound change took place several hundred years ago. The three combinations above are only found in the *middle* of words and are often taught as part of affixed endings.[22]

We might generalize as follows about these three combinations.

**The letters *ci, ti,* and *si* often decode as /sh/ as in such words as pre*ci*ous, fic*ti*on, and mi*ssi*on.**

You may want to make and study these three cards before proceeding further.

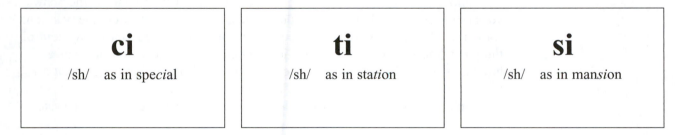

| **ci** | **ti** | **si** |
|---|---|---|
| /sh/   as in spe*ci*al | /sh/   as in sta*ti*on | /sh/   as in man*si*on |

(22) George Bernard Shaw, who disliked the English writing system and offered money to anyone who would improve upon it, once suggested that *ghoti* could be read as *fish*. This is not so, because the consonant digraph *gh* only decodes as /f/ at the *end* of some words, *never* at the beginning. The *o* in *ghoti*, he claimed, could decode as short /ĭ/ as in *women*. The word *women* is the only instance in which *o* has this sound, the word having gone through spelling changes. Also, the *ti*, which he claimed would decode as /sh/ as in *nation*, is equally incorrect. The combination *ti* is *rarely* found at the end of words. A foreign adopted word such as *spaghetti* is pronounced differently.

You have now completed what you should know about phonics generalizations. If you can pass the sectional review test and the final phonics review test, you may proceed with ways of teaching decoding strategies that use phonics principles.

**Chapter 1, Sections 3, 4, & 5:**

**Review and Self-Check**

First review your cards from Sections 1 and 2. Group cards from Sections 3, 4, and 5 and review them. Then try this short test for the last three sections.

1. The letter *y* may function in different ways. Group the following words according to that function, identifying each group: *gym, they, yam, dry, play, yellow, cycle, employ, key, royal.*
2. The following four vowel + *r* combinations can be classified similarly: b*er*th, m*ir*th, p*ur*se, w*or*th. Explain.
3. Three digraphs frequently precede *r* with accompanying sound changes. Explain.
4. Explain what has happened to the sounds encoded by combinations such as *ti, si,* and *ci.* Name other grapheme combinations that encode the same sound.

## SUMMARY

The introduction summarized the ongoing discussion regarding phonics instruction and the whole language approach. Findings by Chall and Adams and many others continue to demonstrate the efficacy of the use of early instruction with phonics. For young students, understanding the relationship between sounds and symbols provides a foundation for seeing how much of our written language decodes.

At the same time, whole language, with its philosophy of placing children's literature at the core of the reading curriculum, and with its emphasis on much writing and publishing within a collaborative environment that integrates the disciplines, continues to shape the classroom curriculum.

The scope of the written English language system for reading teachers may be more easily understood by dividing it into categories that include within the consonant group: single consonants, consonants that vary, blends, and digraphs; and among the vowel group: short, long, and third vowel sounds, the schwa, vowel digraphs, and diphthongs. Additionally, the letter *y* has a unique position, sometimes functioning as either a consonant or vowel. The letter *r* may control the preceding vowel sound when it is encoded by a single vowel or a vowel digraph. As with all word identification strategies, *phonics works best when used in combination with other strategies that provide clues.*

Table 1.2 describes and divides the major areas of the English writing system.

**TABLE 1.2** Overview of English orthography for the teacher.

| CONSONANTS | | VARIANT CONSONANTS | | DIGRAPHS WITH h | | DIGRAPHS WITH FIRST SILENT LETTER | | BLENDS-INITIAL | | BLENDS-FINAL | | SPECIAL COMBINATION OF CONSONANT AND VOWEL | |
|---|---|---|---|---|---|---|---|---|---|---|---|---|---|
| b | bat | c, g, s | | ch | chair | ck | deck | r | break | ld | sold | ci | special |
| d | dent | | | | scheme | gn | gnome | l | clean | lk | walk | si | mansion |
| f | fall | | | | chandelier | kn | knife | s | skate | nd | send | ti | station |
| h | hit | | cat | gh | ghost | wr | write | | scrap | nk | thank | | |
| j | jam | | city | ph | pharmacy | | | tw | twirl | nt | meant | | |
| k | kite | | | sh | ship | **DIGRAPH CLUSTER FOLLOWING A SHORT VOWEL** | | | | | | | |
| l | land | | got | th | thick | dge | bridge | | | | | | |
| m | mat | | giant | | these | tch | stitch | | | | | | |
| n | name | | | wh | what | **ADDITIONAL DIGRAPH** | | | | | | | |
| p | pan | | us | | who | ng | | | | | | | |
| qu | quite | | his | | | | | | | | | | |
| r | road | | sugar | | | | | | | | | | |
| t | top | | | | | | | | | | | | |
| v | vane | | | | | | | | | | | | |
| w | well | | | | | | | | | | | | |
| x | box | | | | | | | | | | | | |
| z | zebra | | | | | | | | | | | | |

**VOWELS**

SINGLE - SHORT
- ă act
- ĕ end
- ĭ it
- ŏ olive
- ŭ upon

SINGLE - LONG
- ā able
- ē even
- ī icy
- ō omen
- ū unit
- ū and ōō rude

SINGLE - 3RD SOUND
- a ä always
- o ōō do
- u ŏŏ push

| SCHWA ə IN UNACCENTED SYLLABLES | | DIGRAPHS/DIPHTHONGS WITH a | | | DIGRAPHS WITH e | | | CLUSTER WITH i | | DIGRAPHS AND DIPHTHONGS WITH o | | | DIPHTHONGS THAT ENCODE /oo/ | |
|---|---|---|---|---|---|---|---|---|---|---|---|---|---|---|
| a | about | ai as /ā/ | maid | | ee as /ē/ | sleep | | igh as /ī/ | sight | oa as /ō/ | coat | | ui | fruit |
| e | ticket | ay as /ā/ | stay | | ea as /ē/ | leaf | | | | oi as /oy/ | oil | | ue | blue |
| i | pencil | au as /aw/ | vault | | | /ĕ/ | head | | | oy as /oy/ | boy | | ew | stew |
| o | apron | aw as /aw/ | draw | | | /ā/ | great | | | oo as /ōō/ | moon | | | |
| | | | | | ic as /ē/ | relief | | | | | /ŏŏ/ | look | | |
| | | | | | | /ī/ | lie | | | ou as /ow/ | around | | | |
| | | | | | ei as /ē/ | (after c) receive | | | | | /ŭ/ | young | | |
| | | | | | | /ā/ | vein | | | | /ō/ | soul | | |
| | | | | | | /ē/ | donkey | | | | /ōō/ | group | | |
| | | | | | ey as /ā/ | prey | | | | ow as /ow/ | cow | | | |
| | | | | | | | | | | | /ō/ | low | | |

| y AS A CONSONANT, VOWEL, DIGRAPH, DIPHTHONG | CONSONANT AT THE BEGINNING: yellow<br>VOWEL: mystery, apply, carry<br>DIGRAPH: play, obey<br>DIPHTHONG: employ |
|---|---|

| r WITH SINGLE VOWELS: | r WITH a: | r WITH o: | r WITH DIGRAPH ae: | r WITH DIGRAPHS: |
|---|---|---|---|---|
| her fir purse worse<br>/er/ /er/ /er/ /er/ | fär câre | stôre doctar | hear learn bear<br>/e-r/ /er/ /ar/ | ai　ee<br>hair　peer<br>/âr/　/ē-r/ |

## Chapter 1:

~~~~~~~~~~~~~~~~~~

## Final Review

Now apply what you know. Place the words that contain related phonics features in the proper column. Some words may appear in more than one column. Underline the feature particular to that column. (You will be able to place all the words except one.)

| scheme | flight | edge |
| world | now | coast |
| bridge | relative | chaise |
| receive | back | athlete |
| treat | surprise | hair |
| afraid | streamlined | earn |
| destroy | about | stitch |
| coaching | breath | physics |
| toil | spoon | fewer |

| Words with Consonant Digraphs[23] | Words with Blends | Words with Vowel Digraphs | Words with Vowel Diphthongs | Vowels with *r*-Control |
|---|---|---|---|---|
| | | | | |

(23) Also include special consonant combinations.

# The Role of Phonics in Word Recognition

## READING READINESS

Parents play a tremendously important role in preparing children for the school's formal reading program.[1] During the preschool years, shared experiences with books lay the foundation for beginning instruction in the school and are invaluable in preparing children to read (Hewison, 1983).

Reading readiness can be divided into learning readiness and actual reading readiness. Learning readiness refers to a creative language environment that enhances and leads to reading readiness. Reading readiness involves teaching reading—specific skills such as the sounds encoded by the letters of the alphabet. Research in this area has established the superiority of specific readiness over learning readiness (Sippola, 1985) and is supported by the report from the 1985 Commission on Reading.* This report suggests, however, that the child who is least ready for systematic reading instruction needs language activities with a light touch: opportunities to listen and to discuss stories that build vocabulary, and also to begin to write—"a balanced kindergarten, not an academic boot camp."

A long-time controversy in readiness extends to letter names. In beginning reading, should these names be learned or not?

Ehri's (1983) lengthy research indicated that if letter names were taught simultaneously with phonics, the integration of the two favorably affected reading acquisition (Groff, 1984; McGee and Richgels, 1989). Adams (1990, 1991, 1995) concluded that instruction with letter names and phonics should also include phonemic awareness (the ability to recognize that a spoken word consists of a sequence of individual sounds).

A continuing interest in this subject may be the result of studies such as Readence and Baldwin (1989), which conclude that "children who learn to read early remain superior in reading achievement when compared with a sample of non-early readers."

## Prereading and Beginning Reading Tasks

As schools introduce the primary reading program, *whether their philosophy is traditional or whole language,* there is a lot of overlap with readiness. Activities are initiated that help children learn to discriminate among letters and help them develop a memory for some of the more common and regular sound-symbol relationships. To do this, teachers create language-rich environments. Many books are

(1) A later section discusses the role of the parent in more detail.

* Anderson, Richard C., Elfrieda H. Hiebert, Judith A. Scott, and Ian A. G. Wilkinson. *Becoming a Nation of Readers: The Report of the Commission on Reading.* Washington, DC: National Institute of Education, 1985.

shared, songs are sung, poetry is read, and lots of "stories" that teachers read or write or that children write (or dictate) are used to learn to discriminate among letters and sounds, to build vocabulary, to understand about capital letters and periods in sentences, and to begin a left-to-right eye sweep.

Most popular today are the use of oversized, large-print picture books called Big Books for both readiness and beginning reading (see Cowley, "Joy of Big Books," 1991). Many of these easily-read books can be made by the teacher. Lyrics of a song children know can be laminated and bound. Pictures of each child in the room can be mounted, and predictable sentences can be written for each page, such as, "This is Jane. She is five years old. Hello, Jane."

Commercial Big Books, with actual stories, are part of many basal programs. *(A basal program consists of the graded reading books used at each grade level.)* In using Big Books, the process can be broken down into three stages: the book stage, the word stage, and the letter-sound stage. This approach gives decoding strategies the attention they deserve within an enriched language or literature setting. As the book is read aloud in front of the class, children see their teacher reading from top to bottom, left to right, and then making the return sweep at the end of the line. Many words are repeated, and eventually some children come to recognize some of these words. As they begin to do so, they can be directed to recurring letter-sound relationships. Following is a more detailed explanation from Cunningham and Allington (1991).

### The book stage

Here language and language concepts are stressed. The book is read by the teacher several times and predictive types of questions encourage children's discussion. Since many of the children are familiar with the story, some "pretend" to read it with the teacher. Later they can dramatize the story, listen to a tape of the book, compare a character with another, or engage in any activity that develops a very clear understanding of the events in the story.

### The word stage

The purpose here is to reinforce reading terms *(letter, word, sentence, top-bottom, left,* and *right.)* The teacher duplicates on cards some of the more commonly used words in the story that are easily discriminated, such as *dog, sailboat,* and *mother.* (A bibliography of some excellent stories with a minimum word count may be found in Appendix E.)

The teacher passes out the cards with the words and points out the differences in their shape and size. As the teacher reads the story and reads the sentence with the target words, children hold up their cards, matching the word. (They can stand or clap their hands also.) Follow-up activities can have children illustrating a word/words or completing a sentence with their word. Each day a word or two can be added until each child has about a dozen words. Together with the student, the teacher writes and reviews the new words daily and reviews other words learned previously.

### Letter-sound stage

Children begin to learn sounds by association and understanding from some of the key words in stories they hear. The teacher may initially use two words from a story, such as *dog* and *mother,* whose beginning sounds are quite different and whose differences can be felt as they are said—/d/ and /m/ for example. The two words, *dog* and *mother,* can serve as key words for these letters. They can be placed on bulletin boards and other initial *m* and *d* words added daily until most children begin to understand the difference in these letter sounds. Gradually other letters can be added as phonemic awareness begins to develop.

## Readiness Activities

### The importance of rereading

In her whole language classroom, Swendal (1993) believes in considerable rereading of Big Books in order for children to look for more connections, patterns, and meaning. A favorite question she poses is, "What did you notice that you want the rest of us to see, hear, or think about?" Insofar as word recognition skills, children can discover rhyming words, alliteration, repetitive phrases and words, and typographic variations in print. This discussion, she states, provides authentic reasons for rereading the text. As a result of several rereadings, students begin to "memorize read" the entire text as a group. By rereading several times, they can focus on the letters, words, and phrases they had not noticed the first few times. Sharing Big Books through rereadings, Swendal believes, promotes a high level of active engagement and learning because there is a simultaneous focus on common print and the spoken word.

### Using familiar songs and chants

Another method used by some whole language teachers is a more defined use of familiar songs and chants (*Learning,* April/May 1995, p. 69). Songs are printed on large posters and children read along as they sing their favorite songs. They point out words they know after the song has been sung, discussed, and enjoyed. A songsheet is then passed around and children circle words they have learned. The songsheet is placed in a song folder. Songs are periodically reviewed and vocabulary and phonics skills work takes place. A learning center contains tapes of the songs and song charts are attached to hangers on a rack so children can choose the song they wish to practice or share with others.

### The daily message

Another favorite practice in both whole language and traditional classrooms is the daily message. (Pearce, 1995). When children come into the kindergarten/first grade classroom they may find a message on the board such as:

Good Morning.
Today is Tuesday, September 8.
The weather is pleasant and sunny.
Pizza will be served at lunch.

The teacher reads the message with the class, pointing out the sounds of some of the letters and encouraging children to sound out some of the words. Children may dictate a sentence of their own and add it to the message. They can try to spell a few words as the teachers helps them match the sounds they hear in the words to the way the words are spelled. The message is reread, and each word is underlined so children learn where one word stops and another starts. Some teachers add a sentence or two, leaving out particular words that students then predict and fill in, such as *Have a nice _____.*

## A strictly phonetic approach

In some kindergartens, kindergartners start off with an intensive 10-week phonics program in which they learn the 40-plus sounds in English and the 26 letters that represent those sounds. Only after children are equipped with these phonetic tools do they begin to try to read books. Some teachers believe the phonics program helps children learn to read much more quickly because it gives them a systematic way to work out simple words for themselves. (See Pearce, 1995).

## A Prereading Inventory

An inventory (Agnew, 1982) to check whether a child understands beginning reading terms such as *sentence, word, letter, sound, begins and ends with* follows. The children's recorded dictation is used with these procedures but no actual reading is done. The object is to discover whether reading instructions will be understood.[2]

Task 1. *Word*

Ask the child to point to any word on the chart story, then to "cup" his/her hands around the word. Repeat the task with three or four other words.

Ask the child to match an individual word card with the same word in the chart story. If the word occurs more than once, ask the child to locate the word in another place in the story. Repeat the task with several other word cards.

Task 2. *Sentence*

Ask the child to match a sentence strip with its counterpart on the chart story. Repeat the task with three or four other sentence strips.

Task 3. *Letter*

Show the child an individual word card and provide him/her with individual letters that can be assembled to spell out the word on the card. Ask the child to "build" the word using separate letters. Ask the child for the names of the letters. Probe understanding of the difference between letters and words. Repeat the exercise with two or three other word cards.

Task 4. *"Begins with" and "Ends with"*

Point to and identify a word in the chart story that begins with a single consonant. Ask the child to think of a word with the same beginning sound. Repeat the task with four or five different words.

Ask the child to point to the place in the chart story to answer such questions as:

1. Where is the *beginning* of the story?
2. Where is the *end* of the story?
3. This word is _____. Where is the beginning of the word? Where is the end of the word?

(2) A record form for these needed tasks may be found in Appendix B.

4. This word is _____. (Point to a word in the story and name it.) Here are two word cards from the story. One of them is *different* from _____. (Repeat the word that was just identified in the story.) Point to the word that is different from _____. (Repeat the word just identified.)

Task 5. *Line*

Run your finger under a line in the story. Ask the child to show you several other lines.

Task 6. *Top and Bottom*

Ask the child to point to the top of the page. Ask the child to point to the bottom of the page. Ask the child to point to the top and bottom of letters.

## Other Readiness Factors

Teachers use both formal and informal methods in determining students' readiness to read. Commercial tests like the Metropolitan screen for letter and sound discrimination and are very popular. Some schools, however, develop their own reading readiness tests based on the school's student body.[3] Teachers, in addition to testing for discrimination abilities, consider many other areas such as the child's maturity, social responsibility, background, language proficiency, and motivation to read. Eventually teachers plan definite instruction and introduce letters for identification visually and auditorily, and students write them. Some programs introduce a number of sight words and draw phonics generalizations from these. Other programs introduce definite sounds and directly teach a few sight words so children may begin reading sentences immediately.[4]

## Invented Spellings

Attention in readiness has focused for some time on invented spellings. For example, a child's invented spelling of "KT" might be acceptable for the word *cute.*

Hansen (1987) states that students "gradually build up their phonics skills via invented spelling." She compares invented spellings to children's early stick figure drawings. The drawings, she states,

> are not interpreted as signs of . . . problems. They are greeted as a display of intelligence and emerging proficiency. . . . Readiness workbooks place several children in the position of studying all the sounds . . . [and since] we score them for correctness, [this] implies that a child is wrong if he [she] is still in the process of learning something.

Parents, especially, worry when their children bring home creatively spelled sentences and stories instead of a spelling list of words to memorize. One teacher turns parents' keen interest in spelling to her advantage. She uses her students' writing in invented spelling as a diagnostic tool, and she lets parents in on the process. (*Instructor,* May/June 1995). For example, after reading this sentence with a parent in September, she shared that Jenny, her daughter, knew:

I CAN ROL BLAD *

* I can rollerblade.

(3) See an example reading readiness inventory in Appendix B.

(4) For a Scope and Sequence Chart of the Phonics Strand of the 1990 Scott Foresman Reading Series, see Appendix B. Study the chart to note the progression of teaching sound-symbol relationships. Not all basals use the same sequence, but the phonics progression is quite similar.

- Text goes from left to right.
- A story has a sequence.
- Considerable letter/sound correspondence occurred in just one sentence.
- Jenny is ready to learn her lower-case letters and is ready to learn to read.

The purpose of invented spellings in the beginning reading stages is to let children do lots of writing. You, as a teacher, will have to consider the guidelines of your particular school system and your own philosophy in this regard. While it may be acceptable in the beginning stages of reading, most school systems take a more traditional approach to spelling accuracy as children enter a more formal reading stage.

Later in this chapter, a section on spelling and its relationship to word recognition skills further expands this brief introduction.

## Beginning Handwriting

The handwriting examples I have seen in my own classrooms and in those I have visited give rise for concern. While handwriting is fast becoming a lost art, given the computer age, *writing reinforces reading;* therefore, the ability to form letters correctly should be taught. Children whose writing is not legible often find it difficult to read their *own* handwriting, leading to their frustration and to a distaste for the reading/writing process. Although it is often difficult, after students are beyond the primary grades, to teach important skills such as holding a pencil properly, slanting the paper correctly, and forming letters accurately, it can be done! Share this information with your students. To write properly:

1. Sit up straight, hips against the back of the chair, and lean forward a little.
2. Slant the paper so that your writing arm and the side of the paper are parallel.
3. Hold the pencil between the thumb and third finger with the index finger on top. Fingers should be rounded, not stiff.
4. Hold the paper with the nonwriting hand.
5. The pencil should lie against the index finger just above the knuckle and point over the shoulder.

Handwriting programs vary, but this skill needs to be monitored not only in early writing, but throughout the elementary grades. Check the students' writing positions (see Figure 2.1) and letter formations, and remind them of the proper method when in error. The program you use will suggest what to say if you initially teach how to form the letters (see Figure 2.2). As a teacher, your own handwriting should be exemplary and serve as a model. I have had many student teachers tell me they could not possibly improve their own handwriting, and yet with board practice for only 15 minutes, there was always considerable improvement. Since the pre-service teachers had to write reasonably well on the board in order to pass my reading courses, improvement in their handwriting always took place rapidly!

Students need to know how to form lower-case letters correctly. These manuscript letters begin with a circle or circle part: a, c, d, f, g, o, qu, and s. These letters begin with a line: b, e, h, i, j, k, l, m, n, p, r, t, u, v, w, x y, z. Students also need to know how to form all the capital letters correctly. When cursive writing is taught in the second and third grades, they will need to know how to form these letters correctly. See the models in Figure 2.3.

**FIGURE 2.1**   Handwriting positions.

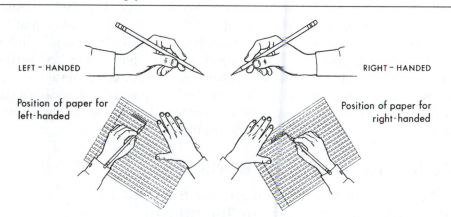

From R. B. Spalding, *The Writing Road to Reading,* Wm. Morrow, N.Y. Reprinted with permission.

**FIGURE 2.2**   Manuscript letters (lowercase).

From Mary Minor Johnston, Senior Author, *Total Reading.* © 1995. P. O. Box 54465, Los Angeles, CA. Reprinted with permission.

**FIGURE 2.3**   Lowercase and capital cursive letters.

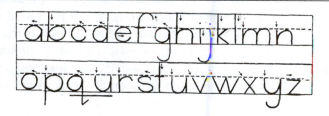

From *The Laubach Way to Cursive Writing,* 1983, New Readers Press, Publishing Division of Laubach Literacy International, used by permission.

Left-handed children need special attention. The side of the paper must be parallel to their left-handed writing arm so that their paper is placed opposite of that for right-handed children. A strip of scotch tape pasted near the top of their desks can show the slanting direction. The top of the paper of left-handed children should parallel the scotch tape; this will prevent them from turning their papers to look like that of right-handed students. Their writing hand should always be below the base line, and the letters can be formed straight up and down *without* a slant. Usually, an extended forward slant for a left-handed writer forces the hand into an awkward hooked position and should be avoided.

## BEGINNING TO TEACH PHONICS

### A Teacher-Directed Procedure for Introducing a Beginning Sound-Symbol Relationship

Beginning readers usually rely heavily on phonics clues to identify words because of a limited ability to use context. How are these beginning sound-symbol relationships introduced in the school instructional program?

In general each phoneme (sound) and its related symbol (letter/s) are introduced within the context of familiar short words. When the sound introduced is the first sound in the word, it is easier to hear. (Most difficult is the medial position.) Some instruction proceeds from identification of beginning sounds in words, to ending sounds, and last to medial sounds. Because some programs are concerned with directionality, they teach the sounds in order such as *b, e, d, bed.*

#### A strategy to teach beginning sound-symbol relationships

1. Students identify the capital and small letter that encode a particular sound, presented by the teacher in a novel way that emphasizes the relationship (step 1).
2. Students next select words containing the specific sound from words containing related sounds. Students suggest words with the specific sound (step 2).
3. Students write the capital and lowercase letters that represent the specific sound (step 3).
4. Students participate in purposeful activities applying the knowledge of the relationship between the letter and sound (step 4).

***Step 1.***    The teacher begins by having an activity in which students identify the sound-symbol under consideration such as *l* /l/. For example, s/he might ask them to watch his/her mouth because s/he is going to look like a singer. (Teacher sings the words *let, like, love, lend,* and *land,* exaggerating the /l/). At the same time s/he writes these words on the board, making one word a short sentence as *Let me go* to use a capital letter. (The words are written on the board so the written word will emphasize the symbol associated with the sound.)

***Step 2.***    The teacher helps students notice how they open their mouths when they say this sound at the *beginning* of words. Then s/he has them identify from words s/he says those that begin with /l/, such as *lion, lazy, maze, left, Brian, lift.* Sometimes pictures with distractors are used, such as a picture of a lamp, a pencil, a lightbulb, a crayon, or a lemon. The teacher helps students think of words beginning with /l/ by asking riddles such as "What can you draw with a ruler?" (line).

***Step 3.*** Prior to writing them without a clue students often trace the letter over dotted lines, with arrows indicating the direction of each stroke. This is so the lines and circles they make are drawn from left to right, or in the same direction as they read.

***Step 4.*** The teacher passes out "little lollipops" for them to "lick," and enjoy. Students are to find and think of other words beginning with /l/. Meanwhile, words used by the teacher and students throughout the day that emphasize the /l/ sound are written on a list and displayed. Children may write a simple sentence such as "I love. . ." and take their choice of words from those they may know, illustrate the word, or use one supplied by the teacher.

## Beginning Reading Workbook Activities

Workbook activities and handouts proliferate in these beginning reading stages. Some of the more common types of these activities follow (remember to use only as needed):

1. Circling the letter/word that is the same.

| m | | m | w | m | n |
|---|---|---|---|---|---|

| and | | ran | and | and |
|---|---|---|---|---|

| N | | N | M | N | W |
|---|---|---|---|---|---|

| Nan | | Nat | Nan | Nan |
|---|---|---|---|---|

2. Using rebus forms so children "read" more elaborate sentences.

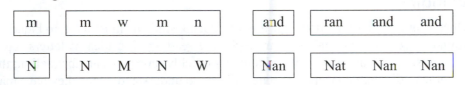

The ⬭ was big.    The 🐰 sat on the mat.

3. Circling those pictures on a page whose name begins with the phoneme under study.

M

4. Circling the correct word on a handout from a matching list read by the teacher.

sun        run        fun

5. Using puzzle sentences such as:

Which can you sit on, a tap or a lap?

What keeps you cool, a fan or a pen?

6. Filling in the correct letter of the word that names the picture.

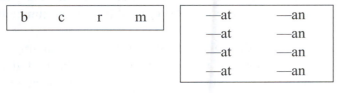

(c)up            (b)at            (h)en

7. Making words grow by adding the appropriate letter.

| b | c | r | m |
|---|---|---|---|

| —at | —an |
|---|---|
| —at | —an |
| —at | —an |
| —at | —an |

8. Supplying the right word in the blank.

*cake     cane     race*

The man ran the —————————.

In most basal programs, the first words children learn to read usually contain regular grapheme-phoneme correspondences or occur in children's classroom materials written by adults. Studies, however, indicate that when children are asked what words they want to learn to read, the words are much more imagery-loaded than some of the early basal ones (Hiebert, 1983). In Ashton-Warner's (1963) classic studies, typical "reading" words selected by children included *pizza, frisbee, Frankenstein, valentine, gorilla, kiss,* and *Star Wars.*

While we would not advocate a haphazard approach in teaching decoding strategies, it is nevertheless important to use some high interest vocabulary with personal meaningfulness to individual children so that reading can be viewed as purposeful and enjoyable.

## Blending

Once sound-symbol relationships are introduced, students must learn to blend the sounds together, a crucial stage in beginning reading. The idea of letters representing sounds that must be glided together quickly represents an abstraction; this becomes a difficult concept for some children to understand. Once they have mastered blending together a few sound-symbol relationships and can apply the principle, they progress far more rapidly.

Rosenshine and Stevens (1984) found that time spent in blending activities at the first and second grades resulted in higher scores on achievement tests. The Commission on Reading's report (1985) corroborates this: "Teachers who spend more than average amounts of time on blending produce larger than average gains on reading achievement tests."

A major disagreement exists in the area of blending as to the presentation of the combined sounds that make up words. Many reading educators feel that sounds must never be presented in isolation; that is, to have the teacher say /c-c-c-a-a-a-t-t-t/ and then blend this to *cat* is tantamount to dooming children to lifelong remediation! They feel that children will blend combinations together by noting when words begin and end the same and noting that a one-letter change in a word makes a different word.

Part of this blending controversy comes from particular consonant phonemes known as "stops," /p/ /b/ /t/ /d/ /k/ /g/ /ch/ and /j/, that cannot be said in isolation. An /uh/ sound always follows when saying these sounds alone. They argue that children would sound a word such as ball as /b-u-all/ and that blending isolated phonemes distorts the true sound of the word.

Other educators argue that this is the only way some children will learn to read new words in the early stages; that is, the teacher saying the sounds in isolation as /c-c-c-a-a-a-t-t-t/, then blending them together, and showing students the combinations that "make" such a word. After sounding the isolated phonemes, teachers have students say them faster and faster until they approximate the spoken word.

Some educators adopt a middle-of-the-road attitude about blending and suggest a procedure such as follows: With the word mat, they have students pronounce the vowel sound alone /a/; add the consonant sound /m/, blended together as /ma/; and then add the /t/ to form /mat/. Others suggest that when blending, students identify the ending sounds /at/ first, and then add the /m/ to form /mat/. In these latter methods the movement is from right to left and can interfere with directional eye sweep, since reading is from left to right. Nevertheless, these methods are still used quite successfully, as are the two blending methods previously mentioned.

A method that differs from all of those just mentioned introduces the abstraction of blending by combining compound word parts. Children are shown parts of compound words such as *base* and *ball, side* and *walk*. They are asked to blend the two parts together to form the words *baseball* and *sidewalk*. Many other compound word parts are used to encourage understanding of the blending concept.

A motivating blending game is "What is it?" The teacher shares with the class that she is thinking of an insect. (Use any category, even correlating with a current unit.) The teacher gives a clue—the separate sounds in the word. For example, for *ant,* she tells the class that the insect is an "/a/-/n/-/t/," articulating each of the sounds separately. Children then must blend the sounds together to discover the insect the teacher is thinking about.

To increase motivation, use picture cards and face them away from the children. Give the segmented clues, then turn the picture around once the children have guessed. Or use a toy box or grab bag, peeking inside and saying, "I see a toy /p/-/l/-/ā/-/n/ in here. Who knows what I see?"

A summary of ways to blend sounds follows:

1. No sounds are isolated. Children reason that changing one phoneme changes the word. *Mat* becomes *sat.*
2. Individual phonemes are pronounced, then blended together. Teacher pronounces each phoneme separately as m-m-m-a-a-a-t-t-t, repeating the sounds faster and faster until they approximate the word.
3. The vowel is pronounced first, followed by the first consonant sound, then the final sound.

    ă        mă        mat

4. The ending phonogram is pronounced first, then the beginning consonant sound.

    ăt        mat

5. Compound words are broken into their respective parts and blended together.

As with other reading issues, this one is far from settled. Children can profit from some formal instruction in blending—the method used is not as important as the children's ability to apply the skill to new vocabulary. To teach initial consonant blending, teachers can use common household products, such as *Sc*ope, *Gl*ad, and *Pr*ide, and cereal boxes, such as *Fr*uit Loops and *Fr*osted *Fl*akes. (See also Eeds-Kneip, 1981.)

## Problems with Vowel Sounds

Vowels cause many problems. The following suggestion may help minimize some of them. Use a mirror to reinforce the sounds under study as students produce the sounds and watch the shape of their own mouths in the mirror. The visual sensation, plus the kinesthetic sensation—how the mouth, tongue, and cheeks feel while creating the sounds—help to underscore the differences. Instead of a mirror, students may place their hands on their mouths to sense the difference as they pronounce the sounds.

Many vowels become more distinguishable through this visual or kinesthetic system. Long /ō/, /o͞o/, /ī/, /ē/, and /ā/ differ greatly in the mirror. Diphthongs *oi* and *ou* differ from each other and from other sounds because visually the mouth changes shape during production. The visual distinction among short vowels is slight but the tongue and teeth position can be of help in discrimination (Ahmann, 1982).

Following is a typical lesson in the review of short vowel sounds.

### A teacher-directed lesson in reviewing the short vowel sounds

An excellent way to review short vowels is through the use of familiar names (and shortened names such as M*a*tt or P*a*t, P*e*g or M*e*g, L*i*l or W*i*ll, B*o*b or T*o*dd, and R*u*ss or G*u*s), in rhyming sentences such as those below. First, volunteers read the names (they have been written on the board) and either the teacher or child underlines the vowel to be sounded. The teacher points again to the underlined letter and repeats the sound.

Teacher: These letters stand for the short vowel sound in these names. Let's practice listening for these short vowel sounds. I'll say the words, and you can echo them back to me.

Use rhythmical speech (some teachers use a "rap" style) or any "tune" with which you are comfortable.

Teacher: Matt, Matt, Matt, lost his hat, hat, hat. (Emphasize the words with the short /ā/ sound.)

Students repeat the sound. The teacher continues with other sounds and sentences:

Teacher: Peg, Peg, Peg hurt her leg, leg, leg. Lil, Lil, Lil saw the hill, hill, hill.

Follow-up may include having a volunteer recall the word that rhymed with a name and then having the teacher or student write that word under the appropriate name. Some of the more advanced students might erase a beginning consonant and substitute another to make a new word appearing in the text just read or to be read. For example, removing *h* from hill and supplying the letters *m, p, s,* and *d* would lead to the words *mill, pill, sill,* and *dill.* You may ask students to infer and state the generalization based on the lesson that "a vowel letter between two consonants often has a short sound" or state the generalization yourself before further application in reading or reviewing part of a story.

### Explicit (Synthetic), Implicit (Analytic), and Linguistic Phonics: Different Teaching Approaches

When working with sound-symbol relationships or new vocabulary, the teacher may follow one of three procedures: (1) guiding the lesson so she *tells* the sound-symbol relationships, and students memorize certain rules (explicit phonics); (2) guiding the lesson so students conclude what the sound-symbol relationship is after studying particular known words (implicit phonics); or (3) presenting words with regular spelling patterns such as *man, tan, fan, ran, can* (linguistic phonics).

Critics of the explicit approach cite the following:

1. Students rely on the letter-sound relationships too much, paying no attention to context and meaning; hence, the term *code-emphasis.*

2. Memorizing rules does not mean they will be applied.

3. Many readers discover the rules and relationships themselves, and class instruction with these rules and sounds can be wasteful.

4. Prolonged work with phonics diverts students from getting meaning.

Advocates of the explicit approach are adamant that:

1. Children see very early that there is a relationship between letters and sounds, and quickly decode words instead of depending on surrounding context.

2. Children become independent readers, decoding many difficult words on their own and taking great pride in doing so.

3. Beginning readers can attend to meaning since they are not frustrated by unknown words.

4. The method systematizes and teaches the needed sound-symbol relationships.

Therefore, advocates' basic argument is that the explicit approach—structured, sequential, and comprehensive—will eliminate the student's foundering with unknown words and will therefore actually enhance meaning. They believe their approach not only helps to break the code, but also ensures that meaning (comprehension) will take place.

Like the explicit approach, the implicit approach also has a great deal of variety, but usually begins with words students are familiar with at sight. Sometimes consonant sounds are identified first in these words and then the vowel sounds. Often, there is a combination approach. Note is made of parts of words that are similar and parts that are different. Then a phonics analysis (hence the term *analytic*) of the words may be made, and phonics principles deduced. A point of difference exists even among those favoring the implicit approach; that is, whether it should be systematic or incidental. Advocates of the latter argue that since there is not agreement as to the order in which the elements should be taught, instruction with phonics should take place only when the need arises and be strictly incidental. It should be obvious, however, that the explicit approach would be favored by traditional teachers, and whole language teachers would prefer an implicit approach.

Following are two example lessons for students in perhaps a third-grade reader that help to clarify some of the stated differences in the two approaches. In actual practice, they do not have to be, nor are they, mutually exclusive.

## The explicit approach

Teacher: Today, we are going to learn about a new letter combination (teacher holds up a card with *ph* printed on it). This letter combination is *ph* and it stands for the sound of /f/. Here are three words you have probably seen with this combination: *Phil, telephone,* and *graph.* (Teacher writes them on the board or has them on transparencies.) Note that this combination may come at the beginning (points to *Phil*); middle (points to *telephone*); or end of the word (points to *graph*). (Teacher stresses the /f/ sound in the words.) (With slower children the teacher might want to show only the combination in the initial position.)

Students: (Teacher calls on different students to read the three words.)

Teacher: I have another group of words here. (Words are as follows.)

| | |
|---|---|
| dolphin | elephant |
| phonograph | Daphne |
| photograph | pictograph |

Will someone underline in each word the two-letter combination that stands for the /f/ sound?

Students: (One or more may underline the *ph* combination.)

Teacher: Let's read these words together, and then see if there are any that you want to talk about. (Continues.) Who thinks they know what a *pictograph* is? (Discusses the word, parts, and the word's meaning and that the word refers to picture writing used in some countries.) Let's try these words in sentences to make certain they are in your meaning vocabulary.

Students: (Offer sentences using the words.)

Teacher: (May call attention for review to other known phonics elements.) What three words do you notice with the *gr* blend? (Continues.) Let's compare these words (points to words on the board) with words that have the consonant *p* alone. Let's read these words. (Stresses the difference between the two sounds as follows:)

| | |
|---|---|
| *p*ill | *Ph*il |
| *p*ant | *ph*antom |
| *p*easant | *ph*easant |

(If necessary, the teacher might decide to review the *ea* digraph as in p*ea*sant and ph*ea*sant.)

Students: (Read words and place them in sentences orally.)

Teacher: On a piece of paper number from 1 to 12. I will read several words to you, all beginning with the letter *p*. You know some of these words from previous lessons. Tell me whether the first sound should be written as just *p* or as *ph*. (Reads *pantry, posture, phonograph, phase, protest, phantom, photograph.*) (Continues discussing words and sounds, assigning some follow-up work if needed.)

### The implicit approach

Teacher: I noticed yesterday we had some difficulty reading words with the letter combination *ch*.[5] One of the words is in this sentence: *The scheme failed, and they left.* (The sentence should not be read but may be either on the board or on a transparency.) Before we look at the sentence, let's look at these words that you do know. Teacher reads *chair, inches, beach,* emphasizing the known sound of /ch/.

Teacher: (Continues) What sound does the *ch* stand for in these three words?

Jane: The sound of /ch/.

Teacher: Good. Give me some examples of other words with this sound.

Tim: *Chip, champ*

Mary: *Attach*

Teacher: Good. (Teacher writes next to the original three words /ch/ to show the sound and at the same time underlines each one of the *ch* combinations:

(5) As mentioned, some teachers tell children that the *ch* is a digraph, while others never use any terminology. Again, always think in terms of your students and their ability.

THE ROLE OF PHONICS IN WORD RECOGNITION

| | |
|---|---|
| *ch*air | /ch/ |
| in*ch*es | /ch/ |
| bea*ch* | /ch/ |

Now, we'll read some other words that also have the letter combination *ch*, but in these words notice something different about the sound that *ch* stands for. (With brighter students, one of them may know the words and can read them.) (On the board or on a transparency the teacher displays another group of words:)

*ch*aracter        a*ch*e        stoma*ch*

What sound do you hear as we read these words together?

John: Is it the /k/ sound?

Teacher: That's right. Will you read the words for us again? (S/he may do this several times to enforce the concept.)

Teacher: Who wants to try to read the sentence on the board now? The word we had trouble with was this one. (She points to the word *scheme*.)

Sue: *Their scheme failed, and they left.*

Teacher: Right. What other word can you think of? It's a holiday, and it contains a *ch* that stands for the /k/ sound.

All: Christmas!

Teacher: Right. Where do you go every day to learn?

Students: School!

Teacher: Right. Most of the words with *ch* that stands for the /k/ sound come to us from the Greek language. Therefore, when we have such a word we know it is of Greek origin. Let's look at this exercise, and use our dictionaries if we need to, and try to find the *ch* word with the /k/ sound that could complete each sentence.

The ——————————— on the car has rusted. (chrome)

I like the ——————————— holiday. (Christmas)

The children sang in the ——————————— (chorus)

(Always apply what has just been learned.)

## Linguistic phonics

Some educators consider the linguistic approach to teaching reading to be language experience, while others consider the linguistic approach to be patterned phonics. Since some of the terms in the field of reading are not standardized, these differences in interpretation persist. The more traditional interpretation of the term "linguistic phonics" is the language experience approach. Here, students either dictate stories to the instructor or write simple stories themselves, and based on these, the teacher may choose to give instruction in letter-sound relationships, or phonics.

Other educators consider linguistic phonics in early reading to be a highly structured patterned approach. This is primarily because research by linguists has shown that certain patterns in English appear with greater frequency. Basal readers that employ this method of teaching word recognition skills use a tightly controlled and systematic method of introducing phonics patterns and emphasis is placed on the recognition of minimal differences in words that follow similar patterns, such as *mat-met, rang-rung,* and *pat-bet.* Beginning readers read sentences such as *Dan ran* to the *tan van.* Three popular linguistic readers include the *Let's Read Series,* the *Palo Alto Reading Series,* and *SRA.*\* A basic criticism of this approach is that linguistic readers use a stilted, unnatural language because of the tight control of phonics patterns. In speech a variety of sentence patterns are used, and if reading is "talk written down," then controlling the pattern creates an artificial language. Nevertheless, some teachers are quite successful in using these linguistic readers, especially with students who seem unable to learn to decode in other ways.

## Classroom Programs

We have noted that teaching phonics can be done explicitly (directly taught); implicitly (letting students discover relationships); or linguistically, using a patterned approach. The classroom teacher might use one of these methods or a combination of methods in any of the following classroom programs.

1. A program that uses a basal reading series as the core curriculum. Most basal series have a built-in decoding strand. (See Appendix B, pp. 170–172 for an example.)
2. A balanced whole language program using children's literature as the core curriculum. Many of the word recognition skills are developed through language activities. There may or may not be a sequential decoding strand.
3. A commercial reading program with its own materials, trade books, and literature, with an intensive phonics program.

### The basal text

Before proceeding with further examples, we need to clarify the present controversy over the use of the basal text in the classroom. Many proponents of the whole language approach do not use a basal because they believe it is too structured, has too many worthless activities, and does not meet the needs of students (Goodman, et al., 1988). They believe state adoptions are part of the problem and "preclude teachers from using other materials . . . few districts are willing to forgo state textbook funds. . . . In most classrooms, the instruction will be driven by a basal reading program" (p. 31). Farr, Tully, and Powell (1987) state, "In most cases the selection of a basal is tantamount to selecting the reading curriculum" (p. 268). Criticisms of the basal are many—the language is synthetic; they only test and teach; the tests are flawed; and use leads to passive students.

In contrast, support for the *wise* use of basals comes from McCallum (1988):

1. Basals have changed over time and translate research into practice.
2. Basals provide on-the-job training for reading teachers.
3. Basals provide a management system for coordinating reading instruction. Good teachers are good managers.
4. The majority of reading teachers do not have the time, energy, or expertise to develop the materials and activities required to meet the goals of instruction.

Today, basals are different, and many reflect research that shows an advantage to an early literature-based reading curriculum with meaningful reading and

---

\* Linguistic Reader Publishers: 1. Clarence L. Barnhart, Inc., Box 250, Bronxville, NY 10016; 2. Harcourt Brace Jovanovich, 757 Third Avenue, New York, NY 10017; 3. SRA Science Research Associates, Inc., 259 East Erie Street, Chicago, IL 60611.

writing language activities. At the same time, a structured sequential decoding system is still an important part of most of these readers.

See Figure 2.4 for a typical basal lesson on decoding for use in the second grade. The basal, of course, includes many stories for practice reading, comprehension questions, and suggestions for creative activities.

**FIGURE 2.4**   Basal lesson on decoding.

| INTRODUCE | Decoding: vowel digraphs |
|---|---|

**Introduce the concept of vowel digraphs**

**1** **LINK**  Write **paint** on the chalkboard. Say:

1. This is a word from the story "Look Out!" What is the word?
2. Look at the word. How many vowels do you see? (Underline **ai**.)
3. Say the word. How many vowel sounds do you hear? (1)

Conclude with children that sometimes two vowels stand for one vowel sound.

**Introduce new vowel digraph ai (tr<u>ai</u>n)**

**2** **LEARN**  Display this Picture Word card: train

Name the picture and read the word with children. Write **train** on the chalkboard under **paint**. Ask children:

1. What letters are the same? (ai)
2. Say the words. What sounds are the same? (vowel sound)
3. What do you call the sound that ai stands for in paint and train? (long **a** vowel sound)

Conclude with children that **ai** stands for the long **a** vowel sound in these words.

**Read more words with vowel digraph ai (tr<u>ai</u>n)**

Ask children to find out whether **ai** stands for the long **a** vowel sound in these words

rain      rail      pail      paid

**Introduce new vowel digraph ai (pl<u>ay</u>)**

Display this Picture Word card: play

Name the picture and read the word with children. Ask children to listen to you say **train** and **play** and tell what they hear that is the same. (long **a** vowel sound) Conclude that **ay** and **ai** both stand for the long **a** vowel sound. Have children verify this by reading these new words. Underline **ay.**

pay      say      day

**Use words with vowel digraphs to answer questions**

**3** **GUIDED PRACTICE**  Write these words on the chalkboard:

maid     pay
jail     day
mail     stay

Read them with children. Tell children to find the word that answers your questions. As each answer is identified, have a child circle the letters that stand for the vowel sound.

1. I am a person who cleans houses. I rhyme with paid. Who am I? (maid)
2. I am where people are sent when they break the law. I rhyme with pail. What am I? (jail)
3. I am the opposite of night. What am I? (day)
4. I am what comes in an envelope with a stamp. I rhyme with sail. What am I? (mail)

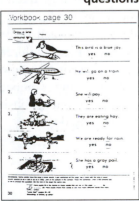

*(continued)*

**FIGURE 2.4** Continued.

5. I am what you do with money when you buy something. I rhyme with say. What am I? (pay)

6. I am the opposite of go. I rhyme with way. What am I? (stay)

**INDEPENDENT PRACTICE** Tell children that they will read more words with **ai** and **ay** on Workbook page 30. Go over the directions and the sample item with children before they complete the page independently.

Write rhyming words | **4** **APPLY** Review the word **play** and the vowel digraph **ay**. Give children the word part __ay and have them write other words that rhyme with play. (bay, clay, day, gray, hay, lay, may, pay, ray, say, slay, stay, tray, way)

D. C. Heath & Co. 1996: "Cats Sleep Anywhere"; "Look Out."

## Whole Language and the Decoding Skills Approach

How would teaching decoding skills vary from the whole language approach? In practical terms, Mills, O'Keefe, and Stephens (1992) cite the differences. Whole language teachers begin with words very familiar to students, such as the names of their classmates. Children are encouraged to note similarities and differences. For example, teachers encourage children when the children point out that *Sally* and *Sara* have common letters and sounds and with teacher support draw generalizations from these similarities. Children may detect other patterns, such as noting that Ray, a classmate, has his name embedded in the word c*ray*on. Jenny may call attention to the fact that Cheryl and Sherri's names sound alike at the beginning yet are written differently. Students call attention to exceptions in the written language such as when the final *e* has no sound. Student names written on a large chart every day may become a book used for reading. Whole language teachers believe children refine and expand their understanding of sound-symbol relationships while using language to communicate. Therefore, there would be continuous oral exchanges, classroom writing, and book making, with teacher assistance where needed. For example, daily messages written on paper are bound and become a classroom book. Sentences that students write daily, adding to the message, are bound and form a book. Much journal writing and sharing takes place. Surveys are conducted by children in areas such as sports. This would be followed by writing and publishing the results.

In the whole language approach, children share their knowledge of reading and writing with classmates in a much freer environment than in a traditional classroom. Unlike some of the more structured classroom environments, whole language classrooms encourage children to collaborate and ask each other for comments, corrections, and assistance during their writing activities. Children are encouraged to use multiple cue systems when reading, to do a lot of predicting from context. The whole language philosophy is simply that learning is embedded within authentic literacy events, with children writing, editing, and publishing, and developing important understandings about language as they do so.

Comments such as the following are common.

Sally made this observation about the word _____.

David used this strategy to figure out what this word says. David, share your strategy.

Tom, look how closely you have spelled the word. All you need to do is place an *e* at the end of the word. Let's look for words that might have a silent *e* in your story.

The classroom environment might look different (*Instructor* 1992). Since the teaching is more child-centered than teacher-directed, you may find pointers for children to use to underscore words when they read and recite. (Drumsticks from the music department work very well.) You might find an "author's chair" for the author of the week or a camera to take photographs of classroom happenings that will be springboards for writing projects. You may wish to use lots of individual chalkboards for creative play, such as taking pretend restaurant orders and creating labels for block structures.

Below are examples of the types of activities found in many whole language classrooms. Their purpose is to develop within children a greater facility with language. This facility will enable them to develop word recognition skills that lead to better reading and writing. As mentioned previously, there is nothing exclusionary about any of these activities. Some of them may be employed in traditional classrooms. However, it must always be remembered that fluent reading comes about only as a result of much reading, when words are part of a large and growing *sight* vocabulary. Those who advocate a strong phonetic approach believe children master what they need more easily by being shown directly what sounds are encoded by which letters or letter combinations. Others believe that children are not ready for the abstractions represented by letters and the English encoding system.

## Activities Used in Whole Language Classrooms to Develop Language Facility

### Building word recognition

*AD WORDS:*   Students bring in examples of words from common advertisements, such as Brillo, Dove, Jello, and Cheerios. These words may be used in many ways, such as on bulletin boards that are read in "ad" scrapbooks or in the game simple lotto. (Simple lotto is played much like bingo. In this game, words are used instead of numbers. Students write their ad words on a "lotto card" similar to a bingo card and provided by the teacher. Each student card will be different as children place the words in different boxes. The ad words are called out and the first one who covers a line of words wins).

*CLASS CALENDAR:*   Use a large poster calendar and calendar cutouts. Each month, have a theme for words—science words, clothing words, election words, words from a familiar story. Write one word on a calendar cutout. Each day, place new words on the calendar. Discuss words as to their definition, spelling, and structure. Review past words by methods such as every other word, words beginning with "s," all the Sunday words, etc.

### Games

*NAMING THE ALPHABET:*   On a bulletin board close to a door, randomly place letters of the alphabet. As students line up, they have an airline checkout. They name the letters randomly placed on the board. There are many variations of this activity, such as selecting a category such as food. Each student in line must, according to the alphabet, name a food: apple, banana, cider, etc.

*POEMS AND SONG AND SHARING:*
Echo Chant: Students echo the teacher line by line.
Alternate: Teacher and students alternate lines.
Dramatize: Students dramatize certain parts.

*RING AROUND THE ROOM:*   Children take turns reading everything around the room. Teachers can bring in different items and label them for this activity. A useful activity for beginning readers.

*WORD GROUPS:*   Teacher and students decide on several categories, such as sports, travel, health, animals. Students find one word for each category. Words are written and placed in bags if children are young. Older children can sort and categorize the words, placing them in the appropriate bags.

## Writing/publishing

*BOOKMAKING:   Alphabet Books.* Younger children collect words beginning with each successive letter of the alphabet, and the class makes an alphabet book. Older children brainstorm interesting words beginning with a particular letter and then try to write an alliterative sentence that uses many of the words. For example, they can use a model, *Aster Aardvark's Alphabet Adventures* by Steven Kellog.

A class Tooth Book helps children celebrate the loss of baby teeth and their emerging writing skills. A tooth-shaped book is prepared complete with laminated oaktag covers and blank pages bound with loose-leaf rings to add extra pages as needed. Students record their tales of tooth loss and share their tooth tales with the class.

Create childrens' favorite characters in their Monster Books. Use the classic *Where the Wild Things Are* by Maurice Sendak for motivation. Discuss that while monsters are not real, they can be made happy, sad, funny, scary, big, little, fat, tall, or short. Using paper and crayons, the children create their monster pictures. Have each child dictate something about their monster or write something about the monster. Assemble the book and have one student design a cover. Discuss the dedication page and the author page, which should include the names of all the children in the class.

Use the books *Grandmother and I* and *Grandfather and I* by Helen E. Buckley to motivate the children to write their own Grandparent Books. This type of book may be integrated with social studies, as many grandparents live in other cities and states.

*DOUBLE ENTRY JOURNALS:*   Students copy a sentence from a book on one side of the page and mark the page number. On the other side, they react to the sentence. For example on one side they might have a sentence such as, "The lion made a terrible noise." They might write about a terrible noise that frightened them.

*KNOW THE AUTHORS:*   Organize a center with one author or a group of authors. Students make oral and written responses to these authors. Try to arrange for local authors to come to the classroom.

*LETTER LIT:*   Divide the class in two. Have one side write a letter as if they were a character in a book. Have the other half of the class answer the letter. Share in class.

*LITERARY YEARBOOK:*   Bring in actual yearbooks for children to look through. As a class make a list of some of the features of a yearbook: clubs, superlatives,

**FIGURE 2.5**  Vowel Code Chart

VOWEL CODE

| | |
|---|---|
| a | ăt |
| a | bā by |
| a | fä ther |
| e | ĕn ter |
| e | wē |
| i | ĭn |
| i | fī nal |
| o | nŏt |
| o | sō |
| o | tö |
| u | ŭp |
| u | ūse |
| u | püsh |

From Mary Minor Johnston, Senior Author. *Total Reading*. © 1995. P. O. Box 54465. Los Angeles, CA 90054–0465. Reprinted with permission.

honors, and individual class photos. Then spend some time listing and briefly discussing the books your class read together this year, or books they've read outside of class and shared. Part of the class yearbook will be the names of the special books they have read or heard, with written comments about each one.

*MINI LIBRARY:*   Children have their own book carrier, a box containing the books they are reading, books they have written, books they will publish, and word collections.

## Commercial reading programs

Among many commercial reading programs that may be used, *Total Reading** is a program that incorporates many whole language features while maintaining an intensive decoding strand. There is emphasis on written and oral creativity with trade books and children's literature representing the core reading material. *Total Reading* can be a complete language arts program for students in primary grades and for those who have not mastered decoding skills in upper elementary and junior high. The decoding approach is multisensory and includes reading, writing, spelling, and speaking. Each step is preceded by oral readiness, with strong vocabulary growth. Reading is individualized.

The decoding system is one of intensive phonics so that within the first four weeks of school, children learn to write and say the sounds of all the single letters. They are then introduced to the vowel chart in Figure 2.5.

Knowledge of just single letters and the vowel sounds enables students to write and decode hundreds of words. A structured dictation method is used to teach students how to read, write, and encode words. Much writing is done, first

* Mary Minor Johnson, Senior Author. *Total Reading*. P. O. BOX 54465. Los Angeles, CA 90054–0465. 1995.

with words, then sentences and stories. Stories are removed from workbooks, colored with crayons, and taken home to read to parents, whose support is an integral part of the program. All spelling is corrected, and the final writing paper must be accurate. Figure 2.6 below is a typical lesson in decoding that would be used at the end of the first grade.

Much preparation precedes dictation and writing. Despite a major difference in how decoding and spelling are taught, *Total Reading* and whole language have much in common. Children's literature forms the core of the reading material. There are provisions for individualized reading, vocabulary development, poetry reading, and writing of poetry and stories. There is integration with social studies and science. The major difference with *Total Reading* is that vocabulary, decoding, and spelling are directly taught. High standards in both writing and spelling are expected from the students, even in the early grades.

## When the Decoding Process Breaks Down

Regardless of which reading approach you use, you will find that the development of some students' decoding skills is not progressing the way it should. Our goal must be for the students to develop independent word recognition skills. A consideration, therefore, is whether students already have the skill or lack it at the text reading level, the word level, or discrimination level (Wisconsin Department of Public Instruction, 1985).

- *Text reading level.* Student's oral reading gives the clues. If the student cannot use the skill at this level, check the skill at the Word Level.
- *Word level.* This can be observed quickly in oral reading or determined from a worksheet. If the student understands the skill at the word level, but fails to use it while reading, s/he needs help in *applying* the skill. Suggest (a) reading the rest of the sentence, (b) looking at the elements or parts of the word, (c) using the skill to see if the word as decoded makes sense.
- *Discrimination level.* If the student cannot recognize and use the skill at the word level, check the discrimination level. Can the student visually identify the letters or spelling pattern of the word? If so, s/he can receive instruction at the word level. If not, begin with the discrimination level.

In other words, you want to see where the decoding process seems to break down for the student, and then take steps to address it.

## Alternate Methods

You may select any of the following methods when teaching word recognition skills or use some of them together. (Teachers provided very few explanations about skills and infrequently modeled or demonstrated them for students [Blanton and Moorman, 1990]). Although these methods are simplified here, more examples should be provided with frequent student responses and reinforcement. (We will use as an example the word *blaze.*)

### Model

Show how you, the teacher, would recognize the word.

Teacher: First, I note the initial consonant blend *bl* and know the vowel is long since the word ends in final *e*. Therefore, I know this word is *blaze.*

**FIGURE 2.6**   Lesson in decoding for first grade.

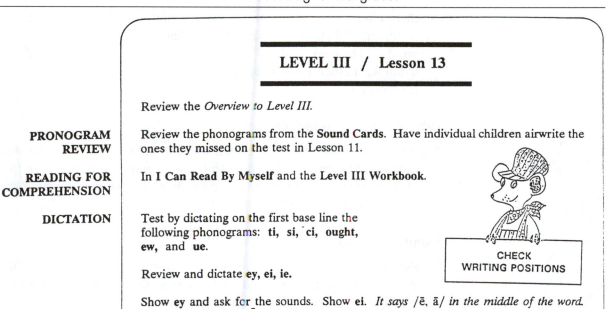

### LEVEL III  /  Lesson 13

Review the *Overview to Level III*.

**PRONOGRAM REVIEW**

Review the phonograms from the **Sound Cards**. Have individual children airwrite the ones they missed on the test in Lesson 11.

**READING FOR COMPREHENSION**

In **I Can Read By Myself** and the **Level III Workbook**.

**DICTATION**

Test by dictating on the first base line the following phonograms: **ti**, **si**, **´ci**, **ought**, **ew**, and **ue**.

Review and dictate **ey**, **ei**, **ie**.

CHECK WRITING POSITIONS

Show **ey** and ask for the sounds. Show **ei**. *It says /ē, ā/ in the middle of the word.* Show **ie**. *It says /ē, ī/ but it is spelled ie.* Teach the rule: i before e except after c and when it says ā. Illustrate the rule on the board. Write: *vein, ceil ing, bē lieve.* Point to the phonograms above. *After c do we use ei or ie?* Spell these phonograms rather than saying the sounds.

Dictation Words

| püt | each | sŏon | shōw | rē cēive | bē liēve | thēir | fiēld |
|-----|------|------|------|----------|----------|-------|-------|
|     |      |      |      | Rule #1a * | silent e 2 * | * | * |

\* Special Comments:

| receive | After the **c** do we use **ei** or **ie**? |
| believe | Do we use **ei** or **ie**? |
| their | Listen to the sound /ā/. Do we use **ei** or **ie**? |
| field | Do we use **ei** or **ie**? |

In each word ask whether we use **ei** or **ie** and why.  (Rule 11)

**CREATIVITY**

Make a new bulletin board display of the Final Copies of the sentences and illustrations. Choose a few to be read aloud by the authors.

POETRY APPRECIATION

Teach a *Level III* Poetry Appreciation Lesson with the Follow-up Activity for the Class Poetry Book.

**EASY TO READ LITERATURE**

See *Overview* and Mid-afternoon Schedule.

From Mary Minor Johnston, Senior Author, *Total Reading*. © 1995. P. O. Box 54465, Los Angeles, CA 90054–0465. Reprinted with permission.

### Rule approach

Teacher: Who can read these two words, *rat* and *rate?* Why are these two words different? (Show other examples.) What is the rule for final *e* in many words? (Then ask students to pronounce the words correctly and find other examples in their texts. They should read the words in meaningful phrases or sentences.)

### Whole word comparison

Teacher: Here are two words. (Teacher writes them: *glad blaze.* Direct students to note the difference in the blend and vowel sounds. You may wish to add the "rule approach" above also, and even "model" how you would discriminate among them with other examples.)

### Family method

Teacher: Let's examine these four words: *gaze, maze, daze,* and *blaze.* (Direct students to note the pattern and find others in their reading. In summary, you could, or have students, state the final *e* rule.)

At higher levels, you would also use affixes (discussed in the next section) as an approach to word recognition strategies.

## Teacher-Designed Materials

In addition to teacher instruction, discussion, and the student reading more extended language with these sound-symbol relationships (always the most important), there are many teacher-designed materials with phonics and many commercial materials used in teaching these skills.[6] A number of different formats are used, and variations of these formats make up the myriad number of activity books, workbooks, games, puzzles, and manipulatives that are used to extend and reinforce phonics principles. Following are listed some of these materials/activities in three broad categories. Because there is a good deal of overlapping and combining, the lists are somewhat arbitrary.

| Game Activities | Puzzle Activities | Manipulatives |
|---|---|---|
| Open gameboards | Matching shapes | Foldovers with answers |
| Filling the correct slot/cup/box, etc. | Concentration activities | Plastic pockets with inserts |
| Pinning/sticking/ taping on the correct response | Solving riddles Cards | Wheels with spinners or windows |
| Line/group games | Bingo variations | Tachistoscopes, single and double |
| | Domino variations | Flipbooks |
| | Solving anagrams/ crossword puzzles | |

Some abbreviated suggestions for carrying out these activities or for constructing these materials follow. They may often be extended to include more than one skill area. For example, instead of having an activity to identify just beginning consonants, the activity could be extended to include ending consonants,

(6) See Appendix E, p. 200 for an annotated list of commercial materials.

medial consonants, blends, digraphs, and vowels. Also these ideas should always be adapted to your own particular classroom situation and your own particular students.

## Game activities

1. *Objective: To identify lowercase and capital letters in various type sets.* Display a letter such as *b*. Have pupils look at it. Then remove. Ask them to search for the same letter in the room. When located, pupils stand by the letter and say, "I spy." After several turns, the original *b* is displayed. Students check to see if they are correct.

2. *Objective: To identify lowercase and capital letters rapidly.* Place particular review letters on a table in random order. Ask pupils to find a letter in response to verbal directions such as, "Find the capital *M*. Find the small *h*." Have pupils give the directions after a while.

3. *Objective: To identify beginning sound-symbol relationships.* Give pupils an index card. Have them write the letter name you are introducing or reviewing (both capital and lowercase) on one side. The other side is to be blank. Call out words. If the word begins with the letter on the card, pupils turn the card toward you with the letter displayed. If the called word does not begin with the letter, pupils display the other side. Variations include (a) having pupils clap hands softly if the word is correct, (b) pretending they are jack-in-the-boxes and jumping up if the word is correct, and (c) showing a smiling or an unhappy face. (A smiling face denotes the word is correct.)

4. *Objective: To build and expand vocabulary.* Set a timer. Students write as many rhyming words as they can from a given stimulus word. Starter words could be *man, pat,* or *tag.*

5. *Objective: Changing phonetic elements.*

    *came*    Add one letter and get a word for an animal.

    *close*    Add one letter at the end and get a word for a place for clothes.

    *flow*    Add two letters at the end and get something you put in a vase.

    *hear*    Add one letter at the end and get a part of your body.

    *plane*    Add one letter at the end and get another word for Mars.

    *tin*    Add one letter at the end and get a word that means "very small."

6. *Objective: Practice with any needed skill.* Teacher stands in the center of a circle. As the ball is bounced s/he says a word. The student who receives the ball must name the letter that begins the word, ends the word, is the vowel, or indicates the number of syllables, etc.

7. *Objective: Practice with digraphs.* Teacher or students construct "digraph-show" cards by dividing a paper square into four sections, labeling each with a particular digraph such as

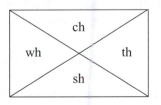

The teacher reads a word from a list. Each player holds up the card with the correct digraph at the top. Points are awarded for correct answers. (For slower children, use four separate cards.)

8. *Objective: Review and reinforcement of the magic* e. Cut 40 cards. On 20 of these write words such as *kit, pan,* and *shin* that change to other words with the addition of final *e.* On 10 cards write words that do not form a new word by adding *e,* such as *jam, stem,* and *slip.* On the remaining 10 cards write *magic e.* Place cards in a brown bag and shake. To play, each child draws a card and reads the word. When unable to read the word, it goes back into the bag. When a *magic e* card is drawn, it may be added to a word card to form a real word or saved to play later. Count each word/*magic e* combination as 5 points and other words as 1 point. *Magic e* by itself receives no points. Bags may be labeled and decorated.

## Puzzle activities

1. *Objective: Recognize letters of the alphabet.* Prepare an egg carton by writing a letter of the alphabet in each of the cups. The child places a marble or a penny in the carton, closes the lid, and shakes the carton. After opening the lid, the child names the letter upon which the marble or penny has landed.

2. *Objective: Recognize letters of the alphabet.* Pour glue on construction paper in the shape of a letter. Pour fruit gelatin over the glue. Shake to remove excess. When dry, have children touch and smell the letter. Proceed with other letters. When children know a certain number, have a "jello party."

3. *Objective: To identify beginning sounds of words.* Make a small chest from a box and cover it with paper. Place several items beginning with the same sounds, such as a nut, nail, necklace, nickel, and napkin, in the chest. Also include items such as a ring and a crayon. Pupils remove objects one at a time and tell whether or not they start with the /n/ sound.

4. *Objective: Recognize beginning sounds.* The Matched Pair Game: Use two colorful boxes. Select four to six pairs of familiar objects small enough so that one of each pair can be placed in a box. The names of these objects should begin with consonant sounds to which children have recently been introduced such as *m*ittens, *s*oap, *f*eathers, and *p*encils. Patterns and colors may differ. To play, have the group name the four or six kinds of objects, as one member of each pair is put into each bag. Select one child to be the Sounder and another the Matcher. The Sounder and the Matcher each receive one of the bags. The Sounder looks into the bag, reaches in, grasps one of the objects, keeping it hidden. S/he utters just the initial consonant sound of the object. The Matcher, having heard this initial sound, grasps the object that begins with the sound and lifts it into full view. The Sounder then raises into view the object s/he was holding for the dramatic test: Do the initial consonant sounds of the two objects match? Choose two other children to be the Sounder and the Matcher. (See Lewkowicz, 1994, for details.)

5. *Objective: Recognizing long and short vowel sounds.* Cover bulletin board with light-colored paper. Use thick felt-tipped pens to draw three or four short shelves on the left side of the paper and three or four longer shelves

on the right side. Students flip through old magazines cutting out pictures of objects whose names contain long or short vowel sounds. The pictures should be of items that would actually fit on a shelf. Then have the students paste their chosen objects on the appropriately labeled shelf (longer shelves are for long vowels and shorter shelves for short vowels). Print the name of each object by the picture.

6. *Objective: Adding consonants to make words.* Make four or five pictures of a clown carrying balloons. Print a common word part on each clown, such as *-ake, -et, -all.* Cut out colored circles the size of the balloon shapes; print a consonant on each. Students make words by combining the initial consonants on the balloons with the endings on the clowns.

7. *Objective: Practice in reading blends and digraphs.* Make flowers for the *r, l,* and *s* blends that the students have learned, such as *cr, gl,* and *sp.* Then make many bees with ending patterns on them, for example, ——————*ad,* ——————*ate;* ——————*ell.* Each child is instructed to place a bee and flower together, using a correct blend to form a word. If the word is incorrect, the child gets "stung" by the bee. (This puzzle match has many variations.)

8. *Objective: Expanding vocabulary.* Create a grid similar to the one below. List various phonetic elements across the top of the grid. General categories are listed at the side of the grid. Duplicate a grid for each student. Have students fill in the grid with words that correspond to both categories. Allow students to consult books and dictionaries to find appropriate words. Have them share responses with the class. Students score one point for each word correctly completing a square. Play individually or in groups.

|  | ai | ay | ee | ea |
|---|---|---|---|---|
| things | train | *clay* | *cheese* | *lead* |
| action words | *sail* | play | *freeze* | *spread* |

## Manipulatives

1. *Objective: Reinforcing words through sensory experience.* Distribute individual letter cards to the students displaying such letters as *a, d, e, h, l, p, m, n, t, A, H, M, N.* Make word cards such as *am, man, mat, help, Nat, Ted,* and *Nan.* Place them face down in a stack. Choose and display word cards. Students with these letters are to stand next to each other to form the word. A student is then asked to read the word aloud. Continue until all the words are read.

2. *Objective: Practice with the final letter e.* Cut 16 slips of paper into 6-by-3-inch strips. Fold over about $1\frac{1}{2}$ inches of one end of each slip. Copy a word with one short vowel onto the larger portion of each slip of paper. Write an *e* on the back of the folded portion. When the *e* is flipped back only the short vowel word can be seen. When the *e* is flipped forward it changes the short vowel sound of these kinds of words to a long vowel sound. Suggested words: *cut, cap, tap, fat, hat, mat, past, rat, rod, tub, pan, man, sit, rob,* and *grip.*

3. *Objective: Practice with letters or words using teacher-made or commercial flip books.*[7] On the back of letters place little pictures for self-checking. These flip books can also be made for CVC (consonant–vowel–consonant) words with beginning blends and digraphs, and for final *e* words.

4. *Tachistoscopes* (teacher-constructed of oaktag or cardboard, or purchased commercially). For those that are teacher-constructed, a strip of paper is fed through the slits of a fun-type figure (see examples below). The student reads each word as it appears. The object is to increase the rate of speed and to learn the words as sight words. Sometimes two slits of paper are used to teach generalizations such as the final *e* changing the preceding vowel.

Example
Tachistoscopes

## Materials Inundation

On the market today are a variety of computers and software programs. There are *Controlled Readers* for increasing the eye sweep, with the line of print adjusted for rate of speed and size of type. Additionally, videos, films, filmstrips, cassettes, and records are available, all promising to teach word recognition skills. There are kits that combine cassettes, filmstrips, and books; programs with animal and cartoon cutouts, posters, and all manner of motivational gimmicks, all purporting to teach and improve word recognition skills.

Confronted with so many materials, activities, and ideas for teaching these sound-symbol associations (and many of these are suggested in teaching other word-recognition skills too), teachers often engage students in these activities to the exclusion of actual reading. Phonics or skill instruction becomes the end, instead of the means to an end (Anderson and Fordham, 1991).

Dixie Lee Spiegel (1990) examined many materials that purported to reinforce phonics skills, and found:

(7) Commerical flip books may be purchased from Jane Ward Co.

There were many problems with the amount of reinforcement and transfer poten-tial of the materials. Often several letters were introduced at one time. . . . In many cases the skill/strategy was practiced only with spelling and only with isolated let-ters. . . . Serious content validity problems were found. Pictures were often unin-terpretable . . . inappropriate rules were introduced. . . . Other problems included visually cluttered pages, tasks beyond the level of the child, and activities requir-ing too much teacher direction.

Because phonics skills, in varying degrees of intensity, are usually empha-sized in early reading, it is important to stop a moment to consider some guide-lines to help keep the teaching of phonics in proper perspective.

## Guidelines for Teaching Phonics

1. The purpose of teaching phonics skills in reading is to help students develop the ability to recognize *at sight* large numbers of words.
2. Periodic evaluation of students' skill needs must be made through both in-formal and formal assessment.[8]
3. Students must, after the beginning reading stages, apply what they have learned through follow-up activities/lessons that involve *actual reading*.
4. Students must be taught to rely on contextual and other visual clues, togeth-er with phonics.
5. Individual differences must be considered. It is not unusual to find reading levels spanning six years in a single elementary classroom.
6. A teacher must know the skills thoroughly so that what is taught is not only correct, but appropriate and necessary.

As a teacher ask yourself, "What is my objective in engaging in this activity? Is it necessary for all students? (Durkin, 1990) Would John, May, and Suzy, who seem to know and use these skills so effectively, need this exercise/activity?" Not only is it a waste of time for many students who already know and use the skill ef-fectively, but many materials commonly used in classes are confusing and have no real reading transfer value!

Often the directions for completing skill activities are so difficult that if the children could read them in the first place they wouldn't need the activity. Then too, as children become more mature readers, many activities can be completed without the child actually reading, but merely telling which word has a short *a* or a short *i*, the number of syllables, or the accent.

For the reasons mentioned above and because phonics is such a controversial area, teachers frequently ask questions about it.

## Questions Teachers Ask Concerning Teaching Phonics

1. *How much phonics do children need?* Many educators flippantly say, "As little as possible." This answer is quite misleading. Initial reading can be frustrating and overwhelming if too many words are introduced too rapidly without considerable phonics review and reinforcement. On the other hand, too much phonics for competent readers is a waste of time. *Periodic careful*

(8) A survey test for diagnosing students' decoding skills may be found in Appendix D.

*diagnosis,* coupled with teacher observation to determine who needs what, is the key.

2. *Should the phonics lesson be taught before the reading lesson, after, or during a separate period?* In beginning reading it must be part of the lesson, but after children begin reading more fluently by the second grade, a separate period is necessary. This is because group reading should be primarily concerned with comprehension, interpretation, and enjoyment in order to foster a love of reading.

3. *What do I say when a generalization doesn't work?* Tell students that generalizations are merely starting points. Emphasize that they must remain flexible when decoding and that when letters combine in different ways, they sometimes encode different sounds.

4. *Should I try to induct generalizations?* It depends. What must be kept in mind is that the goal of phonics instruction is teaching children to learn to decode quickly. Sometimes inducting generalizations takes a long time.

5. *What is a reasonable skill sequence?* Because there is greater consistency between consonant letters and their respective sounds than there is between vowels and their respective sounds, most instructional programs begin using the consonants to initiate learning some sound-symbol associations. In general, a few letters are introduced (no two programs agree), together with the short *a*, followed by additional consonant letters, and some of the other short vowels. Gradually a few blends and consonant digraphs are introduced, followed by the long and special third sounds of certain vowels. The more difficult *r*-controlled vowels, vowel diphthongs, and special combinations are taught later. (See Appendix B for a basal skill sequence.)

6. *Should I tell children to try the short vowel sound if they are undecided?* Yes, especially with troublesome words, because short vowel sounds occur more frequently than long vowel sounds do, except with the two sounds of /o͞o/ where the long sound predominates.

7. *What correspondences are worthwhile teaching?* It all depends. In order to learn to read, some children need intensive instruction in almost all the correspondences, while others, through a kind of osmosis, seem to soak up these relationships without any explanation. Again the key is diagnosis.

8. *Should children state the rule?* The inability to state a phonics rule did not seem to hinder children's efforts to analyze unfamiliar words. They used the generalizations without being able to state them. (Rosso and Emans, 1981). The important thing, therefore, is their ability to *apply* the rule. The teacher, however, should be able to state a generalization *since s/he must verbalize it to the student.*

9. *Should students use the terms* blend *or* digraph? As in the previous example, this is not essential but depends on the teacher's philosophy and the type of class. Students need to understand that blends are pronounced very rapidly, while digraphs encode only one sound. Some programs use the term *phonogram* to apply to any two-letter combination. The teacher may use these terms as s/he is responsible for definitions.

10. *What should I do when children who are first learning to read continually ask for help in decoding words?* Help them begin to develop a word-pronunciation strategy and suggest they do something similar to the following:

a. Try the first sound of the word, noting whether it is a single consonant letter, a letter combination (blend or digraph), or a vowel.

b. Continue reading the sentence to see if further clues are within the sentence to help decode the word.

c. Reread the sentence to see if the word as they have decoded it makes sense.

As children mature, their strategy must expand. Initially they will profit from using the sound patterns and context, while later they will need to learn how to use the structure of words, context, and sound patterns.[9] They must also learn to use the dictionary.

## SPELLING: ITS RELATIONSHIP TO WORD RECOGNITION SKILLS

Reading and spelling are alike in that they both develop in stages, and to some extent both rely on phonics and other visual clues. They are, however, different processes. We know this because a few students in each class will be excellent readers but poor spellers, and conversely some excellent spellers will be poor readers. Why this is so continues to be a matter of debate. Nolan (1995) suggests that for some students who use the computer for writing, the spellcheck may not only help them to spell correctly but also teach them the importance of some of the patterns and visual clues they have not internalized.

The good speller, however, not only understands the patterns in the encoding of words, but also has a photographic imprint of the word so that it looks correct when it is spelled. This is the goal in teaching spelling—that students will have a rich storehouse of words as in reading, calling upon it in their writing and knowing how to spell the words correctly.

### Teaching Spelling: A Balanced Approach

While it is true that immersion in reading and writing with many practice opportunities will result in some fine spellers, most students will profit when spelling patterns and generalizations are made more explicit for them (Adams, 1990; Clay, 1991; Routman, 1993). As with the continuing debate in reading and whole language, the teaching of spelling is moving to a more balanced approach. As mentioned previously, invented spellings used by children in kindergarten and first grade are not supposed to mean that "anything goes" but are a useful way of freeing children's writing creativity.

After the beginning reading/writing stages, children need to be accountable for certain standards (Snowball, 1993; Novelli, 1993; Routman, 1993; and Adams & Bruck, 1995). They should take pride in their work and, even in daily journal or story writing, be expected to use legible handwriting, correct spelling of frequently used words, and correct punctuation (capitals and periods). They should also be expected to reread their draft, checking for spelling, punctuation, and meaning before asking a partner to read what they have written or before having a conference with their teacher.

(9) Context and structure of words will be discussed in later sections and an expanded decoding strategy suggested.

The student should also be able to read the draft with ease. This puts greater responsibility on the student and makes him/her aware that the spelling, if not perfectly correct, should be reasonably so. For example, a child who spells *president* as *pt* needs to think through the word more carefully, listen to the sounds, and approximate it more closely (Snowball, 1993).

## Direct Teaching

The *Total Reading* approach to teaching word recognition skills asserts that even very young children profit from an introduction to certain consistent English spelling generalizations that reinforce their decoding skills. *Total Reading* directly teaches 12 of these generalizations beginning in the first grade, as children write words the teacher is dictating. These generalizations are reviewed and reinforced during the primary years, together with more advanced generalizations, along with much creative writing practice as in whole language. Again, a *balance* is achieved. As the teacher dictates a group of words to children, the spelling patterns within the words are discussed so that the generalizations are internalized and understood, not merely memorized by rote. Questioning of the students by the teacher as they are writing helps them to think through the pattern. By the end of the first grade, children are taught the following generalizations:

1. the rules for long vowels.
2. the five reasons a word may end in a final long *e*.
3. the reasons *c* and *g* have two sounds.
4. the letter *y* can function as the long vowel *i* or *e* at the end of a word (*i* in a one-syllable word: *cry*) and *e* in a two-syllable word (*la dy*).
5. the /er/ sound can be written five ways.
6. *l, f,* and *s,* are often doubled at the end of a one-syllable word.
7. *ay* is used to write long *a* at the end of a word.
8. *dge* is used to write /j/ at the end of a word.
9. *i* precedes *e* except after *c* or when *ei* "says" long *a*.
10. *ti, si,* and *ci* are used to write /sh/ at the beginning of a two- or three-syllable word.

Learning these generalizations reinforces the decoding of words as children write the words that exemplify these generalizations.[10]

## Activities to Reinforce Spelling

### Finger spelling

To help students master frequently occurring words of three to five letters, Foss (1995) uses a finger spelling procedure. The teacher begins by telling children that there are five (or three or four) letters in the word and holds up his/her hand, spreading the fingers. The left hand is used, the palm facing the students so that directionality is correct. The teacher points to the thumb and asks, "What is the first letter?" The children give the first sound as perhaps *t*. The teacher agrees, pointing to the thumb, and then pointing to the second finger. She asks, "What do you hear next?" If the children mention a letter in the word, but not in the sequence, the

(10) See Mary Minor Johnson, *Total Reading,* Primary Teacher Manual, Levels I–III, pp. 41–42.

teacher shows them where in her hand the letter belongs, and then asks, "What else do you hear?" This helps some children begin to understand the sequencing of sounds. (An alternative method is to draw a hand on the chalkboard and place letters correctly as they are called.)

## Making words

Cunningham and Cunningham (1992) suggest a strategy called "Making Words" in order to enhance the spelling-decoding connection. In this fifteen-minute activity, children are individually given a combination of letters to use in making words. During the activity, children make twelve to fifteen words beginning with two-letter words and continuing with three-, four-, or five-letter, and longer words until the final word is made. The final word, a six-, seven-, or eight-letter word always includes all the letters used that day in class. In this hands-on manipulative activity, children discover letter-sound relationships and learn how to look for patterns in words.

In a beginning lesson (abbreviated below) children have one vowel letter (always in red) and know they must use the vowel card in every word. Additionally, they would have the consonant letters *g, n, p, r,* and *s.* Here are some of the steps the teacher might use, although other combinations are possible:

1. Take two letters and make *in.*
2. Add a letter to make the three-letter word *pin.*
3. Change just one letter, and turn your *pin* into a *pig.*
4. Now change just one letter, and your *pig* can become a *rig*—sometimes we call a big truck a *rig.* (Other intermediate words with teacher instruction and explanation follow: *rip; rips; nips; spin; snip; pins; sing.*)
5. Now, change just one letter, and change *sing* to *ring.*
6. Now, we will make a five-letter word. Add a letter to change *ring* to *rings.*
7. Has anyone figured out what word we can make with six letters?
8. Take all six of your letters and make the word *spring.*

Many children are amazed to learn that more than one word can be made with the same letters and that you can make a different word simply by putting the same letters in different places.

"Making Words" with two vowels offers children opportunities to work with vowel digraphs such as *ea.* It also may be used with intermediate children and older remedial readers.

"Making Words" works well because of the endless possibilities it offers children to see how our alphabetic system works. (See the original article for many letter combinations to use, for words to be constructed, and for patterns to be learned.)

## Classroom spelling explorations

The author recalls a spelling exploration in a sixth-grade class that did not provide the answer, but proved to be a rewarding learning experience for the students. The class was having trouble spelling words that ended in either *ant/ance* or *ent/ence* and decided to see if there was a rule for using the appropriate form. Actually there are some so-called "rules" for these endings, but they are quite complicated. While the students did not discover any definitive patterns, they did decide that the *ant/ance* form appeared much more frequently than the *ent/ence* form. In the meantime they had learned to read and spell many words with these endings.

Additionally, they wrote letters to the various lexicographers of the most popular intermediate children's dictionaries and asked for their insights regarding these forms. The lexicographers then responded that it was a matter of discipline to learn them!

As Snowball (1993) advises, these spelling explorations should arise in the context of the children's writing so it is relevant to what they are learning. Here are some strategies that could be used to explore the long *e* sound with primary-grade children:

1. Select some of the words the students are trying to write that contain the long *e* sound. Write the students' attempts on a chart.
2. Read the words from the chart and discuss that all these words have this long *e* sound. Students may like to suggest various ways they think their words could be spelled.
3. Read from a story and ask the students to listen for words with the long *e* sound: *thief, queen, be, mean, he, donkey.*
4. List the words and identify the part of each word that represents the long *e* sound.
5. Ask the students if they know or can find any other words with the long *e* sound. Add these to the class list: *believe, sleep, scream, money.*
6. Have the students work in small groups with their word cards to see if they can find various ways to group the words. Share these ideas and eventually group the words according to their spelling patterns.

| be | thief | queen | mean | donkey |
| he | believe | sleep | scream | money |

Try to elicit from the students generalizations such as: The long *e* sound can be written in many ways. In spelling words with this sound, we need to attend to the letter(s) that encodes the long *e* sound.

With older students, it might be useful to explore a generalization such as how to add the suffix *ed* to a base word:

1. Choose a story the class has read. Ask the students to search for words ending in *ed*. Have them find many other words with this pattern.
2. Have students list the words with the base word and then group them according to their pattern. (This is an abbreviated list.)

| claim/claim*ed* | paint/paint*ed* | play/play*ed* | relieve/reliev*ed* | nap/napp*ed* |
| mail/mail*ed* | treat/treat*ed* | journey/journey*ed* | change/chang*ed* | rob/robb*ed* |
| train/train*ed* | thread/thread*ed* | spray/spray*ed* | rule/rul*ed* | tug/tugg*ed* |

Ask students what they noticed about the way the base word changed when *ed* was added. Did all the words change? Try to elicit from the students generalizations such as these:

1. For words such as *claim, mail,* and *train,* ending in *m, l,* and *n,* merely add *ed*.
2. Words ending in *t* and *d* add *ed*. *Ed* becomes an extra syllable when the word is pronounced: *paint-ed, treat-ed, thread-ed.*

3. Do not drop the letter *y* when adding *ed: played, enjoyed.*

4. With words ending in *e,* drop the *e,* and add the *ed* or *ing: rake, raked, raking.*

5. *One*-syllable words ending in *one* consonant, preceded by *one* short vowel, as in *rob,* doubled the final consonant when adding *ed: robbed.*

### Spelling dictionaries

Angeletti (1993) suggests two types of spelling dictionaries, one for the class, and a personal one that each student develops. The class spelling dictionary is divided into three sections. In the first section, a page is included for each letter of the alphabet. Students identify high-frequency words from their classroom lessons, then list them under the appropriate letter. In the second section, word lists are grouped according to selected patterns. For example, after a lesson on the *dge* pattern, the students enter newly learned words on the *dge* page. A third section can have word categories—animals, countries, cities, important people, etc.

The personal spelling dictionary is modeled after the class dictionary. It can be as simple as a part of a page for each letter of the alphabet, with separate sections for word patterns and word categories.

Students should enter high-frequency words from their writing and reading into the alphabetized section. Do not expect young children to alphabetize correctly, but help them alphabetize to the second letter. At the end of the year or when they are ready, they can make new dictionaries with words alphabetized to the third letter, or even with appropriate guide words for each page.

## SUMMARY

Reading readiness was discussed, and the importance of a language-enriched environment was stressed. Terms essential for students to know before beginning more formal reading instruction were outlined. The use of invented spellings as a way for children to understand the relationship between sounds and symbols in beginning reading was described. The controversy over invented spellings continues with some schools adopting a more traditional approach. Suggestions on beginning handwriting that stressed the importance of legibility completed the readiness section.

A method to teach beginning sound-symbol relationships was suggested, with examples of classroom materials and activities. A very important part of beginning phonics instruction is work with blending sounds, and several methods were suggested. Three examples of instruction with phonics—explicit, implicit, and linguistic—were detailed, with examples of each type of lesson, and as in the case of blending techniques, the method used depends on student maturity and ability and on teacher preference.

A typical decoding lesson using a basal was included as well as a typical decoding lesson from *Total Reading.* Suggestions concerning how decoding instruction would differ in a whole language classroom were given.

Students' decoding skills may break down at three levels: the story level, the word level, or the discrimination level. Ways to correct these were detailed. Differing teacher approaches in teaching word recognition skills were suggested.

Ways of teaching, extending, reinforcing, and reviewing sound-symbol relationships were presented. The inundation of materials on the market necessitates consideration before use and care that these materials do not take the place of actual reading. As students begin and continue to learn to read, it is important through formal and informal assessment to identify their skill strengths and weaknesses and plan appropriate lessons accordingly.

Questions asked most frequently about teaching phonics with suggested answers were included. When teaching phonics is purposeful and helps children learn to decode words and read them at sight through meaningful activities, then teaching phonics has a definite place in today's elementary school classroom and at higher levels where needed.

A section on spelling and its relationship to decoding skills examined some creative ways to teach spelling generalizations to children. Twelve spelling rules were outlined that more traditional spelling programs would include.

Tests to check phonics and other decoding skills of the teacher are included in Appendix D, as well as an evaluation of decoding skills for students.

## Chapter 2:

## Final Review

1. a. What are some factors considered in reading readiness?
   b. What terms should children understand?
2. What would be a strategy for introducing a beginning sound-symbol relationship?
3. a. How many different ways may students be taught to blend sounds?
   b. What are these ways?
   c. Which would you use and why?
4. a. What is the difference between implicit, explicit, and linguistic phonics?
   b. Why are these terms confusing?
5. a. What are the levels where students may show difficulty in decoding?
   b. What are some remedial procedures?
6. What are four approaches teachers may use in teaching word recognition skills?
7. What are some game and puzzle activities that teachers may use in teaching, extending, reinforcing, and reviewing sound-symbol relationships? What are some writing activities they may use?
8. Why is the "inundation" of materials that teach phonics a problem in schools?
9. What should be the major goal in teaching phonics to children?
10. What is the best way to know what and when particular decoding skills should be taught?

# Developing Additional Word Recognition Skills

## SIGHT WORDS

In reading, a group of "heavy duty" words, such as *at, the, be, of,* are referred to as sight words and are encountered with great frequency. It would be difficult to read any extended passage without meeting a large number of them. As they must be recognized at sight instantly, the term *sight words* is used when discussing them. Percentages for the frequency of these words are often given, and these range from 50 to 66 percent. The difference in occurrence is due to the nature of the text, with simpler reading materials usually containing a higher percentage.

A good number of these high frequency words contain irregular spellings, therefore limiting the effectiveness of teaching them through phonics and consequently providing another reason for teaching them as "sight" words. As students in early reading learn both sight words and sound-symbol relationships as part of word recognition skills, they will see them in proper perspective and will avoid relying completely on either one.

## Sight Word Lists

One of the most popular of these high frequency sight word lists is the Dolch list, which contains a total of 220 words. There are a number of others, including the Harris-Jacobson, the Dale Johnson, and the Durr. Two of these lists, the Dolch and the Harris-Jacobson, are included in Tables 3.1 and 3.2, respectively.

There are four levels to the Dolch list, with the words arranged in increasing levels of difficulty, although these divisions are somewhat arbitrary. There have been many attempts to update this list since Dolch first compiled it in 1936, but nevertheless it retains its original popularity. A later revision is a list by Johns (1978) in which 189 of the Dolch words have been retained and changes made in the others.

In a later study, Palmer (1985) checked the Dolch list against four series of basals: Ginn's Reading 720; Holt, Rinehart & Winston; Houghton Mifflin; and Scott Foresman. She found the Dolch words made up between 57 percent and 82 percent of the vocabulary in the passages and levels, with the average being 60 percent.

You will notice that there are no nouns in Table 3.1 because the nouns used in any passage are determined by the subject matter and vary enormously. In contrast, most of the words included in this list occur repeatedly in reading materials, regardless of reading level. The Harris-Jacobson core list (Table 3.2), which is quite a bit longer, does include some very common nouns.

**TABLE 3.1**  Dolch Basic Sight Word List.

| PREPRIMER | PRIMER | FIRST GRADE | SECOND GRADE | THIRD GRADE |
|---|---|---|---|---|
| 1. a | 1. all | 1. after | 1. always | 1. about |
| 2. and | 2. am | 2. again | 2. around | 2. better |
| 3. away | 3. are | 3. an | 3. because | 3. bring |
| 4. big | 4. at | 4. any | 4. been | 4. carry |
| 5. blue | 5. ate | 5. as | 5. before | 5. clean |
| 6. can | 6. be | 6. ask | 6. best | 6. cut |
| 7. come | 7. black | 7. by | 7. both | 7. done |
| 8. down | 8. brown | 8. could | 8. buy | 8. draw |
| 9. find | 9. but | 9. every | 9. call | 9. drink |
| 10. for | 10. came | 10. fly | 10. cold | 10. eight |
| 11. funny | 11. did | 11. from | 11. does | 11. fall |
| 12. go | 12. do | 12. give | 12. don't | 12. far |
| 13. help | 13. eat | 13. going | 13. fast | 13. full |
| 14. here | 14. four | 14. had | 14. first | 14. got |
| 15. I | 15. get | 15. has | 15. five | 15. grow |
| 16. in | 16. good | 16. her | 16. found | 16. hold |
| 17. is | 17. have | 17. him | 17. gave | 17. hot |
| 18. it | 18. he | 18. his | 18. goes | 18. hurt |
| 19. jump | 19. into | 19. how | 19. green | 19. if |
| 20. little | 20. like | 20. just | 20. its | 20. keep |
| 21. look | 21. must | 21. know | 21. made | 21. kind |
| 22. make | 22. new | 22. let | 22. many | 22. laugh |
| 23. me | 23. no | 23. live | 23. off | 23. light |
| 24. my | 24. now | 24. may | 24. or | 24. long |
| 25. not | 25. on | 25. of | 25. pull | 25. much |
| 26. one | 26. our | 26. old | 26. read | 26. myself |
| 27. play | 27. out | 27. once | 27. right | 27. never |
| 28. red | 28. please | 28. open | 28. sing | 28. only |
| 29. run | 29. pretty | 29. over | 29. sit | 29. own |
| 30. said | 30. ran | 30. put | 30. sleep | 30. pick |
| 31. see | 31. ride | 31. round | 31. tell | 31. seven |
| 32. the | 32. saw | 32. some | 32. their | 32. shall |
| 33. three | 33. say | 33. stop | 33. these | 33. show |
| 34. to | 34. she | 34. take | 34. those | 34. six |
| 35. two | 35. so | 35. thank | 35. upon | 35. small |
| 36. up | 36. soon | 36. them | 36. us | 36. start |
| 37. we | 37. that | 37. then | 37. use | 37. ten |
| 38. where | 38 there | 38. think | 38. very | 38. today |
| 39. yellow | 39. they | 39. walk | 39. wash | 39. together |
| 40. you | 40. this | 40. were | 40. which | 40. try |
| | 41. too | 41. when | 41. why | 41. warm |
| | 42. under | | 42. wish | |
| | 43. want | | 43. work | |
| | 44. was | | 44. would | |
| | 45. well | | 45. write | |
| | 46. went | | 46. your | |
| | 47. what | | | |
| | 48. white | | | |
| | 49. who | | | |
| | 50. will | | | |
| | 51. with | | | |
| | 52. yes | | | |

**TABLE 3.2**    Harris-Jacobson Core Words for First Grade.

### CORE PREPRIMER LIST

| | | | | | | |
|---|---|---|---|---|---|---|
| a | come | get | is | not | stop | who |
| and | daddy* | go | it | play | the | will |
| are | did | green | little | ran | this | work |
| at | do | have | look | red | to | you |
| ball* | dog* | he | make | ride | up | |
| blue | down | help | me | said | want | |
| call | fun* | here | mother* | see | we | |
| can | funny | in | my | something* | what | |

### CORE PRIMER LIST

| | | | | | | |
|---|---|---|---|---|---|---|
| about | cake* | him | may | run | thank | yellow |
| all | car* | his | new | saw | then | yes |
| around | eat | home* | now | say | they | your |
| ask | fast | house* | of | she | too | |
| away | father* | into | on | show | train* | |
| bike* | fish* | jump | one | sit | tree* | |
| birthday* | from | know | out | so | two | |
| boat* | goat* | let | paint* | some | us | |
| book* | good | like | pet* | soon | want | |
| but | has | man* | put | take | word* | |

### CORE FIRST READER

| | | | | | | | |
|---|---|---|---|---|---|---|---|
| after | build* | find | hen* | more* | read | these | window* |
| again | bus* | fire* | her | morning* | ready* | thing* | wish |
| airplane* | by | first | hill* | must | right | think | won't* |
| along* | cage* | five | hold | name* | road* | those | would |
| am | came | fly | hop* | never | rocket* | three | zoo* |
| an | can't* | food* | horse* | next* | sang* | time* | |
| animal* | cat* | found | how | night* | sat* | told* | |
| another* | catch* | four | hurry* | nothing* | school* | tomorrow* | |
| any | children* | fox* | I'll* | off | seen* | took* | |
| as | coat* | friend* | ice* | on | shoe* | town* | |
| baby* | cold | game* | if | old | should* | toy* | |
| back* | color* | gave | it's* | or | sing | truck* | |
| bag* | could | girl* | just | other* | sister* | try | |
| balloon* | crow* | give | kind | our | sleep | turtle* | |
| bark* | cry* | gone* | kitten* | over | sound* | TV* | |
| barn* | cut | goodby* | last* | own | stay | under | |
| be | dark* | got | laugh | pan* | step* | very | |
| bear* | day* | grass* | leg* | party* | still* | wagon* | |
| bed* | didn't* | had | letter* | peanut* | stopped* | walk | |
| bee* | does | hair* | light | penny* | store* | was | |
| before | don't | hand* | live | picnic* | story* | water* | |
| began* | dress* | hear* | long | picture* | street* | way* | |
| behind* | drop* | hello* | lost* | pig* | sun* | were | |
| better | duck* | hand* | made | please | surprise* | wet* | |
| bird* | fall | happy* | many | pocket* | talk* | when | |
| black | far | hard* | maybe* | pony* | tea | where | |
| box* | farm* | hat* | men* | prize* | than* | which | |
| boy* | fat* | head* | met* | rabbit* | their | white | |
| bring | feet* | hear* | miss* | race* | them | why | |
| brown | fight* | hello* | money* | rain* | there | window | |

For a rationale of the list and the list itself, see Albert J. Harris and Milton D. Jacobson, *Basic Elementary Reading Vocabularies* (New York: The Macmillan Co., 1972), pp. 60–82. Also see Albert J. Harris and Edward R. Sipay, *How to Increase Reading Ability* (New York: David McKay Co., 1975), pp. 362–363.

*Words that are not on the Dolch Basic Sight Word List.

Students who do not experience reading problems will have learned most of these words by the end of the second or third grade. However, problem readers, even some junior and senior high school students, have not mastered them. Appendix B includes a list of basic sight words for older readers that incorporates frequently used words at upper levels.

## Teaching Sight Words

Mastery of a core vocabulary such as the Dolch list is necessary in order for children to become fluent readers. Teachers sometimes check students individually on their ability to recognize these words, with mastery defined as the "instant" recognition of 90 to 95 percent of the words in any list. Reading words in a list, however, is always more demanding for poor readers than reading these same words in a story (Krieger, 1981).

To master many of these words, some students learn them in context by merely reading a variety of interesting stories and articles (the best way). Other students need simple introduction to the words followed by a little practice, engaging in some of the following activities for learning these words. There are others who need a more structured program. Each word must be carefully introduced by perhaps placing it in a pocket chart and asking such questions as:

1. How many letters are in the word?
2. With what letter does the word begin?
3. What is/are the letter/s at the end of the word?
4. Read the word.
5. Read the word in this phrase. Now read the word in this sentence.

With a more structured program, the introduction of each word is followed by lots of review and practice as suggested in some of the following activities. Before describing them, it is important to sound a note of caution. When learning any word recognition strategy, children need to know that words spoken in isolation are frequently stressed differently than when they are spoken in sentences. Sight words are particularly vulnerable in this respect. For example, the word *an* would be pronounced and accented as /án/ in situations in which it is spoken in isolation, but it would be unaccented as /ən/ when spoken in the context of a phrase as /ən áppl/. For this reason, whenever possible, present these words as parts of phrases and sentences. Remember, too, that most of these words have a variety of meanings depending on the context in which they are used. For example, notice the various meanings of up in these phrases: *add up, shape up, dress up, eat up, clam up, slip up, fold up, mess up,* and *frame up.*

## Activities for Teaching Sight Words

The objective for the following activities is to help students who experience difficulty with particular sight words:

1. With easily confused words such as *on* and *one,* have students identify the letter that causes the difficulty. Place several students' names on the board with the particular letter, such as *e*—*J*er*ry*, T*ed, Jane.* Ask the student to identify the "demon" letter in the names. Practice with phrases that include the easily confused words.

2. Trace words in sand that are repeatedly missed and point out the salient feature. Have the student repeat the tracing, verbalizing the difficult letters as s/he does so.

3. Construct a slotted stand-up frame to hold "My Word for the Day." Insert words needed for practice.

The following activities are for review and extension:

1. Drill with phrase and sentence cards. (See Table 3.3.)

| | |
|---|---|
| jump up | He jumps up. |
| Example: Phrase Card | Example: Sentence Card |

2. Prepare pairs of phrase or sentence cards. Start with about 5 pairs, or 10 cards, turning them upside down. Students must read the word or phrase card as they turn it over and attempt to find the matching pair.

3. Cards (phrases or sentences) may be passed out. The teacher says such things as, "Whoever has the phrase *will do* stand up, get in line, or whistle."

4. Have about a dozen pairs of phrase cards ready. Take one set and distribute the remaining cards among a small group of students. Place one card in the pocket chart and say, "All those who have this same word or phrase card may place it in the pocket chart with mine." Continue with the rest of the cards.

5. Have each student develop a "word bank" that includes a file of words known and a file of words that need to be learned. These may be kept in alphabetical order.

6. Use the ever-popular bingo format with words or phrases as shown in these examples.

| and | must | see |
|---|---|---|
| big | FREE | he |
| what | yes | play |

| I can | for me | is it |
|---|---|---|
| to run | FREE | what went |
| my new | to him | come down |

7. Use a muffin pan or plastic egg carton. Write sight words on the bottom of each section with a felt pen. Make copies of these sight words on cards. Students sort and place them in the appropriate section, reading the word.

8. Use well-known short nursery rhymes, such as *Humpty Dumpty,* that contain lots of sight words. Write the words on the chalkboard or on a chart. Read them aloud. Ask students to read them along with you several times until the words are well known. Then make word cards for each sight word

**TABLE 3.3** Phrase unit, based on the Dolch Basic Sight Vocabulary.

| PHRASE | PHRASE | PHRASE |
|---|---|---|
| about it | he went | of their own |
| are big now | help me | one or two |
| as I do | here is an | only one |
| ask him | his green one | our yellow one |
| at the | how much | out came three |
| ate his | | out came two |
| | I am | |
| be good | I can | please let |
| be just right | I do | pretty while |
| before long | I have | pull us out |
| best of all | I like | |
| but I do | I want | ran fast |
| | I will | ran to stop |
| came because | if he goes | read and write |
| can always see | into the | run away |
| can buy | is cold | |
| can find | is full | saw her |
| can fly | is going | see how small |
| can laugh | is not black | see my green |
| can use | it came from | shall both talk |
| carry her | it is | shall know soon |
| come and play | it is going | she gave eight |
| could not grow | | she has five |
| | jump up | sit down |
| did not | jump upon | so am I |
| do not | just then | |
| do you | | take hold |
| does not | keep him | talk at once |
| don't you | know which | tell me |
| draw a green | know why | tell them |
| | | thank you |
| for a walk | let me | that big yellow |
| four little yellow | let us | the first one |
| | like to ride | the funny one |
| get on | like to show | the hot |
| give up | live in | the kind of |
| go to | long, long drink | the light |
| go together | look after | their brown |
| | look at | there are |
| had not been | look for | there are ten |
| had to clean | look under | they called |
| have found | look up | they said |
| he could see | | this is |
| he got | made a blue | to cut some |
| he looked around | made him white | to drink |
| he never saw | may I sing | to eat |
| he put new | must be warm | to keep those |
| he ran | my big | to make |
| he said | my red one | to play |
| he saw | | to play with |
| | not very far | to sleep |
| | | to work |

you want them to retain from the rhyme. Shuffle the cards and spread them face down. Taking turns, the children choose a card and read the word. The card is then kept if read correctly. If a player misreads the card, s/he must keep it until the next round and then read it correctly.

## When Sight Words Are Especially Troublesome

Cunningham (1980) described sight words as "four-letter" words because of the connotation of "bad" and the fact that many include four letters such as *were, with,* and *what.* She stated:

> Since sight words have no tangible meaning and their function is to connect other words, children are often unaware of their existence as separate words. The word *what* is often used in "Whatcha doing?" *Them* is just pronounced "m." Some children do not even realize these are separate words such as *big, truck* and *elephant,* nor are they clear as to their function (p. 160).

Weisendanger and Bader (1987) concluded that most problems are created by those sight words of low visual imagery that are easily confused, such as *their* and *then, what* and *when.* To remediate, they suggest teachers should subdivide the task, first teaching each word as a separate unit. Only after the words are learned separately, should they be presented together in order to discriminate between them. If a comparison between "easily confused words" is done too early, they believe children will become confused.

For students needing lots of practice, Higdon (1987) creates "sticker" books from stickers donated by parents. Each book contains about eight pages with a sticker on each one and a predictable sentence written about the sticker that includes sight words. Each book follows a format and uses a specific problem sight word, such as "I *want* a banana, an apple, a peach, etc." Smelly stickers add an extra sensory experience. (Many concepts can be taught using this method, such as toys, food, numbers, and insects.)

One final suggestion: Some teachers construct sight word rings. They place unknown sight words, written on index cards, six to twelve on a ring. When a child can read the sight word correctly three times, cut off one edge of the index card. When a child can spell it correctly, cut off another edge. When a child uses it correctly in a sentence, cut off a third edge.

## Sight Word Storehouse: The Goal in Reading

The sight words listed and discussed previously differ from the sight words acquired weekly, monthly, and yearly by students as they progress through the grades. By repeatedly encountering words (the number of times varying for different students), words are recognized immediately without any form of analysis. The goal in reading should be that words read are all part of a growing, expanding sight vocabulary. The vast storehouse of sight words accumulated by expert readers makes it possible for them not only to read rapidly, but also to pay full attention to thinking about what they are reading.

## Sight Words for the Computer Age: An Essential Word List

Today's children need to familiarize themselves with words used in the computer environment. Table 3.4 represents a core of major procedural and feedback words

**TABLE 3.4** Essential words for computer-assisted instruction in the elementary grades, based on a sample of 35 programs.

| | | | |
|---|---|---|---|
| activity | different | lesson | ready |
| adjust | directions | letter | regular |
| again | disk | level | remove |
| another | diskette | list | repeat |
| answer | display | load | return* |
| any | document | loading* | rules |
| arrow* | down | match | save |
| audio | drive | memory | score |
| bar | edit | menu* | screen |
| before | effects | monitor | select |
| begin | end | move | selection |
| bold | enter* | name* | sound* |
| button | erase | need | spacebar* |
| catalog | escape or <esc>* | no | speed |
| change | exit | number* | start |
| choice | find | off | team |
| choose* | finished | on | text |
| colors | follow | options | then |
| column | format | paddle | try |
| compete | game* | password | turn |
| complete | good | picture | type* |
| command | help | play | up |
| computer | hit | player | use |
| continue* | hold | please | video |
| control or <cntrl> | incorrect | point | wait |
| copy | incorrectly | practice | want |
| correct | indicate | press* | which |
| correctly | insert | print | win |
| cursor | instructions | problems | word |
| delete | joystick | program* | work |
| demonstration | key* | quit | yes |
| description | keyboard | rate | your |

*Words present in at least 10 of the 35 programs.

in the samples of programs reviewed (Dreyer, Futtersak, and Boehm, 1985). These words need to be introduced early in computer classroom instruction in the context of phrases or sentences in which they actually occur in programs, such as:

> hold down
>
> sound effects
>
> video monitor
>
> Loading . . . please wait.
>
> Type your name.
>
> Do you want instructions?
>
> Press spacebar to continue.

While teaching these words, point out to students that the same terms may appear in different forms in different programs. Command key names, for example, are sometimes presented in capital letters such as RETURN, within angle brackets as in <RETURN>, abbreviated as in <esc > or <ESC > or ESC, or highlighted on the screen.

---

1. Examine the following list and place a check mark next to the sight words:

   did      pepper
   from     for
   dragon   matching
   about    once

2. What is the name of the most popular sight word list?
3. What would be a structured approach to teaching sight words?
4. What is the best way for children to learn sight words?
5. What are some activities that may be used to teach sight words?

---

## CONTEXT CLUES

The words, phrases, or sentences that appear on either side of a specific word are called the context. Clues may be obtained from the context around an unfamiliar word, provided the material is not too difficult for the student. This is one of the best ways to decode unfamiliar words and gain meaning, the result being a faster and more efficient word identification process than is available through any other single technique. It is important to remember, however, that word identification is usually most efficient when various techniques are used in conjunction with one another.

### The Problem Reader

Problem readers, who generally have limited vocabularies, are frequently unmotivated or unable to do the amount of contextual reading required to extend their vocabularies (Blachowicz and Lee, 1991). They lag behind able readers in the use of strategies that allow them to gain new word meaning from context (McKeown, 1985). With problem readers, especially, guided instruction in the use of context is necessary (Jenkins, et al., 1989).

Two excerpts taken from the story, "Time for Andrew"[1] might be used in the following activity in teaching context. The strategy was formulated and used by middle grade teachers and is called $C^2QU$ (Blachowicz, 1993). The acronym stands for the procedures following the excerpts.

> "To summarize," he said at last, "you disobeyed me. First, you endangered our lives on the train trestle. Second, you fought with your cousin a week to the day after I punished you for the same offense. I told you then, and I'll tell you now, I will not *tolerate* such behavior." (p. 132)

> Then he rocked the chair *vigorously.* When that didn't get the attention, he sang, "I've Been Working on the Railroad" at the top of his lungs. (p. 140)

$C^1$: The teacher gives the target word in a broad but meaningful *context.* Students form hypotheses about it and share why they believe the meaning to be as they state.

(1) Mary Downing Hahn, *Time For Andrew,* Clarion Books, New York, 1994.

$C^2$: The teacher provides *more explicit context* with the word, asking students to reflect on their original choices and refine them.

Q: The teacher asks a *question* that involves semantic interpretation of the word and asks students to try to approximate the definition.

U: The students *use* the word in a sentence, often in summation or in writing about some part of the book or a lesson.

Instruction involves using a transparency on which components of the lesson are revealed one at a time, engaging students in a dialogue similar to the following:

T: ($C^1$) Will you read this sentence with this italicized word for me? "Then he rocked the chair *vigorously* . . ." (Student reads.) T: What could *vigorously* mean? (Students discuss.)

$S^1$: Maybe a whole lot.

$S^2$: Rocked it very hard.

T: ($C^2$) Read this sentence: "She shook the little bank so *vigorously* that all the coins fell out." Teacher poses this question: Does this match up with what we thought at first?

$S^3$: Well, yes, she had to use lots of energy.

$S^4$: She had to use lots of force.

T: (Q) Well, how about this. Can people speak *vigorously?* Can they walk *vigorously?* What might be some other things they could do *vigorously?* (This is a good time to show that words only permit themselves to be used in certain contexts.) Let's see if we can agree on a definition and check it with our dictionary. (End of the lesson should result in a working definition.)

T: (U) Suggests ways students should *use* the new word in their writing.

## Two Broad Areas of Context Clues

There are two types of context clues: (1) semantic, which provides lexical or meaning information, and (2) syntactic, which provides grammatical information. When readers understand the meaning of other words in the surrounding context, they use their semantic knowledge to help decode the unknown word. Their syntactic understanding, or their sense of the English sentence (and they must have this or they would be unable to speak), can help them deduce what type of word (noun, verb, adjective) would fit in a particular slot.

Since these two types of clues, semantic and syntactic, are interdependent, readers tend to use the two together to anticipate and confirm what they believe the word will be. For this reason, most reading programs combine the two types under the umbrella term *context clues.*

## Types of Context Clues

Many teachers claim that students do not use context to its full advantage (Cunningham, 1979). They need help in judging whether context can be an aid or whether the dictionary will have to be used. Sometimes there are extremes—some students consulting a dictionary at every instance and other students rarely bothering. Neither procedure is good and should be discouraged. Few students, however, are aware of the variety of ways context can help unlock unknown words and give meaning to them. The following are some examples of these many different ways.

***Direct explanation clue.*** Often authors realize students will not know a word and place it in an explanation to help them.
Example: *Lobbyists* got this name because they used to stand in a lobby or hall outside the room where the laws were passed. They try to influence the laws that are made.

***Experience clue.*** A student's own experience can help unlock an unknown word. Example: In any team, the members must *cooperate* by working together.

***Words in a series.*** Often unknown words in a series can be decoded from clues. Example: There were marigolds, pansies, and *chrysanthemums* among the flowers.

***Restatement.*** To clarify, authors often repeat what they have stated.
Example: In some places where fresh and salt water meet, as at the mouth of a river, the water is *brackish*. Brackish water is in between fresh water and salt water in saltiness.

***Contrast and comparison.*** Words such as *but* often give clues to word meaning. Example: Jerry smiled at Tim, but looked *disapprovingly* at me.

***Inference.*** Surrounding words or sentences provide clues.
Example: It was necessary to make sure that the coin was as old as the date said it was. Any *artifact* with writing on it is very important to historians.

## Advantages and Limitations of Using Context Clues

As with all types of word recognition strategies, there are advantages and limitations to using context clues.

### Advantages

1. Words can be identified in context that cannot be identified in isolation.
2. Readers who can use context clues become independent decoders more quickly. They learn to be good predictors of what the word will be, confirming or rejecting it, based on whether or not it makes sense in the context of what they are reading, and then they quickly read on.
3. Students who have difficulty with phonics skills that require closer attention to visual features may perceive unknown vocabulary more easily in this way.
4. Words that do not follow consistent sound-symbol relationships may be more easily generalized.

### Limitations

1. Beginning readers have difficulty using context, as their reading vocabulary tends to be limited.
2. There are many synonyms in English and these could make sense in a given context; therefore, when context is used solely, apart from other word recognition strategies, it does not result in exact word identification. When the exact word is required, readers must reinforce this clue with other word identification clues.

3. The surrounding context may be insufficient or provide misleading information about the word.

## Guidelines for Teaching Context Clues

1. Young readers are not always as successful in using context clues as older, more successful readers for two reasons: First, older readers have had more experience; they have heard, seen, and read more; they have accumulated larger vocabularies; and they have stored more information to draw upon. Second, because of maturation factors, they have developed greater reasoning skills. These enable them to put certain facts together, to become more successful at decoding unknown words through context.

2. Unfamiliar words that students are initially unable to decode in a selection are often decoded later as the student meets these words in varied contexts throughout the selection. Information in a selection is often accumulative; there is usually more semantic (meaning) information at the end of a sentence than there is at the beginning, and more information at the end of a paragraph than at the end of a sentence.

3. Materials that are too difficult present students with a disproportionate number of unknown words. This precludes the students' use of context because they cannot gather enough semantic information to bring the unknown word into focus.

4. Reading materials must be significant and interesting enough for readers to make use of context clues. They must be involved in what they are reading, because if they are not, they will be unaware of the semantic clues available, concentrating instead on individual words.

## Sentence Context Clues Will Vary

Note the following three groups of context clues. Some sentences provide all the clues needed; some limited clues; and some no clues whatever.

GROUP I.  *Context does the work for the student.*

1. "It's cold in here. Shut the w_ _ _ _ _ .
2. When I take an u_ _ _ _ _ _ _, it never rains.
3. They have one d_ _ _ _ _ _ _ and two sons.
4. On the day David became 10, his Mom had a b_ _ _ _ _ _ _ party for him.
5. There is no e_ _ _ _ _ _ _ so you'll have to climb the stairs.

GROUP II.  *Context clues are present here too, but they do not provide as much constraint as the former sentences. More reading than just the sentence is needed.*

1. How many p——————— are in the book? (pictures, pages)
2. Her coat was tan and bl———————. (blue, black)
3. They like to play in the b———————. (ballpark, basement, band)

GROUP III.  *Some sentences provide no context clues.*

1. That is a s——————— statement.
2. The l——————— is here.
3. Have you ever p———————?

While a given sentence may lack context clues, the help needed may be in the sentence that precedes or follows it in a paragraph. Context is always more than just a single phrase or sentence.

## Activities to Help Students Become Aware of Context as a Decoding Aid

To help students become aware of context, the teacher may begin by writing a simple sentence containing one unknown word on the board.

She *ambled*  slowly down the path.

Discuss with the students possible meanings that make sense in the sentence. Show them how the context limits the word choices they may have.

Suggest to students that when they come to an unknown word they continue reading the complete phrase, sentence, or paragraph. This may help them infer the meaning of the new word. Then, see if they can supply the meaning of the word and find out if it makes sense to them.

Even when students use structural or phonetic analysis to unlock a new word, the final check for accuracy must be the context in which the word is originally found. This is of great help in correctly placing the proper accent and the vowel sound.

I *objéct* to the rule.

She will *condúct* the orchestra.

The *óbject* could not be seen.

Her *cónduct* in the class has improved.

There are other activities the teacher may use to create awareness of context:

1.  a.  Read a sentence aloud and omit an "unknown" word, but tell the students the beginning sound. Ask students what they think the word is and why they came to that conclusion.

    b.  Discuss the "why" of the choices. Other students will be aided by the how-to-do-it of their peers.

2.  Provide examples showing that context clues may precede or follow the unknown word.

    *Preceding the unknown word*

    People who write about famous persons, places, and events of the past are called *historians.*

    *Following the unknown word*

    Among them are *antibodies.* These fight germs.

3.  Provide examples showing that a context clue may be a phrase, sentence, or paragraph.

    *a phrase*

    The day was *sweltering,* too hot for any fun.

    *a sentence*

    She *announced* loudly to everyone that she was leaving.

    *a paragraph*

    He held the *questionnaire* in his hand. "I need your help," he stated. "I don't know how to fill out the answers to all these questions. Why are they asking so many?"

4. Have students search through some of their favorite books to see how skillfully authors provide many context clues.[2]

   a. But that quietness had been shattered by the coming of Mrs. Scallop, whose voice now *intruded* . . . every morning. (p. 5)

   b. People put out rat poison in their barns to kill the *vermin*. (p. 127)

   c. The old man's voice, its *exasperated* tone, showed Ned he was tired of the cat. (p. 137)

5. Have students write sentences to exchange with their classmates where the context explains the word and where choices are provided.

   a. Mr. Barrows had a way of making the most difficult things seem easy. His *lucid* explanations lit up every subject and helped us understand it.

       interesting            relaxed            clear

   b. The *prototype* of the automobile was a clumsy three-wheeled carriage invented in 1770 in France. It was propelled by steam and produced to haul cannons. Though its speed was three miles an hour, it was the forerunner of the swift cars of today.

       original model            prospect            production

   c. The first task of a cub pilot on the Mississippi was to learn the *elusive* shape of the river since the shape of the river was constantly altering forever beyond the grasp of the cub pilot's mind and hand.

       complicated            basic            baffling

## Dos and Don'ts for Students' Use of Context

### Do . . .

1. try reading to the end of the sentence to try to figure out the unknown word.
2. search for clues and make certain the meaning "clicks" with what you have been reading.
3. use context when you need a general sense of what you are reading, such as in a story for pleasure reading or to get a general idea of a topic.

### Don't depend completely on context . . .

1. when you need the exact meaning of a word.
2. when clues suggest several meanings and you do not know which one is right.

**Quick Self-Check 14**

1. Why do poor readers have difficulty with context clues?
2. What are the two broad areas of context clues?
3. What are some different types of context clues?
4. How may teachers help students learn to use context clues?
5. Why are older readers more successful in using context clues?

(2) Excerpted from Paula Fox, *One-Eyed Cat* (New York: Bradbury Press, Inc., 1984).

# STRUCTURAL ANALYSIS: AN IMPORTANT DECODING STRATEGY

Thus far, three decoding strategies have been discussed: phonics analysis, instant recognition of high-frequency words, and context clues. Structural analysis, which entails identifying meaningful subunits within words, becomes increasingly important in decoding strategies as children move through the grades and on through high school. It consists of recognizing big word "chunks," such as compound words, prefixes, suffixes, and roots, and understanding certain principles of syllabication, thereby having the ability to "break apart" words quickly (Blachowicz, 1987; White, Sowell, and Yanagihara, 1989; Peterson and Phelps, 1991).

Children begin reading words with these structures as early as first grade when they are introduced to verb units such as *ing* and *ed* and plural endings such as *s* and *es.* Prefixes such as *re* and *un* are sometimes introduced as early as second grade, while work with more complex affixes (prefixes and suffixes) and roots usually begins in the middle grades and continues through high school.

The effectiveness of using structural analysis depends in large part on the extensiveness of a student's reading vocabulary. Those students who have internalized the phoneme-grapheme relationships of English, and have additionally a rich storehouse of sight words and word roots, are in the best position to profit from this kind of instruction.

## Compound Words

Compound words are simply a combination of two base words and are fairly easy to decode. English abounds with compound words (seatbelt), and their number is increasing all the time. As a matter of fact, about 60 percent of the new words that come into our language *(countdown, software, cyberspace)* are compound.

Students may be informed that in most cases the meaning of the compound word is a combination of the two joined words. Sometimes, however, it is not, as in the word *blackboard,* referring to a green chalkboard. Students should also know that because of wide usage some compound words are thought of as single words. Examples: *windshield* (shield from the wind) and *sidewalk* (walk by the side of the road).

### Activities for teaching compound words

1. *Objective: To practice combining two base words.* Write words on the board that can become part of a compound word, such as *dog, plane, thing, some, house, noon, man, air, after.* Ask children to choose two of the words to form a compound and write the word on a slip of paper, later sharing their word/words by using them in sentences. There are many variations of this activity.

2. *Objective: Review and extension.* Use a folder with pockets. On one side place the first part of almost a dozen compound words. On the other side place the second part of these words. Students combine these pieces. Answers are on the back of the folder for self-checking.

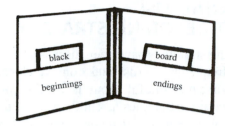

3. *Objective: Extending knowledge of compound words.* Construct a large wall chart with five headings such as *People, Places, Things, Animal Life,* and *Time* at the top. Ask students to find compound words that fit under the headings. The list can be quite extensive as the following chart indicates:

| PEOPLE | PLACES | THINGS | ANIMAL LIFE | TIME |
|--------|--------|--------|-------------|------|
| anybody | anywhere | airplane | butterfly | afternoon |
| chairman | barnyard | broomstick | goldfish | bedtime |
| everyone | bedroom | birdhouse | horseshoe | birthday |
| fisherman | doorway | boxcar | starfish | daylight |
| grandmother | downstairs | baseball | watchdog | lifetime |
| grownup | downtown | basketball | wildlife | playtime |
| housewife | driveway | cardboard | | springtime |
| milkman | farmhouse | campfire | | |
| nobody | farmland | dollhouse | | |
| policeman | fireplace | doghouse | | |
| postman | highway | doorbell | | |
| runaway | outside | firewood | | |
| salesman | playground | eyesight | | |
| shoemaker | roadside | football | | |
| | schoolyard | footsteps | | |
| | sidewalk | flashlight | | |
| | storeroom | greenhouse | | |
| | upstairs | houseboat | | |
| | workshop | moonlight | | |
| | | mousetrap | | |
| | | newspaper | | |
| | | raindrop | | |
| | | snowman | | |
| | | sunburn | | |
| | | sunlight | | |
| | | snowball | | |
| | | steamship | | |

**Quick Self-Check 15**

1. What generalizations about compound words can be drawn from the words *carseat* and *firewood?*
2. What three words are compound and have recently entered the English language.
3. Can you suggest two activities to teach compound words?

**Review**

A. Write the four digraph/dipthongs with the letter *a.*
B. What two letter combinations, a consonant and the vowel *i,* can decode as /sh/? There are three of these combinations.

## Contractions

In discussing compound words, some instructors also introduce the concept of contractions. These forms are frequent in the conversation of characters in stories read by children. Confusion occurs because sometimes more than one letter of a contraction is omitted and also because some forms have similar sounds but differ in meaning. A list of some common contractions follows:

| | | | | | |
|---|---|---|---|---|---|
| I am | I'm | I have | I've | I will | I'll |
| You are | You're | You have | You've | You will | You'll |
| He is | He's | She is | She's | It is | It's |
| We are | We're | We have | We've | We will | We'll |
| They are | They're | They have | They've | They will | They'll |
| cannot | can't | could not | couldn't | have not | haven't |
| would not | wouldn't | | | | |

One of the most common errors young students make (and also older students!) is in writing the phrase "would of." It should be written as *would have* but because it sounds like a contracted form, students shorten the *have* to a *v* sound and write the word *of,* since this is what they hear. *Would of* is always incorrect.

## Prefixes, Roots, and Suffixes

### Prefixes: definitions and dilemmas

Defining a prefix for the teacher is not the same as defining it for the student. Linguists begin to define prefixes as morphemes. Simply defined, a morpheme is a minimal unit of meaning. A morpheme differs from a syllable. (For example, the /t/ written as *ed* in *jumped* is a separate morpheme; therefore, the word *jumped* consists of one syllable, but two morphemes.)

By definition, prefixes, being bound, are *dependent meaning-bearing elements* attached at the beginning of independent words. Therefore *un* as in *unable* is a prefix, but *un* as in *until* is not (because *til* is not an independent word). By definition, therefore, *pre* as in *presume, in* as in *insult,* and *dis* as in *disturb* are not prefixes, again because they are not attached to independent or base words. Words such as *presume, insult,* and *disturb* have historical roots, but as the language changed, these words changed or they were taken directly into English as whole words from Latin or French. Some educators refer to these kinds of related prefix syllables, attached to nonwords, as "absorbed" prefixes.[3]

The above information and definition is, of course, for the teacher and much older students. Certainly young children should not be burdened by such an explanation; instead, the teacher may proceed by instructing a third or fourth grade class with the following lessons as suggested by White, Sowell, and Yanagihara (1989). They believe in explicitly defining and teaching the concept of a prefix by presenting examples and nonexamples. Thus, after discussion, the teacher would write, "What is a prefix?" on chart paper and, below it, the following:

1. A prefix is a group of letters that go in front of a word.
2. The prefix changes the meaning of a word.

(3) While these absorbed prefixes do not change the word meaning, the prefix does affect the accent or stress pattern of the word. Absorbed prefixes are often unaccented syllables.

3. When you "peel off" the prefix, a word must be left. (This is demonstrated by contrasting genuine prefixed words such as *unkind* and *refill* with non-example words such as *uncle* and *reason*.)

They believe students taught in this way begin with a clear idea of what a prefix is.

Three prefixes taught early are *un, re,* and *dis*. Generally, exercises such as the following are used so that students can see the difference when the prefix is added. You will note that an independent base, a clearly recognizable whole English word, is used to minimize confusion.

| re | + | pay | repay |
|----|---|------|-------|
| re | + | state | restate |
| un | + | able | unable |
| un | + | sure | unsure |
| dis | + | like | dislike |
| dis | + | trust | distrust |

Students encounter words such as *disdain, determine,* and *result* in which there is a decodable common beginning syllable. Should they use their phonics/syllabication skills to help decode these words if they are unknown? Certainly! Clues are important. But students should gradually be instructed about these absorbed "prefix" forms after first having exposure to the more traditional prefix plus whole word combination, as shown above. This does not mean that children cannot learn to read and understand words with absorbed prefixes while doing a lot of independent reading.

## Roots and suffixes

Since suffixes are attached to roots (or bases), defining *root* at this point for the teacher seems appropriate. A root is defined as a basic unit having a semantic connection with other words. For example, in the words *lighted, lightning,* and *enlightening, light* is the root word. More specifically, the root is that part of a word, neither prefix nor suffix, that conveys the major portion of the word's meaning. (Linguists use the term *base*.) Again, much of this information is provided for the benefit of the teacher and the older student. For the young student, a simple definition such as "a root carries the main meaning of a word" should be sufficient.

As with prefixes, defining a suffix can also present difficulty. A suffix (again, not necessarily a syllable) is a "meaningful" language unit or morpheme, bound, as with a prefix, and affixed to the end of a root or base word. While other aspects of meaning are involved, a primary function of a suffix is to indicate the part of speech of the word; that is, how it functions in a sentence. Although there are some cases in which the suffix does not change the part of speech (for example, *race* and *racist)* in general, there are four types of suffixes, and these may form nouns, verbs, adjectives, and adverbs. In addition to often changing the part of speech, some suffixes also change the lexical meaning of roots, such as *colorless* and *colorful* or *doubtless* and *doubtful*.

Suffixes are of two types: inflectional suffixes as defined in list *A* (the sum total) and derivational suffixes as exemplified in list *B* (only a few of the many that exist in the English language).

*A*
### *Total Inflectional Suffixes*

| | |
|---|---|
| *s* (es) plural | boys, brushes |
| *'s* (s') apostrophe | boy's, boys' |
| *s* third person singular | sings |
| *ed* past tense | grabbed |
| *ing* present participle | singing |
| *en* past participle | (has, have) eaten |
| *er* comparative | taller |
| *est* superlative | tallest |

*B*
### *A Few Derivational Suffixes*

| Root Word | Part of Speech | Suffix | Affixed Word | Part of Speech |
|---|---|---|---|---|
| base | n. | ic | bas*ic* | adj. |
| correct | adj. | ly | correct*ly* | adv. |
| fool | n. | ish | fool*ish* | adj. |
| allow | v. | ance | allow*ance* | n. |
| person | n. | al | person*al* | adj. |
| attract | v. | ive | attract*ive* | adj. |
| clever | adj. | ness | clever*ness* | n. |
| agree | v. | ment | agree*ment* | n. |

The suffixes in list *A* (a closed group of only eight) do not usually change the part of speech of the word. These suffixes also represent some of the first ones taught to primary children. It is much easier to understand the word changes in list *A* than it is to understand those in list *B*. (There are many, many derivational suffixes.) Not only are there alterations in the meanings of the words in list *B*, but in addition, the parts of speech change.

A simple definition such as "a suffix is a letter or group of letters (a unit) that comes at the end of a word" would be sufficient for most students. With older students, you could add "and that often change the part of speech."

The concept of a suffix can be taught at upper elementary levels similarly to the prefix. After discussion and examples, the teacher would write, "What is a suffix?" and below it, the following:

1. A suffix is a group of letters that comes at the end of a word.
2. The suffix often changes the part of speech of a word. For example, verbs can be changed to adjectives, such as the word *accept* (a verb) + *able* (an "adjective" suffix) can become *acceptable* (an adjective).
3. When you "peel off" the suffix, a word is usually left.

## Further complexities of affixed words

It is not difficult to decode a suffix, provided that the student recognizes the letters or syllables as a unit. The difficulty arises when the suffix has changed the part of speech or changed the word concept to such a degree that students do not recognize the meaning of the affixed word. Being familiar with the noun *person* and then

**TABLE 3.5**   Selected list from Dale's "The Words We Know."*

| | |
|---|---|
| active (4)—activate (12) | information (6)—informant (10) |
| break (4)—breakage (10) | injury (4)—injurious (8) |
| competing (6)—competitive (10) | migrate (6)—migratory (10) |
| decision (6)—decisive (12) | nice (4)—nicety (10) |
| demolish (6)—demolition (10) | nominate (4)—nominee (8) |
| deprive (6)—deprivation (10) | note (4)—notation (10) |
| elephant (4)—elephantine (12) | opportunity (6)—opportune (12) |
| erase (4)—erasure (8) | part (6)—partition (12) |
| error (6)—erroneous (12) | penalty (6)—penal (12) |
| escape (4)—escapade (10) | persuade (6)—persuasive (10) |
| evacuate (6)—evacuation (12) | pollen (6)—pollinate (10) |
| habit (4)—habitual (10) | population (6)—populace (12) |
| infant (6)—infancy (10) | simple (4)—simplify (8) |

*Edgar Dale and Joseph O'Rourke, *Techniques of Teaching Vocabulary* (Palo Alto, CA: Field Educational Pub., Inc., 1971), p. 183.

having to shift to a phrase such as a *personal matter* may take some understanding. Studies show that students do not always make these shifts in meaning. While the root word is known, the affixed form may not be understood until much later. Table 3.5 provides pairs of related words with their grade level scores as found in the Dale nationwide study, "The Words We Know—A National Inventory."

Added to the problem of a shift in the part of speech of the word, which affects syntax and meaning, the suffixed word sometimes undergoes shifts in spelling as in *prescribe/prescription*. The same suffix is often spelled differently, such as *tion/sion, ant/ent, ance/ence, ar/er*. These differences are of historical origin, but have nothing to do with meaning or pronunciation. There are also shifts in some of the vowel pronunciations as *cave/cavity, crime/criminal, supreme/supremacy*. Even more puzzling, some suffixes denote words as either adjectives or adverbs: *kindly* (adj.) and *quickly* (adv.). And then, there are words like *hardly*, which has nothing to do with *hard*. Since oral language has far fewer derived words than does written language, many children have not had exposure to these affixed forms. TV programs, which monopolize much of children's time today, have a paucity of these kinds of words.

Added to these complexities is the difficulty of understanding the meaning of many of the bound roots. Therefore, it is necessary that the teacher guide discussion in the classroom to clarify the decoding, the meaning, and the related vocabulary of these affixed forms. This is certainly time well spent and is perhaps the most important aspect of teaching these words.

### Spelling and suffixes

A direct link exists between spelling generalizations about suffixes and the reader's ability to mentally separate suffixes from roots in order to identify the total derived or inflected word. The following generalizations are worth knowing:

1. When adding a suffix beginning with a vowel to a word that ends with an *e,* the *e* is usually dropped: *believe + able = believable; secure + ity = security.* In a word such as *changeable,* the *e* is not dropped. To do so would "give" the *g* a "hard" sound.

2. When adding a suffix beginning with a vowel to a word that ends in one single consonant with a short vowel before it, the last consonant is usually doubled: *run + er = runner; knot + ing = knotting.* (This permits us to differentiate between words such as *sloping* and *slopping.*)

3. When adding a suffix to a word that ends with a *y* preceded by a consonant, the *y* is usually changed to an *i; greedy + ness = greediness; fancy + full = fanciful.* Exception: The letter *y* is never changed to an *i* when adding *ing; reply/replying; cry/crying.* This is because English does not permit two *i*'s together, and without the *y,* the words would be pronounced as /repling/ and /cring/.

4. When adding a suffix to a word that ends with a *y* preceded by a vowel, the *y* is not changed: *employ + ment = employment; play + er = player.*

## Affix lists

Although there is a difference of opinion as to which affix list best represents the most common prefixes and suffixes found in the elementary grades, the lists in Table 3.6 were based on an examination of basal texts by the author. Some more common roots are also included. Table 3.7 lists additional affixes.

## How many? Which grade levels?

Much variety can be found in basals and in materials that purport to teach the prefixes and suffixes used in instruction. Johnson and Pearson (1978) presented a list of 19 prefixes for instruction, while White, Sowell and Yanagihara (1989) concentrated on the 9 most common prefixes. They pointed out others only as they arose, such as *sub* in *subarctic.* They suggested these 9 prefixes and 10 suffixes because they believe these are the most common and also because of their high utility. Prefixes: *un, re, (in, im, ir, il,* with a meaning of *not*),[4] *dis, en, non, (in, im* with a meaning of *in* or *into), over, mis.* Suffixes: *-s/es, -ed, -ing* (these are the 3 most common inflected suffixes) and the derivational suffixes *-ly, -er, -ion, -able, -al, -y,* and *-ness.*

While there is some disagreement over which specific affixes to teach, there is broad agreement in the research that emphasizes the importance of knowing how to decode and understand affixed words, especially as students move into more complex reading in the content areas of social studies and science (Beck and McKeown, 1991). A proliferation of commercial materials to teach these skills has also flooded the market. While some of them may have a place in the classroom, we need to always remember the importance of teacher instruction, daily attention to vocabulary, motivating activities that build interest in words, and, most importantly, the benefits that accrue to students who do wide and varied reading, thus learning many of these words through the context of varied selections.

Figure 3.1 includes an example of an abbreviated lesson for students who are in the early stages of learning structural skills and some example lessons for more advanced students.

(4) The prefix *in* has different forms because the final letter assimilates to the root or word: *immature, irregular,* and *illegible.*

**TABLE 3.6**   A list of prefixes, suffixes, and roots for elementary grades.

### COMMON PREFIXES

| PREFIX | MEANING | WORD EXAMPLE |
|---|---|---|
| anti | against | antiwar |
| ex | out of | exit |
| inter | between | intermission |
| in, im, ir, il | not | incapable, impossible, irregular, illegible |
| mis | not | misplace |
| non | not | nonfiction |
| over | too much | overrate |
| post | after | postdated |
| re | again | replay |
| sub | under | submarine |
| super | above | superman |
| trans | across | transworld |

### COMMON SUFFIXES

| SUFFIX | PART OF SPEECH (SUFFIX) | ROOT | WORD EXAMPLE |
|---|---|---|---|
| able | adj. | depend | dependable |
| al | adj. | form | formal |
| er/or | n. | farm/sail | farmer/sailor |
| ful | n. | cup | cupful |
| ify | v. | beauty | beautify |
| ion/tion | n. | rebel | rebellion/condition |
| ish | adj. | self | selfish |
| less | adj. | care | careless |
| ly | adv. | quick | quickly |
| ment | n. | state | statement |
| ness | n. | kind | kindness |
| ous | adj. | courage | courageous |

### COMMON ROOTS

| ROOT | MEANING | WORD EXAMPLE |
|---|---|---|
| cap | head | captain |
| cycl | ring, circle | bicycle |
| dent | tooth | dentist |
| form | shape | uniform |
| geo | earth | geography |
| gram | letter | telegram |
| graph | write | autograph |
| phone | sound | earphone |
| vis | see | television |

**TABLE 3.7**  An additional list of prefixes, suffixes, and roots.

### PREFIXES

| PREFIX | MEANING | WORD EXAMPLE |
|---|---|---|
| ante | before | anteroom |
| mono | one | monotone |
| peri | around | perimeter |
| semi | half | semi-monthly |
| tri | three | trimester |
| ultra | beyond | ultrasuede |

### SUFFIXES

| SUFFIX | PART OF SPEECH (SUFFIX) | ROOT | WORD EXAMPLE |
|---|---|---|---|
| an | n. | artist | artisan |
| ance, ence | n. | resist, depend | resistance, dependence |
| dom | n. | wise | wisdom |
| ent | adj. | preside | president |
| ic | n. | drama | dramatic |
| ism | n. | ritual | ritualism |
| ize | v. | oxygen | oxidize |
| ive | v. | narrate | narrative |
| ity, y | n. | hostile, fidget | hostility, fidgety |
| some | adj. | worry | worrisome |

### ROOTS (FOR UPPER ELEMENTARY AND JUNIOR HIGH)

| ROOT | MEANING | WORD EXAMPLE |
|---|---|---|
| ambi, amphi | around | ambition, amphitheater |
| anthrop | man | anthropology |
| aster, astr | star | asterisk, astral |
| bio | life | biology |
| cav | hollow | cavity |
| chrom | color | chromosome |
| circum | around | circumstance |
| contra | against | contraband |
| demo | people | demonstration |
| derm | skin | dermatologist |
| dict | to speak | diction |
| duc | to lead | induction |
| epi | upon | epidermis |
| gam | marriage | polygamy |
| hetero | different | heterogeneous |
| homo | same | homonym |
| loc | place | location |
| mal | bad | malformed |
| manu | hand | manual |
| mar | sea | maritime |
| mort | death | mortician |
| port | to carry | porter |
| scrib, script | to write | transcribe |
| theo | god | theology |
| vid, vis | to see | vision |
| vinc, vict | to conquer | invincible, victim |
| vita | life | vitamins |
| viv | to live | vivacious |
| voc | to call | vocalize |

**FIGURE 3.1** Sample lessons for teaching prefixes and suffixes.

EXAMPLE LESSON: YOUNGER CHILDREN

Begin by drawing a simple picture of a house, telling children that some words can be compared to a house; that just as you can add on to a house, you can add on to a word (add on to the house as in the example):

Write the words *happy* and *unhappy* on the board (under the house) and ask a student to underline the parts that are alike.

Teacher: What did we add to the beginning of the word *happy? (un)* We call this a prefix. Say prefix. A prefix is not a word by itself, but we add it to a word to make a new word.

Teacher: (writes the two parts under the house) What does *happy* mean?

Children: (respond)

Teacher: (Points out to children how *un* changed the meaning, or inducts the meaning from the children.)

Follow Up: Offers additional exercises with *un* for words such as *untrue, unfair, unlike, unreal,* and *unable.* Children dictate sentences with these words as the teacher writes them on the board or on a transparency. Children underline the root word and draw a ring around the prefix. (The activity may be extended after sufficient practice, and an addition made to the house to introduce the idea of a suffix.)

EXAMPLE LESSONS: ADVANCED STUDENTS

**I. Recognizing Prefixes**

**Purpose:**

Students will recognize certain common prefixes and learn to read them as part of a larger word unit.

**Procedure:**

1. Write the following roots on the board explaining to students that each is a base word to which a prefix may be added. Also impress upon students that our roots, sometimes referred to as stems, are very selective and will only accept particular prefixes. A stem often carries the lexical meaning of the extended word. Read the stems with the students.

   | | | | |
   |---|---|---|---|
   | agree | sight | sense | war |
   | claim | pay | circle | merge |
   | place | play | world | port |

2. Now write each prefix on the board. These are commonly found in reading materials. Have the students pronounce these prefixes. You may want to explain that we have several prefixes that mean something similar to "not" such as *dis, mis, non,* and *anti.* You may want to discuss some of the meanings of other prefixes, although as mentioned, some of these are absorbed prefixes and carry no meaning in and of themselves.

   | | | | |
   |---|---|---|---|
   | dis | in | non | anti |
   | pro | pre | semi | sub |
   | mis | re | trans | ex |

*(continued)*

**FIGURE 3.1**   Continued.

3. Now attach the prefixes to the roots or base words and have the student read the new words:

| | | | |
|---|---|---|---|
| disagree | insight | nonsense | antiwar |
| proclaim | prepay | semicircle | submerge |
| misplace | replay | transworld | export |

4. This lesson should be followed by practice. Place prefixed words on the board or a ditto. Have students identify and pronounce the prefix, identify and pronounce the root or base word, and blend the two together to pronounce the affixed word.

| | | | |
|---|---|---|---|
| unfit | overbid | antifreeze | pro-American |
| degrade | redraw | preschool | supervisor |
| misbehave | transport | forewarn | subterranean |

5. Students will, when asked to offer prefixed words, give examples such as "pro/perty." Tell them these are not prefixes in the true sense of the word but knowing prefixes can aid in pronunciation. This is a good place to learn something about the fascinating history of the English language.

6. Have students verbalize that looking for a prefix can be a first step in decoding polysyllabic words and have them locate prefixed words in their reading materials, identifying the prefix and the base word or root.

## II. Recognizing Suffixes

**Purpose:**

Students will recognize certain common suffixes and learn to read them as part of a larger word unit.

**Procedure:**

1. Write the following stems on the board explaining to students that each is a base word to which a suffix may be added. Again as with the first lesson on prefixes, impress upon students that our roots are very selective and will only accept certain suffixes. The suffix often changes the part of speech of a word, whereas the prefix usually does not.

| | | | |
|---|---|---|---|
| block | dance | music | wise |
| employ | wool | fear | simple |
| poet | act | fool | alarm |

2. Now write each suffix on the board. These are commonly found in reading materials. Have the students pronounce these suffixes. You may want to explain that suffixes may change the part of speech of the word and show them examples of these changes. Point out also that the spelling sometimes changes when suffixes are added to words but does not usually change when prefixes are added to words.

| | | | |
|---|---|---|---|
| ade | er | ian | dom |
| ee | en | ful | fy |
| ic | tion | ish | ist |

3. Attach the suffixes to the root and have the students read the new words.

| | | | |
|---|---|---|---|
| blockade | dancer | musician | wisdom |
| employee | woolen | fearful | simplify |
| poetic | action | foolish | alarmist |

4. Practice with other suffixed words. When students have confidence and show they understand the principle involved, have them locate suffixed words in their reading materials and identify the suffix and root.

## III. Recognizing Words with Prefixes and Suffixes

**Purpose:**

Students will recognize that certain words are composed of a prefix, a stem, and a suffix. Half of the words with prefixes also have suffixes (White, Sowell, and Yamagihara, 1990).

*(continued)*

**FIGURE 3.1** Continued.

**Procedure:**

1. Write the following words on the board. Ask students to identify and pronounce the prefix and then to look at the rest of the word. If they cannot identify the root, have them check the suffix first and pronounce it, then return to the stem, pronounce it, and then blend all three parts together. Some students will be able to identify the word parts in order after they have had practice and will not need to always locate prefix, suffix, and then root.

| | | | |
|---|---|---|---|
| repayment | exceeding | interchangeable | enrichment |
| enjoyment | unsinkable | unknowing | reboarded |
| undesirable | inaction | removable | preheated |

2. Have students locate words in their materials with prefixes, suffixes, and roots. Practice with these word parts, trying to build other words with these structural parts.

Always remind students that after identifying the word parts of unfamiliar words as the prefix, suffix, and root, and blending them together, the next step is to place the word in context to see if it makes sense.

## Turning incorrect answers into learning experiences

Collins (1987) suggests some procedures to turn incorrect answers into learning experiences. While her suggestions were for comprehension questions, the same procedures can be adapted while working with affixes.

***Think once again.*** If you believe a student has the background to answer correctly say something like, "Take just a little more time. I believe you do know the answer." (You have asked the question, "Name two prefixes that mean 'not'.")

***Paraphrase the question.*** By rephrasing the question to, "Name two prefixes that mean 'not,' and that change the meaning of a word," you include a needed clue.

***Help with a prompt.*** Offer a small piece of relevant information to help students such as, "If you understand something, it is clear. If you do not, (pause for a moment to let students supply the answer) it is unclear," and let the student supply the word.

***Expand the answer.*** Repeat the part of the answer that was correct as "Unclear, that's correct." Now add, "Now, what is the prefix?"

***Asking for clues.*** In some classrooms you might call on other students to give clue words or suggest some yourself such as "unable, unbeaten, unusual." You may also ask a student who missed the question to call upon a classmate to help with clues. The student could offer words such as misprint, misconduct, inaction, invalid, dislike, disregard.

***Making students accountable.*** If students give two incorrect answers to the same question, tell them you will ask the question again to give them the incentive to remember. Return to the students before the period ends and ask the same question.

***Nonexamples.*** The writer once had a young student offer "dis-a-minute" as a word with a prefix. Giving a clue such as "Do you like candy? (always receives a "yes" answer) "How about spinach? Do you like it or do you ___ it?" helps the student supply a correct word.

***Wait time.*** If students do not raise their hands after a suitable time, tell them what the answer is not. This allows time for thinking and, at times, can introduce a little humor into the lesson.

## Activities with affixed words

When teachers believe students would profit from drill activities with affixes and roots, some of these types of exercises might prove useful:

1. Showing change of meaning when prefixes are added.

    | | |
    |---|---|
    | dis | interest |
    | dis | agree |
    | dis | approve |

2. Using roots to form new words and then discussing their meaning.

    | | |
    |---|---|
    | phone | phonograph, phonics, telephone |
    | graph | graphics, telegraph, photograph |
    | geo | geology, geologist, geography |

3. Reviewing affixed words.

    a. Write two columns of words such as the following on the board. (This list should be more extensive, with review words from their texts.)

    | | |
    |---|---|
    | movement | believable |
    | payment | excitement |
    | usable | portable |
    | readable | agreement |
    | equipment | lovable |

    b. Divide students into two teams.

    c. A student from the first team selects a word from the first column, reads it, and uses it in a sentence.

    d. If the second team agrees that the word is correct, both in pronunciation and meaning, team one erases the word. The procedure continues, and a member of the second team selects a word from the second column, reads it, and uses it in a sentence. The first team that erases all the words wins.

4. Creating visual-auditory links (Peterson and Phelps, 1991). Select roots such as *script* (to write) and *audi* (to hear). Locate a picture with which to associate the meaning of the word part. (Libraries have copies of reproducible artwork, or use magazines and cartoons.) Students or the teacher create a slogan that helps recall the root's meaning. For example, *Scriptus, the writer,* is the auditory link for the picture (the visual link) of a rabbit *writing* on a chalkboard. Transparencies can be used for reference. Worksheets for other roots can eventually become small booklets for students as they collect their words, finding and enlarging their word families. Always share and discuss the words. Refer to Peterson and Phelps for a more detailed explanation.

Audi's all ears          Scriptus, the writer

5. Practicing reading words with a particular prefix. Use a tachistoscope with a strip of words.

6. Seeing the relationship between words with similar roots. Use word building whereby students begin with a word and build on this root to form as many new words as possible. With the root *graph*, a "tree" can be constructed with the word *graph* on the trunk, and the related words written on the leaves. Example words might include *geography, spectograph, telegraph, graphic, mimeograph, photograph, polygraph, phonograph, graphics*.

   Another method is to show the relatedness by drawing "bricks" of the meaningful word parts as:

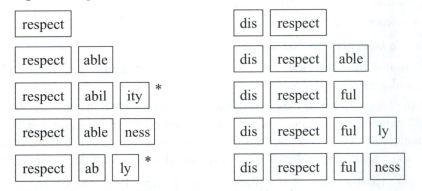

   *Note how the spelling of the suffix is sometimes altered.

7. Gaining an overview of vocabulary in a new unit.
   a. The teacher places a list of words on the board, a transparency, or a ditto. The words are discussed and read. In pairs the students decide what words they will pantomime. These might be such words as *feudalism, nobleman, conquistadors* from a social studies unit about the Middle Ages. (Use about a dozen words.)
   b. In pairs, students pantomime their word and then after a minute or so call on a classmate to spell the word, define it, and use it in a sentence.

8. Engaging in overall practice.
   a. Mimeo bingo cards so that there are a total of 25 blocks. From a list of words on the board or a ditto sheet, students make up their own cards, placing the words in whatever blocks they wish. The teacher (or a knowledgeable student) reads and gives the definition of the word.
   b. Students with limited vocabulary skills may sit with a buddy, and the two-member team then plays with two cards. The caller states whether

the winner must cover five spaces horizontally, vertically, or diagonally. The winner reads the words and may define particular ones. An example card is shown below.

c. Further variations include covering the four corners, the *B* row, the *I* row, etc.

| B | I | N | G | O |
|---|---|---|---|---|
| certainly | dependable | vocalize | autograph | appliance |
| disagree | biology | respectful | television | electricity |
| transportation | countless | free | carefully | intensity |
| subscribe | believable | replacement | selfish | impossible |
| phonograph | agreement | extremely | misplace | submarine |

## Words in the content areas

Words in the content areas, unlike story reading, often have roots and affixed forms. This vocabulary differs from story vocabulary in still other ways (Ambruster and Nagy, 1991). First, in story reading, if some of the words are unknown, the meaning can still be clear. For example, if the setting establishes that the heat was *torrid,* the student who is reading would still get the idea without necessarily knowing the meaning of *torrid.* In contrast, content area vocabulary often represents major concepts essential for understanding. Failure to understand the meaning of *metamorphosis* (the physical change undergone by some animals) means the student has failed to grasp the main idea of the lesson. Second, new vocabulary in content areas often is unrelated to any familiar concept. Not only are students learning new vocabulary, they are also often learning new ideas. Third, there is often a relationship among these words (unlike in story reading), and as much as possible, teachers should try to show what the relationship is; this also reinforces the concept of the word. For example, the student would, along with *metamorphosis,* meet these related words: *transformation, function, appearance,* and *condition.* The relationships among them should be elaborated upon.

Research by Jenkins, Matlock, and Slocum (1989) on vocabulary instruction indicates again that a key appears to be the amount of time devoted to vocabulary instruction. The activity "Possible Sentences" provides a novel way to carry out that instruction.

*Possible sentences (Stahl and Kapinus, 1991).* Select about six words from a content area that might cause difficulty for students; for example, words involving key concepts from a textbook passage on the weather would include *barometer, humidity, meteorology, front, moisture, air pressure.* Place all these words on the board and orally provide a short definition of them. Select another four to six words students would recognize from the passage, such as *rain, clouds, high, changes, weather, snow.* Place these on the board also.

Next, ask students (in groups) to think of possible sentences they might read in such a passage about the weather. The sentences should contain at least two of the words; one word should be a key concept word. After discussion, write their sentences on the board. Accept both accurate and inaccurate "possible" sentences but do not discuss them at this time. Follow this by having the students read the passage from the chapter.

After the reading, the teacher returns to the board, and the class discusses whether or not each sentence could or could not be true based on the reading. True sentences are left whole. The untrue sentences are discussed and modified to become true. (For a more detailed explanation, see the article by Stahl and Kapinus.)

This kind of activity draws upon the student's prior knowledge of the topic, and predicting the sentences forces students to use any partial knowledge they have about the word. The use of two words forces the student to think about the relations between word concepts rather than each word separately. Because of the interaction among the students in discussion, there is better retention of the concepts and word meanings.

### Guidelines for teaching affixed words and more advanced vocabulary

1. Teachers who use activity exercises to reinforce these skills should remember that difficult words with affixes encountered in reading should be *talked about*. Students should say the words aloud to one another and in groups. School language is more easily clarified and reinforced as it is learned initially by frequently meeting and hearing words in meaningful context (Eller, Pappas, and Brown, 1988).

2. Try to encourage students to be "word collectors" with their own personalized list. Set aside a time to share and discuss these words. Have bulletin board displays with particular kinds of words. Bring in books about words. Build *word consciousness* through meaningful language activities.

3. Be certain to schedule time in the curriculum for working with affixed words. Don't assume students will learn to decode and understand them on their own.

4. Emphasize to students that base words are very selective as to which prefixes and suffixes they will accept. For example, *nation, national, nationality,* but not *nationment.*

For extensive word lists of prefixes and suffixes, with a suggested grade level see Appendix C.

### Questions teachers ask about roots and affixes

1. *Should students be taught to search for "little" words in "big" words?* Not really. This is a poor practice because it can lead to all kinds of misinformation. Example: In the word *father,* should it be *fat-her?* The only "little" words students should search for in "big" words are subunits of meaning. There is only one smaller word in *splashed: splash,* not *lash,* or *as,* since they do not represent a meaning unit within the word. Uncovering the root is therefore not the same as finding little words in big words.

2. *Should students be aware of problems in definition? Should they be told why affixed words can present difficulty?* It depends on many factors such as age and maturity. Teachers should understand structural analysis so they are in a

position to answer questions, but avoid burdening pupils with more information about affixes than they can utilize.

3. *What should students focus on when they meet an unknown affixed word?* They should be taught to isolate letter combinations resembling affixes in unfamiliar words and to recognize what remains as a base word, subject to spelling changes *(debate/debatable)*. It is the underlying meaning units that should receive the focus. A strategy such as the following might be employed:

    a. Note the contextual clue. What kind of a word do you think it is?

    b. Separate or "peel off" the prefix and suffix (depending on the word) from the root.

    c. Put the word together. Think about related roots and other affixes for clues to meaning.

4. *Why is work with structural analysis considered so important?* First, because it is particularly useful in identifying word forms not previously encountered in print, such as *dentist/dental*. Second, fluent reading depends on the ability to quickly decode unknown polysyllabic words, many of which are affixed. Third, many of the difficult words students meet in the content areas (social studies and science), beginning in the fourth grade, are often affixed words they have never met before.

5. *Are phonics skills important in using structural analysis?* Yes. This is because once the root is sorted out and recognized, sound-symbol relationships can help a reader arrive at the root's pronunciation. Of course, the ease with which students proceed through this structural reading skill stage depends as mentioned on their accumulated storehouse of a large sight vocabulary.

**Quick Self-Check 16**

1. State the differences between a prefix and a suffix.

2. Identify the two types of prefixes from the following list:

    | | | |
    |---|---|---|
    | recent | insist | dislike |
    | prepay | uncertain | impersonal |

3. Identify the two types of suffixes from the following list:

    | | | |
    |---|---|---|
    | foolish | singing | called |
    | cleverness | jumps | safely |

4. State some of the generalizations students need to know when suffixes are added to words.

5. What is one of the best ways for students to learn to read and understand affixed words?

6. Explain why work with structural analysis is so important.

7. Suggest some activities to teach affixed words.

For a more complete list of active and absorbed prefixes and example words and a more complete list of suffixes and example words, see Appendix C.

## Syllabication[5]

### Teaching syllabication

Good readers tend to learn to divide words into syllables intuitively and to capitalize on this skill to help them decode words. Some students do not have this ability and need considerable practice with syllabication, as an aid to both reading and spelling. They need to understand that a syllable is a *unit of speech* that always contains one vowel sound, and has nothing to do with the number of letters. (*Oleo* has three syllables, while *squashed* has one.) This is because the focal unit of language is the stress given to vowel sounds, with consonant sounds being subordinate to this stress. Therefore, in teaching students to syllabicate in order to decode multisyllabic words, it is necessary to help them understand that the vowel sound is the key unit.

Young children do not have to know the precise rules of syllabication but after some reading instruction, they should have a general idea of how to break a word into smaller units, as aids to reading and spelling. Practice can take place by first working with words they do know to get the concept of a syllable. They may engage in such activities as

1. saying words in syllables.
2. writing words in syllables.
3. sensing the syllables by placing their hands under their chins and saying the word. As their jaws drop, they can "feel" the syllable division.

To begin instruction in syllabication, teachers do not always start with a definition such as "every syllable contains a sounded vowel," but instead often begin in a game-like format. Children are asked to note columns of words in which the vowel sound rather than the number of vowel letters is the key to the word parts or syllables. For example:

Teacher: We are going to play a game. Look at these three lists of words. Let's read these words together. How many parts, or syllables, do you hear? Listen carefully.

| *A* | *B* | *C* |
|------|-------|---------|
| mat | same | can dy |
| talk | spray | rob in |
| short | mail | catch er |
| scrap | coat | but ter |
| duck | tease | may be |

How many vowels do you see in column *A?*

How many vowel sounds do you hear in column *A?*

How many vowels do you see in column *B?*

How many vowel sounds do you hear in column *B?*

How many vowels do you see in column *C?*

How many vowel sounds do you hear in column *C?*

(5) Syllabication does not have to be like the dictionary, as the rules used there are not based on linguistic research but on the arbitrary decisions of typesetters from early days. Dictionary syllabication rules sometimes have little to do with the actual sound patterns of syllables.

The teacher draws conclusions from the students about the three groups of words.

When introducing more formal syllabication instruction, many teachers begin with the concept of the open and closed syllable. By definition, an open syllable has a long vowel sound, and a closed syllable has a short vowel sound followed by a consonant.

| A | B |
|---|---|
| **Open Syllables** | **Closed Syllables** |
| po ny | fin ish |
| pa per | hab it |
| la bel | mod el |
| mu sic | riv er |
| mo tor | sig nal |

The idea is that in list A the "open syllable" as the first syllable in *po ny* has a long vowel sound, while in list B the second consonant sound has "closed" the syllable and the vowel sound is short. In working with syllabication, two syllable words such as those in list B often follow the CVC rule: when you have one consonant, one vowel, and one final consonant (not r), you generally have a short vowel (m*a*t, b*e*d, f*i*g). This rule also holds in multisyllabic words such as *fin/ish, hab/it, mod/el, riv/er,* and *sig/nal* as above. In a word such as *power,* remember that *ow* is a diphthong, and therefore the letter *w* is not a consonant here but is part of a vowel combination and therefore not separated.

In an unknown two-syllable word, however, sometimes there is no way for the student to tell whether the syllable division should be before or after the second consonant. Students must often try both vowel sounds to see which one works. Some reading programs suggest that if you do not find a double consonant in the middle of a word, divide after the first vowel, and it is long. Example: *sha/dy, me/ter.* Obviously, based on list B above, this is not always the case. The writer has found that the "rules" listed below have greater consistency.

After practice and instruction in syllabication with older students, it is a good idea to place categories of words on the board and to draw generalizations about how these words are usually divided, as an aid in decoding. For example:

| **Compound Words** | | **Affixes** | | **Double Consonants** | |
|---|---|---|---|---|---|
| birdhouse | bird/house | kindness | kind/ness | dollar | dol/lar |
| outside | out/side | lovely | love/ly | happen | hap/pen |
| seatbelt | seat/belt | return | re/turn | rabbit | rab/bit |

| **Different Consonants** | | **le Preceded by a Consonant** | |
|---|---|---|---|
| envy | en/vy | icicle | ic/i/cle |
| picture | pic/ture | maple | ma/ple |
| silver | sil/ver | table | ta/ble |

## Dividing words into syllables

Something similar to the following may be realized and charted after the previous discussion. Remember that every syllable must have a vowel sound.

1. See if the word is compound. Examples: *birdhouse, outside, seatbelt.*
2. See if the word has affixes. Examples: *kindness, lovely, return.*
3. See if the word has a double consonant in the middle. Examples: *dollar, happen, rabbit.*
4. See if the word has two different consonants in the middle. Examples: *envy, picture, silver.* Do not divide a blend *(twisting, folding)* or a digraph *(mother, wishful).*
5. See if the word ends in *le,* preceded by a consonant. Place this consonant with the *le.* Examples: *ic/i/cle, ma/ple, ta/ble.*
6. Now try the word in context. Does it make sense? Then read on.
7. If it does not make sense, try the dictionary or ask a group leader.

Putting this all together, a simple syllabication generalization can be as follows:

**Check to see if the word**

1. **is a compound or has affixes.**
2. **has double consonant letters or two unlike consonant letters. Do not divide blends or digraphs.**
3. **ends in *le*; if so, place the preceding consonant letter before it.**
4. **makes sense!**

### Activities for teaching syllabication

1. *Objective: To begin to recognize two-syllable words.* Write words with one and two syllables on the board. Have them read. Then let one pupil read a word, while others clap hands softly to indicate how many parts they hear in the word.
2. *Objective: To teach syllabication of words with medial consonant digraphs.* Write these words on the board: *bucket, washer, cricket, gather, bother, nephew, bishop, leather.*
   a. Ask pupils what the words have in common.
   b. Divide words with a slash mark for students.
   c. Ask pupils what they can deduce from your division.
   d. Elicit from them that a digraph is not to be divided.
3. *Objective: To decode words based on syllabication generalizations (as many as they have learned thus far).* Pass out a worksheet with a number of words as follows:

| | | |
|---|---|---|
| pattern | department | equipment |
| shallow | oatmeal | subject |
| exposed | cardboard | pinhole |
| thickness | complete | darkroom |
| maple | thimble | staple |

On the board, write a word as below that typifies a specific example of each rule.

| *Compound Words* | *Prefixes and Suffixes* | *Double Letters* | *le Words* |
|---|---|---|---|
| sidewalk | largely | butter | angle |

Pupils write each word under the generalization they used. Sometimes more than one generalization is appropriate.

## Language Change

### American and British spelling

In working with syllabication, students sometimes comment that they see words spelled in more than one way. This is because there are some minor differences in the spelling of American and British words. Some of these changes occurred more than 100 years ago when Noah Webster revised some of the spellings of American words in an attempt to regularize the lexicon and have it more closely reflect American pronunciation. For the most part, the British have retained the original spellings of the Samuel Johnson dictionary. Examples of some alternate spellings of British and American "English" are given here.

| *Preferred American English* | *Preferred British English* |
|---|---|
| honor | honour |
| traveler | traveller |
| program | programme |
| veranda | verandah |
| story | storey (of a house) |
| catalog | catalogue |
| center | centre |
| jewelry | jewellery |
| pajamas | pyjamas |
| connection | connexion |
| theater | theatre |

***Language change today.*** As has been mentioned in the section dealing with phonics, language change, though difficult to notice, is always taking place. At present one of these changes affects what we say about syllabication and should be called to the attention of students. Many former three-syllable words are slowly losing the middle vowel sound even though the vowel letter appears in the written word (Burmeister, 1975). An examination of the following words—only a few of the many hundreds—will illustrate this point.

| | | | |
|---|---|---|---|
| sep*a*rate | om*e*let | fam*i*ly | cath*o*lic |
| car*a*mel | cam*e*ra | card*i*nal | iv*o*ry |
| comp*a*ny | int*e*rest | eas*i*ly | mem*o*ry |
| marg*a*rine | bach*e*lor | cab*i*net | hist*o*ry |
| ins*u*lin | nat*u*ral | | |

In some locales and among some groups of people, these vowels will still be pronounced in varying degrees. In other areas of our country these sounds have practically disappeared.

***The "formal" nature of English words.*** Many students comment that English words are written according to a more "formal" English code; that is, words are written as they tend to be pronounced in isolation, and not as they are pronounced in a sentence where stress patterns affect the sounds (minimizing some and doing away with others altogether). Additionally, regional variation affects the pronunciation of words. For this reason, Samuel Johnson, the renowned lexicographer, concluded many years ago that only one pronunciation, a more "formal" one, should be "acceptable" and it should become the standard written form. This makes it possible for the millions of people who speak English, with a variety of pronunciations, to have a valid form of written communication among them.

**Quick Self-Check 17**

1. What is the difference between an open and closed syllable?
2. What is the simple syllabication generalization?
3. What are two procedures teachers may use to teach syllabication?
4. What language change is occurring that affects the instruction of syllabication?
5. What should students know about the nature of our written words?

**Review**

A. Define a prefix, stem/root in language appropriate for students.
B. Define a "sight word list." Explain why these words are important.

For a list of words to aid in teaching about syllables, see Appendix C.

## THE DICTIONARY

As the student moves toward becoming an independent reader, s/he often meets words that cannot be decoded and understood according to the word recognition skills s/he has learned. At these times the dictionary can be an aid, but only if the student is skilled in its use.

Some newer dictionaries include words from major subject areas including computer science. They also include a mini-thesaurus and vocabulary builders (showing students how to make new words out of prefixes and suffixes) and expand understanding by showing regional differences in pronunciation. For a typical page see Figure 3.2.

A brief summary of needed dictionary skills includes:

1. alphabetizing skills.
2. understanding the use of guide words.
3. ability to use the pronunciation key and interpret stress marks.
4. ability to use phonetic spellings for pronunciation.
5. ability to use the proper word meaning through the right definition, sentence example, and illustration.

### Activities to Teach the Dictionary Skill Areas

Words suggested should be modified according to the age group and ability of the students.

#### Alphabetizing skills

1. Write the word sets in alphabetical order.
   a. demon, monster, robot, giant

**FIGURE 3.2** Page from the *School Dictionary 1*.

Reproduced with permission of Macmillan/McGraw-Hill School Publishing Company from *School Dictionary 1*. Copyright © 1990.

   b. mob, magnet, mermaid, million

   c. money, moppet, morning, motor

2. Which word is first? Which is last?

   lightning, light, lighthouse, lightyear

3. Which of these three entry words would be found first?

   birth, birthstone, birthday

4. Which of these entry words would be found last?

   six, sixth, sixteen

5. Arrange the following words according to the way they would appear on a dictionary page.

   termite, test, terrific, tent, tense, tension, testimony, terror, term

## Guide words

1. A dictionary should be thought of as having four sections.

   *Section 1* A-E

   *Section 2* F-M

   *Section 3* N-R

   *Section 4* S-Z

In what section (part) would you find these words?

a. pepper
d. scream
b. black
e. kickoff
c. heroic
f. window

2. Look at the following dictionary page. Write the first guide word. Write the second guide word.

| | |
|---|---|
| can | canteen |
| candy | canvass |
| candle | canyon |

3. The words *grown* and *gulf* are guide words at the top of one page in the dictionary. Select the words that would appear on that page.

gull, guide, grumpy, guard, grab, gulf, guess

4. If you were looking for the entry word *honorable,* with what set of guide words would you find it?

a. hobo        hog
b. hole         home
c. honor       hostess

## Pronunciation key and stress marks

1. When you find the entry *impatiently,* you want to know how the word is pronounced. Use the key that may be placed within your dictionary pages at the bottom of the page or in the front of the dictionary. The important marks to consider follow: long and short vowels; the schwa; *r*-controlled vowels; and ŏo as in *book* and o͞o as in *moon*. Also note that the sounds of *ci, si,* and *ti* are often /sh/. Most importantly, pay attention to the syllable receiving the stress. With the word *impatiently,* you will note the following syllables and diacritical marks:

**im**      short *i* (No mark over the vowel in dictionaries also means the vowel has a short sound.)

**pā′**     long *a* and the stress mark (Long vowels are indicated by a *macron,* a straight line over the vowel.)

**shənt**   schwa (looks like an upside-down *e*) receives an uh sound (the schwa can be likened to the sound you make if you get hit in the tummy).

**lē**      long *e* indicated by the *macron*

When there is difficulty in pronouncing words of many syllables, say the first syllable, then the first and second syllable together, then the first, second, and third syllable, and finally the last syllable. Repeat the word several times to hear the "tune" of the word. Now try to say the word to yourself.

## Phonetic spelling and pronunciation

1. Write the correct word for the following phonetic spellings.

ĕn sĭ klə pē′ de ə       (encyclopedia)

ĕg zo͞o′ bər ənt         (exuberant)

rĭ bĕl′ yən              (rebellion)

**Word meaning**

1. Look up these unusual words and write the dictionary definition.

   cantankerous

   lionize

   greenback

   expatriate

2. Sometimes dictionary words have more than one meaning, and you must decide from the context of the sentence the meaning that is appropriate. Read the dictionary entry below:

   mesh (mesh) n. 1. Any of the open spaces in a cord, thread, or wire network. 2. A net or network. 3. The engagement of gear teeth. v. 1. To entangle or ensnare. 2. To engage or become engaged, as gear teeth. 3. To coordinate; harmonize (masche, maesche) mesh´y, adj.[6]

3. Examine these sentences. What meaning is intended in each?
   a. The mesh in the screen was in need of repair.
   b. The gear wheels do not mesh properly.
   c. The mesh of problems proved to be too difficult.
   d. The plans meshed and they proceeded accordingly.

## Activities for Motivating Students to Use the Dictionary

1. Dictionary background and development

   a. A good brief refresher on the history of the dictionary is Robert Kraske's book, *The Story of the Dictionary*. Older students may read it independently, or teachers may share it with younger students in class. It is a fascinating book in which students learn, for example, that English dictionaries are really quite "young," dating back only about 400 years, and that listing words in alphabetical order was considered a brilliant, novel idea at that time. Students are surprised to learn also that ordinary, commonly used words had to wait many years to win a place with uncommon words in the dictionary list. All the dictionary aids that we take for granted such as word histories, illustrative sentences, pronunciation symbols, syllabication, accents, parts of speech, and usage notes gradually developed as parts of a typical dictionary entry.

   Sharing these insights with students, plus relating short stories about the controversial personalities of Noah Webster and Samuel Johnson, build an appreciation for the dictionary's use.[7]

   b. Teachers who have access to the compact two-volume edition of the *Oxford English Dictionary* can build lots of interest in this study by bringing these volumes into the classroom. The micrography, with 13 volumes compressed in one, and the accompanying magnifying glass will not be easily forgotten by students.

(6) © 1980 by Houghton Mifflin Company. Reprinted by permission from *The American Heritage Dictionary of the English Language.*

(7) See Robert Kraske, *The Story of the Dictionary* (New York: Harcourt Brace Jovanovich, 1975). Also a book that contains a delightful fictionalized dictionary "happening" is Joseph Moses's *The Great Rain Robbery* (New York: Houghton Mifflin, 1975).

2. Creating original dictionary entries
   a. Students create the sounds, syllables, and definitions for made-up words that reflect various dictionary entries. (This, of course, increases their familiarity with the different entry parts and increases awareness that dictionaries differ in what they include.) These words with their respective entries are bound, and constitute the class's "Creative Dictionary."

> Example: stratmous. (strat/moos) Eskimo stew made from venison, water, lichens, and moss. "This is the best stratmous I have ever tasted." Noun. (Stratmous has different ingredients depending on the area.)

   b. Proceed as in the previous instance except this time students use their own names and write the appropriate entry. This also helps familiarize students with entries and pronunciation guides.

> Example: Jane Callaway. (Jān Căll å wāy) 1. Third grade student at Hilltop School. 2. Also actress and musician. 3. Blue eyes, black hair, small and thin. Noun.

3. Dictionary scavenger hunts. Students engage in word quizzes. These are appropriate for middle-graders. Examples:
   a. Can a centaur be found in a zoo?
   b. Is a poetess a man who writes poems?
   c. Is a cherubim a delicious fruit?
   d. Is a grackle a kind of noise?
   e. Was Ceres the same god as Demeter?
   f. Can you wear a waste?
   g. Is a limerick a kind of soft drink?
   h. Is a puffin a small pillow?
   i. Would you rather be a spelunker or a philatelist?
   j. Is a statue a law?
   k. Is an artichoke a disease of the lungs?
   l. Is a goatee a baby goat?

The activities suggested, while introducing students to some of the types of skills needed and engaging students in some creative activities using the dictionary, do not ensure success in locating, pronouncing, and understanding the meaning of an unknown word. Skill in using the dictionary is acquired through frequent and long time use and interest. To motivate such use and interest, the teacher can serve as a good model, showing students that s/he too finds it often necessary to refer to it.

**Quick Self-Check 18**

1. What are the five dictionary skills needed?
2. How might these skills be learned best?
3. What are some activities to motivate students to use the dictionary?

**Review**

A. Why do beginning readers have difficulties using context clues?
B. What four letters may be used in beginning consonant blends?

## Recommended Dictionaries

The following titles for various age groups have been recommended by the American Library Association.[8] As you check this list, you will note that in addition to the traditional use of dictionaries, they may be used also to enhance reading from readiness through mature reading.

### Picture dictionaries (preschoolers–first grade)

Entries are arranged by category instead of alphabetically, using pictures instead of words for the definitions.

*Good Morning, Words!* Scott Foresman; distributed by HarperCollins, 1990. 142 p. Contains 850 words. Initially, the text begins with all the letters of the alphabet surrounded with words beginning with that letter. Under the category "People" are three subcategories: family, work people, and body parts. Special features include information for the parent plus letter recognition on the end sheets, which can be used for reading readiness activities.

*The Macmillan Picture Wordbook.* Ed. Judith S. Levey. Macmillan, 1990. 64 p. Contains 900 words in 30 categories, such as homes, visiting the doctor, and world of fantasy. The purpose is to learn to associate the printed word with the visual clue, which also builds reading preskills. Twelve characters are used throughout the text for continuity. To locate words quickly, a word list is provided.

### Ages 5–9

These dictionaries list entries in alphabetic order. Entries offer the definition and an example sentence.

*Words for New Readers.* Scott Foresman; distributed by HarperCollins, 1990. 312 p. (Also published for classroom use as *My First Picture Dictionary.*) Defines 1,500 words, with more than 1,000 illustrations. In addition to defining the word in a sentence, plurals of nouns and differing verb forms are included.

*My First Dictionary* (Also published as *My Second Picture Dictionary.*) Scott Foresman; distributed by HarperCollins, 1990. 448 p. Includes 4,000 entries and more than 1,000 illustrations with captions. Variations of the word follow the example sentence. Special features include a diagram page entitled "How to Read an Entry;" maps of the U.S. and the world; a page labeled landforms; ideas on conservation of the environment, concepts of eating healthy food; time on clock faces and digital clocks; measurements; calendar words; holidays; the alphabet; and suggested activities to encourage children to categorize, compare and contrast, and even draw conclusions.

### Ages 8–11

Some of these dictionaries include more complex entries with information about pronunciation, part of speech, and syllabication. They may provide interesting reading, such as word histories, U.S. historical events, usage notes, and informa-

(8) Frances Corcoran, "Children's Dictionaries," Reference Books Bulletin, *Booklist,* June 15, 1991, pp. 1,988–1,992.

tion on U.S. presidents. Additionally, some include reading activities, such as finding synonyms for words and using prefixes and suffixes to derive additional words.

***Macmillan Dictionary for Children.*** (Also published under the title *School Dictionary 1*). Macmillan, 1989. 896 p. Includes more than 35,000 entries. Each entry includes a definition, followed by an example sentence, with the part of speech spelled out. The word is then repeated with pronunciation and other forms of the word. Blue boxes contain notes about words and language with word histories given in red boxes. Includes more than 1,000 full-color photographs, illustrations, and maps.

Special features include a section on how to use the dictionary, a history of the English language, maps of the world and the U.S., events in U.S. history, presidents of the U.S., flags of the world, and tables of measurements.

***Webster's New World Children's Dictionary.*** Ed. Victoria Neufeldt. Webster's New World, 1991. 912 p. (School edition is called *Webster's New World Dictionary for Young Readers and Writers* and is available from Silver Burdett/Ginn.) Designed for use in grades 3–5. Includes 33,000 main entries. Homographs (words spelled the same but with different meanings, such as *fair*) are differentiated in the entries. There are entries for all the countries of the world, U.S. state capitals, and major world cities. Biographical entries are also included in the main text. Prefixes, suffixes, and contractions are also given as main entries. Pronunciation aid follows the entry word in parentheses. Final lines show the entry word broken into syllables and variations of the word and its parts of speech.

Special features in boxes abound. There are boxes with lists of synonyms like a thesaurus, "Word Maker" boxes with prefixes and suffixes, spelling tips for difficult words. Features also include maps of the U.S.; a world atlas; portraits of U.S. presidents; and an overview of states, state birds, and flowers.

***World Book Student Dictionary.*** (Also published as the *Childcraft Dictionary.*) World Book, Inc., 1991. 900 p. Includes 30,000 entries with many colorful photos and drawings. Each entry is followed by definitions (numbered when necessary) and example sentences in italics. Following these are the syllabicated word form, pronunciation, part of speech, and inflected forms. Idioms sometimes follow an entry word such as with the entry music (music to one's ear). Includes synonyms, antonyms, and homonyms preceded by a blue dot. Includes "Word Histories," "Word Power," and "Language Fact" in boxes. The latter contains information on prefixes, suffixes, usage, and other topics. Supplementary features include tables for state and national capitals and U.S. presidents.

## Ages 11–14

Except for type size, which is larger, these dictionaries are similar to those used by adults.

***The American Heritage Student's Dictionary.*** Houghton, 1986. Includes 35,000 main entries and more than 2,000 black-and-white pictures in support. Entry words are divided into syllables and pronunciation is enclosed by vertical bars. Part of speech follows and then a sentence or phrase defining the entry word. Idioms are found at the end of the definitions. Outside columns include illustrations, etymologies, pronunciation guides, and geographic and biographical information. As with adult dictionaries, special helps are found within the alphabetic arrangement of the text itself, not in an appendix.

***Thorndike-Barnhart Student Dictionary.*** Scott Foresman; distributed by Harper-Collins, 1988. 1,328 p. (Also published as *Scott, Foresman Advanced Dictionary.*) There are about 100,000 entries, with two-color drawings and black-and-white photographs. Includes 900 synonym studies and more than 18,000 etymologies (history of the word). Both geographic and biographical entries are found in the main word list.

Each entry begins with the word separated into syllables. Pronunciation follows in parentheses, and the abbreviation for its part of speech. Variant forms of the word are given in smaller boldface type after the defining phrases. Usage labels (e.g., "informal") are included. An illustrative sentence appears in italics for some definitions. Idioms are in small boldface type, and brackets set off the etymology of the word.

Special features include puzzles and other aids to help the reader get the most out of the book. The appendices are extensive and include such areas as charts and tables of regions of the atmosphere, the periodic table of elements, geological time, and language families.

It is obvious from this list that dictionaries today can include many activities that motivate students to find out about words in interesting ways. Moreover, as students build their skill in using the dictionary and their vocabulary, they become more confident readers. Few students are aware of the wealth of information their school dictionaries can provide. Motivation for using the dictionary as a valuable tool can be provided by using some of the special features they provide.

## GUIDELINES FOR SELECTING MATERIALS AND ACTIVITIES

Just as with the teaching of phonics, the commercial market also is inundated with materials to teach basic sight words, structural analysis, use of context, and dictionary skills. A few guidelines about these materials (Cunningham, 1981; Spiegel, January 1990) follow:

1. *Will the materials help meet your reading goals?* They should be an integral part of your reading program.

2. *Are the materials flexible?* Good materials should meet a variety of instructional goals.

3. *Do they teach what they say they do?* Close perusal often shows the skill is not what is purported.

4. *Are the skills taught important to reading?* Knowing a word is a noun or verb may be important to language instruction, but that knowledge does not help readers identify words or get meaning from them.

5. *Are the skills taught appropriate for the level of the readers with whom you intend to use the material?* Not all skills are important at all levels. Skill emphasis shifts from word identification to vocabulary and comprehension. If the skills are important, are they important to your particular level of readers?

6. *Are skills taught at the application level?* Do students actually apply the skills or is it expected they will automatically transfer the knowledge to real reading? You may still purchase the materials but recognize you need to provide the application practice and assessment.

7. *Are the materials intrinsically motivating?* Avoid boredom. You may still have to use some extrinsic motivation to get students started working on a piece of material, but if it is interesting, worthwhile, and varied, students' intrinsic motivation system can take over.

8. *What's the ratio of time spent actually reading?* Material where students spend twice as much time doing other things as they do actual reading should get a very low rating.

9. *Is there bias or stereotyping?* Note the questions and illustrations.

10. *Is the material worth the cost?* How durable and sturdy is the material? How many children's needs will it help meet? Are there less expensive materials that meet the same instructional criteria?

Some examples of the kinds of activities that can be useful without costing any money follow.

## DO-IT-YOURSELF MATERIALS AND ACTIVITIES

### Using Cereal Boxes

Cereal boxes may be one of the most overlooked and underused materials. Almost everyone "reads" cereal boxes at the breakfast table—children are also eager to find the free offerings. These boxes are easy to obtain, and the variety can be interesting. Students can use different boxes for the same lesson, a change from the usual way. Adapt the following ideas to any grade level.

**TABLE 3.8** Pros and cons of hand-produced and commercially produced materials.

| HAND-PRODUCED | | COMMERCIAL | |
|---|---|---|---|
| *Pros* | *Cons* | *Pros* | *Cons* |
| 1) Can be designed to meet specific needs and interests of target group. | 1) Durability of the constructed material is sometimes questionable. | 1) Material can be geared to specific needs of children. | 1) May use a too difficult vocabulary or a different approach to skill development. |
| 2) Use an appropriate vocabulary and level of difficulty. | 2) Constant remaking or mending may be required. | 2) Material is durable, legible, and colorful. Looks professional and may be long-lasting. | 2) May be limited in usefulness. |
| 3) Children can be actively involved in game production. | 3) Construction must reflect high standards of neatness and legibility. | 3) A wide variety already available in the marketplace. | 3) Require much time to locate, evaluate, purchase. |
| 4) Kits and activity game files can be expanded as needed. | 4) Directions must be carefully thought out. | 4) If teacher time is a factor, may be less expensive than "homemade." | 4) Lost items are expensive to replace. |
| 5) Favorite "old" games can be easily adapted. | 5) Construction sometimes requires more time than is warranted. | | 5) Frequently considered too expensive. |
| 6) Materials are sometimes more economical. | 6) Easily available commercial materials are sometimes more economical. | | |

1. *Word recognition.* How many words do you see on the box that you recognize? Write these words.

2. *Vocabulary development.* What words do you see that you regularly use as you speak or write? What words do you see that are less familiar? Do you know their meanings? How can we find out what these words mean? Follow this with dictionary exercises.

3. *Grammar.* Find the adjectives (nouns or verbs) on your box. Write them on your worksheet. Compare the adjectives (nouns and verbs) on different boxes.

4. *Suffixes.* Find words that have these endings: *s, es, ing, ed.* Find other suffixed words.

5. *Reading/writing.* What kinds of information are on the front, back, sides, top, and bottom of your box? Write three facts about your cereal. Choose your favorite cereal. Write a letter to the company telling why this cereal is your favorite. Use some of the words on your cereal box. (Labels and brochures may also be used for similar activities.)

## Sports Names

*Objective: Word Recognition*

Read and discuss with students the following examples of sports team tongue twisters:

> The Pittsburgh Penguins pretended to have a particular pathway to the park.
>
> The Chicago Cubs constantly came close to confessing the crisis.

Then direct the students to use the following list of team nicknames to write sentences containing their own creative tongue twisters:

**List of Team Nicknames:**

| *Hockey* | *Baseball* | *Basketball* |
|---|---|---|
| Philadelphia Flyers | Philadelphia Phillies | New York Knicks |
| Pittsburgh Penguins | Pittsburgh Pirates | New Jersey Nets |
| Boston Bruins | New York Yankees | Los Angeles Lakers |

*Football*

Buffalo Bills

Kansas City Chiefs

San Francisco 49ers

## Wordsplash

Write words that tell about you on the lines. Add other words and pictures in any spaces. Trade wordsplashes with a classmate. Take turns using your wordsplash to get to know one another.

| FAVORITE MOVIE | SOMETHING I'M PROUD OF | A TV SHOW I NEVER MISS |
|---|---|---|
| _____ | _____ | _____ |

|  | FAVORITE PLACE | |
| FAMILY MEMBERS | AWAY FROM HOME | FAMILY PET |
| _____ | _____ | _____ |

| A BOOK I'VE READ TWICE | FAVORITE SPORT | SPECIAL TALENT | SOMETHING I'VE ACCOMPLISHED |
| _____ | _____ | _____ | _____ |

A group of pre-service teachers (Snyder, 1981) experimented with producing reading games for fourth to sixth grade children, evaluating whether or not the activities were worthwhile. Their final consensus was that, while purposeful activities and games have a place in the school environment, the "greatest game in town" is still book reading. Hooray!

## SUMMARY

Chapter 3 has discussed additional important word recognition skills as:

1. knowing the basic sight words.
2. understanding principles of structural analysis that include compound words; prefixes/suffixes/roots, and syllabication.
3. using context clues.
4. using the dictionary.
5. using materials to teach these skills.

The importance of early mastery of the basic sight words cannot be overemphasized, as they represent a large part of the running vocabulary of any reading selection. Methods to employ when sight word learning is particularly difficult were presented. As students frequently encounter polysyllabic and affixed words in reading, structural analysis becomes increasingly important as the primary decoding strategy useful to students in and above the fourth grade. The differences between absorbed and active prefixes and inflectional and derivational affixes were discussed. Teachers need to actively involve students in discussions about affixed words, as they are most easily learned, since language is initially learned by actively hearing and using the words in meaningful contexts. More structured lessons for learning affixes for both younger and older readers were presented. Differences of opinion on the efficacy of syllabication principles were discussed, and a simple syllabication scheme was included. The use of context, semantic (meaning), and syntactic (part of speech) continues to be one of the best ways to decode words, and for mature readers represents one of the first clues to use in decoding words. Finally, the use of the dictionary as an aid in decoding strategies was discussed. Throughout, lessons and activities to teach the above skills were presented, with some guidelines for teachers and answers to frequently asked questions. A rationale for selecting materials and the pros and cons of handmade vs. commercial materials were included with the conclusion that reading is still the best game in town.

**Chapter 3:**

**Final Review**

1. Explain why sight words are sometimes referred to as high-frequency words.

2. Suggest some activities to use with students to help them learn these words.

3. Define the phrase "storehouse of sight words."

4. Evaluate this sentence: The meaning of a compound word is always a combination of its two parts.

5. Group the following words according to whether they contain active or absorbed prefixes: *contain, unsure, preclude, exceed, submarine, preview.* (What is the difference between these two types of prefixes?)

6. Group the following words according to whether they contain inflectional or derivational suffixes: *jumping, courageous, smallest, woman's, attention, merriment, draws.* What differences must teachers be aware of in teaching these two types of suffixes?

7. State several important generalizations for students to remember when adding suffixes to words.

8. Discuss the best ways to learn the meanings of roots and affixed words.

9. List the five steps that might be used for a simple syllabication generalization for students.

10. In teaching syllabication, a recent language change should be considered. Write three words that show this change.

11. Suggest several ways teachers may help students see the value of context clues. Define the two types of context clues.

12. Proficiency in the use of the dictionary requires that students acquire certain skills. Identify what these are. How are they best learned?

# Aids in Decoding

**4**

## TOWARD AN IMPROVED DECODING STRATEGY

### Finding the Right Combination

Four decoding strategies are available to the student who meets an unknown word: context, structure, phonics, and the dictionary. For example, in the sentence "The fire burned down the house," the word *burned* may be deduced from the remainder of the sentence, or the context. In a second example, the root of a word or the affixes attached to it may be used as keys to unlock the rest of the word: *unhappy, dislike, hopeful.* Third, the arrangement of the letters in a word, or phonics, may suggest that clusters of letters may encode particular sounds as *igh* /ī/ in *mighty,* or *th* /th/ and *ir* /er/ in *thirst.* Last, the glossary or dictionary may help with the division of a word into syllables and give clues to pronunciation. But this should only be used when previous clues have failed.

After a class discussion, a procedure could be charted, such as the one presented, with steps to follow when meeting an unknown word and could expand the simple word recognition strategy suggested earlier in the text.

*To Unlock an Unknown Word*

1. Try the context first.
2. Then look at the structure to see if the word is a compound and whether it has any roots or affixes.
3. Check for syllable or meaning clues of roots or prefixes.
4. Check for phonics clues.
5. If still unsure, try the dictionary if the word is critical to meaning.

Once students familiarize themselves with these procedural steps, however, they must be led to understand that often a word will necessitate a different sequence for identification. For example, context may be used *after* the word has been partially determined through the use of phonics to make certain the word makes sense in the sentence.

While a series of steps, such as those previously outlined, is useful, the rapid decoding of words, including those met for the first time, becomes essential so that meaning is not lost. The good reader sifts the options available when meeting an unknown word, selecting perhaps one, two, or all three in rapid succession. This is what all students must essentially learn to do: *understand the options available and make use of the best one/ones when decoding unrecognizable words.*

## Presenting Vocabulary to Students

### Direct instruction

While some students are able to zero in on the precise word recognition skill needed for unknown words, other students need direct instruction on how to proceed. With these students it is best to anticipate the difficult vocabulary that will be encountered and place such vocabulary (in a phrase) on the board or on a copy. Words are divided into syllables to teach structural analysis, followed by the teacher or student underlining the particular phonetic features (such as consonant and vowel digraphs) that may present difficulties:

syn *ch*ron ize (our watches)
*launch*ed (the ship)
dis o b *ey* (the orders)
ple*dge* (to keep)
re*ck* less ly (left his watch)
cam p*aign* (every day)

This enables students to see the "why" of how to decode the word and includes both structure and phonics. The phrase also helps with the context. Vocabulary is then discussed from the standpoint of particular decoding strategies.

### Discuss and clarify as needed

Knowing how to decode a word is an important step, but follow that step by discussing and clarifying some of the word meanings. We have more than one million words in English; no other language begins to approach this number! Children meet new words daily as they go through the elementary grades, and many of these words need to be clarified. As much as possible, do so in meaningful contexts with students actively solving the problem of the word's meaning (Beck and McKeown, 1988). Here are some guidelines:

1. Choose vocabulary for instruction from classroom reading.
2. Plan prereading activities so students see and hear the words before reading, especially in the sciences and social studies.
3. Organize them in some way to help students study:
   a. Place each one in a meaningful phrase.
   b. Tie them in with an event or idea.
   c. Use the words to predict what a passage may be about.
4. Involve students in postreading discussion. If words have been chosen properly for instruction, it is difficult not to use them in postreading discussion or questioning. Research suggests little attention is paid to vocabulary after reading (Blachowicz, 1987).
5. Ask students if they know any synonyms and antonyms of particular words.

For words that are still unclear, have students look back at the context to see if now the vocabulary makes more sense. Questions can be posed about the meaning of the new words. "When did you feel wretched?" "How does someone who feels wretched look?" New words can also be used in dialogues as students act out particular scenes from stories they have read or lead discussions on events that incorporate the new words they have learned.

## Suggested Decoding Aid Programs

### Word wonder

Word Wonder is a teaching strategy useful with older children to help with a number of reading skills, among them word decoding and word meaning. In its simplest form, students tell what words they expect to find in a story and then read to find out if they are right. In a more complicated form, the teacher lists words and students decide after decoding the words whether each word is likely to appear in the story, giving a rationale for their decision. The teacher purposely includes words apt to be chosen incorrectly so postreading discussion can center around misconceptions. Postreading discussion can determine whether wrong guesses were "bad" guesses or if the author just didn't choose to use those words. With this method, many students experience and learn to read many new words (Spiegel, 1981).

### Expanded sentences

A more indirect way of introducing vocabulary and simultaneously improving writing is the method of expanded sentences. Selected vocabulary words from the basal or trade books are embedded in dependent clauses (Cudd and Roberts, 1994). Some example sentence stems follow:

> *As a result of the <u>perilous</u> snowstorm, Tim and Jamie*
>
> *Behind the <u>massive</u> iron gate, Mrs. Roberts*
>
> *After Rebecca <u>stumbled</u> across the missing part, she*

After these sentence stems are introduced, the teacher and the class enjoy a brief brainstorming session in which students orally expand the clause into sentences, using their own ideas. The sentences are stated orally in their entirety in order to emphasize the syntax, and the decoding of the target word is discussed. Writing takes place only after the children are comfortable with the varied syntax and the vocabulary words. The abbreviated procedure follows.*

1. Select vocabulary to embed from the basal, trade book, or content area.
2. Embed the targeted vocabulary into sentence stems that, when expanded, will produce complex sentences.
3. Personalize the sentence stems by adding students' names, familiar events, people, or places, drawing on students' experiences.
4. Create two to five sentence stems, writing them on the chalkboard, chart, or transparency.
5. Go over the sentence stems, discussing concepts and eliciting from students ideas for completion. For each idea, it is important that students repeat the entire sentence to reinforce the idea of sentence structure.
6. As students compose their sentences, they work with partners who are their peer editors.
7. Illustrations that add details to the main idea encourage students to elaborate on their own sentences.
8. The resulting sentences may be used to write paragraphs or initiate a story or an article.

* For a more complete explanation, see the article by Cudd and Roberts.

This procedure helps students to better understand the variety they encounter in syntax as they read.

### The ECRI method[1]

In situations in which students have particular difficulties in decoding and fail to see clues, teachers may choose to place each vocabulary word on an individual card and instruct students (in small groups) as to the decoding method that would work best with that particular word. This instruction should be followed with lots of practice, discrimination exercises, and emphasis on word meanings. For example:

Teacher: (Has the word *concern* on a card.) This word is *concern*. It is best decoded by syllables. Say *con/cern, concern*. (S/he follows this by using the word in a sentence to make certain students understand the word): "The parents showed concern over the weather." (S/he asks students to orally offer sentences of their own and then s/he continues.) Write and say the word *concern*, and then check it with this card to see if it is correct.

Students: (They write the word, read it, say the word, and then check it with the model.)

Teacher: (Shows them two words, one is *concern*, and the other is a word similar to it, *conceal*. S/he continues.) Look at these two words. Tell me what is the same and what is different about them.

Students: (They respond by identifying the letters and sounds that are similar and those that are different, somewhat as follows): Well, the first syllables are the same, but the second syllables are different. In *concern*, the second syllable has the /er/ sound plus /n/; and in *conceal*, the second syllable has an *ea* with the sound of /ē/ plus /l/.

Teacher: Now look at these two partially written words. (Show the words *concern* and *conceal*, omitting key letters, such as *con _ _ n* and *conc _ _ l*.) What sound is missing in the first word? Tell me how to write the letters that stand for that sound. What sound is missing in the second word? Tell me how to write the letters that stand for that sound.

By using this method the teacher encourages students to attend to the salient features that make the word decode as it does, showing students the particulars of one word by comparing it with another word. The method also includes lots of timed practice with vocabulary every day.

By initially saying, "This word is decoded best by its syllables," "This word is decoded best by using phonics clues," or "This word is decoded best by looking at the prefixes and suffixes," *teachers illustrate and model for students which word recognition method is most appropriate.* Also, this helps to show them that sometimes more than one type of word recognition skill is used.

## Reading Evaluation

### Developmental problems

Students who exhibit a low level of accuracy in decoding during reading may have a physical problem, but this is usually not the case. Before considering that the student has real problems, see if the problem may be due to (1) the need to read a

(1) For more information on this successful teaching method, write to ECRI Exemplary Center for Reading Instruction, 3310 S. 270 East, Salt Lake City, UT 84106. 1-800-486-5083. You may send for catalog and materials.

little slower, (2) a slight visual recall weakness due to noting only the outer configuration of words, or (3) constructing a version of the author's meaning based on context at a rapid rate, using whole word processing with not enough attention to detail. Their thinking processes run faster than their perceptual and recognition processes for the letters and words. To remediate, Moon and Scorpio (1984) suggest some of the following procedures:

Check to see if the student can read directions accurately and take tests. If so, the lack of accuracy in story reading may simply be an early stage in the development of a more flexible reading rate and the development of strategies for reading. When students fail to maintain high accuracy in situations that demand it, try some of the following procedures:

- Use flash cards for similar words, such as *though, through,* and *thorough.*
- Read in unison with a partner. The goal is to increase the number of words read without error. Keep progress checks.
- Record on cassette while reading. Recheck for errors while listening a second time.
- Ask the student where his/her eyes were when the error was made. Lead the student to see that the voice got ahead of the eyes, which needed a little more time for a more careful look.

Also, be careful to see that the assignment quantity is not causing emphasis on hurrying to get through versus quality. Keep a list of errors to be analyzed for patterns. Often, what may be needed is for the student to simply allow enough time for the eye to stay ahead of the voice so it notices detail in words and then gradually to speed up.

## Reading and self-evaluation

In a speech over a decade ago, William Glasser, author of the classic book *Schools Without Failure,* suggested that

> it is not important for us to spend a great deal of time evaluating other people. That really isn't necessary. What's very very necessary is that we spend time evaluating ourselves and that we set up our schools so that children spend a great deal of time evaluating *themselves.*

There are indications even young students can use self-evaluation techniques effectively, often providing information that could not be discovered in any other way. Moreover, allowing students to evaluate themselves encourages them to take greater responsibility for their activities. Some useful techniques suggested by Coley (1983) follow:

***Structured techniques.*** An introduction to student self-evaluation can start on a small scale. With young children, begin by asking them to put a happy or sad face at the top of their paper to indicate how well they feel they understand the story.

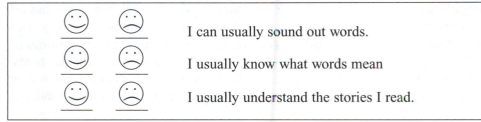

With older students ask them to indicate on a 15 scale how difficult they felt the vocabulary was in a given selection or how well they felt they did on an activity involving syllabication. Once students get used to evaluating small bits of their reading behavior, move them to a task where they look at a more comprehensive picture of their reading. The skills checklist is a useful next step. A skills checklist may be as broad as the following:

| yes | no | |
|---|---|---|
| —— | —— | 1. I know where to divide a v c c v word. |
| —— | —— | 2. I know how to pronounce the vowel in a syllable that |
| ends | | with a vowel. |
| —— | —— | 3. I know . . . etc. |

Checklists can also be specific to a given skill such as the partial checklist above on syllabication.

Another helpful self-evaluation format is the comparison checklist.

| Student Name _____ | | | | | | |
|---|---|---|---|---|---|---|
| | *My Evaluation* | | | *Mr. Jones' Evaluation* | | |
| | Poor | Fair | Good | Poor | Fair | Good |
| 1. vocabulary | | | | | | |
| 2. questions | | | | | | |
| 3. smooth reading | | | | | | |
| Comments: | | | | | | |

***Open-ended evaluations.***    In addition to fairly structured evaluations, use some very open-ended sentences. Students may respond orally or in writing to stems such as:

The hardest thing about reading is . . .

When I come to a word I don't know, I . . .

I like to read when . . .

Data gained from these statements give exceptional insights not only to the students' attitudes toward reading, but to the strategies they employ during reading, and to their reading problems (Coley, 1983).

***A taped reading.***    Students who listen to a tape of their own reading often make important discoveries about their reading strengths and weaknesses.

***Portfolio assessment.***    A method of assessment gaining much popularity has recently been named *portfolio assessment.* This type of evaluation not only uses student self-evaluation but also uses additional items such as taped recordings of student's reading, writing samples of his/her work, a teacher's anecdotal notes, and test scores. These references are excellent if you wish further information in the use of this method: Scott G. Paris, "Portfolio Assessment for Young Readers,"

*The Reading Teacher* (May 1991) pp. 680–682. *Portfolios and Beyond* by Susan Mandel Glazer and Carol Smullen Brown (1993), and *Portfolio Assessment: Getting Started* by Harry Noden and Barbara Moss (1994) are two recent books on this topic.

## Helping Students Develop Flexibility

Since no one word recognition strategy is adequate, students who rely exclusively on one must be led to the use of other strategies. The teacher who wishes to help students become more flexible as they decode should

1. encourage the student to try, to think, to reason, and to solve decoding "dilemmas." Determining words then becomes a personally satisfying encounter, done in a confident way.
2. encourage the expansion of sight vocabulary lists. These hold a significant spot in the reading ability of all readers.
3. get some insight into the student's sequence of decoding by having him/her tell precisely what s/he does when s/he meets an unfamiliar word.
4. help the student develop a procedure for unlocking words and understand that there are alternative approaches and that at times it is a case of trial and error.

## Developing Fluency

Some students appear to have decoding skills when tested on isolated words but seem unable to integrate these word identification abilities with any degree of fluency. In many cases the reading is too slow and labored, lacking the automaticity of decoding that must take place if readers are to enjoy and comprehend what they read. (This *does not* apply to beginning readers, who often read haltingly during the first year or so as they learn decoding strategies.)

### The imitative method

Teachers engage in creative activities to encourage older readers to develop automaticity. To improve fluency, Cunningham (1979) suggested a procedure called the "imitative method," first suggested by Carol Chomsky (1976), a noted linguist.

Briefly, the teacher locates an interesting short story at the student's instructional reading level and records it on a cassette in an appealing and dramatic form. While listening to the tape, the student follows along, reading the story from the book until the story is mastered. Patience is required of both teacher and student because it may take several weeks until true reading mastery of the story occurs, but when it does, the student is encouraged to read the story to parents, friends, and classmates. The story has not been memorized, and the student will need the book, but elements of memorization are certainly present. Nevertheless, this approach to reading enables the student to have the experience of successful, effective, fluent reading for perhaps the first time.

### "Impress"

Cunningham (1979) suggests another method called "impress." A selection at the student's instructional level is located and given to the student to read silently. The student and teacher reread the material together orally, the teacher setting a moderate pace and moving his/her hand along under the lines being read. The teacher sits quite close to the student, practically reading into the student's ear, but adjusting the strength of his/her voice throughout the selection in accordance with the student's ability. This means allowing the student to take the lead when s/he is comfortable with the reading and the teacher moderating his/her voice to a whisper during that period, but then raising his/her voice to move the student along in the selection when the student appears uncertain or falters. The name of the procedure suggests what the teacher is attempting to do—to *impress* the words on the mind of the student through repeated practice.

A modified method is suggested by Eldredge and Butterfield (1986) whereby slower students can be assigned to read with a more skilled student. Students sit side by side reading aloud from one book. The faster student touches each word as s/he reads it and the slower student repeats each word after her/him. The faster reader reads at her/his normal rate with the slower student instructed to follow and repeat the words as quickly as possible. As the slower reader gains skill the more rapid reader reads silently, supplying words only when needed.

## Repeated readings

A third procedure used by Cunningham (1979) and Samuels (1988) involves a method called "repeated readings." Students are given a selection of about 100 words and asked to read and reread it, each time increasing their speed. Initially the passage should be read by the student with no more than five errors (95 percent word recognition), or else it will prove too difficult. The teacher may use this method in a group, listening to one student while others are practicing. Again, the idea is to improve the rate and give the student the feeling of fluency for perhaps the first time.

Two modifications to the procedure are suggested by Lauritzen (1982). These lie in the choice of materials and in the initial method of presentation. Materials chosen should have a singing quality loved by children, with a definite rhyme, strong rhythm, identifiable sequence, and oral literature patterns. These are all prevalent in folk literature such as *Henny Penny,* the *Gingerbread Boy,* and the *Old Woman and Her Shoe.* The teacher first reads the entire selection, and the children follow the print, either from a book or from a copy on a chart or board. Then the children echo-read a line, a sentence, or a paragraph with length determined by the structure of the poem or story. Eventually the teacher and children read the entire selection in unison. The children may read individually, in pairs, or in small groups as many times as they wish. Because the teacher models fluent reading from the beginning, the children imitate it. Difficult material is mastered, and children can be motivated to improve their reading because of success.

Another modification of repeated readings is suggested by Swaby (1982) in what is called an *instructional* repeated reading program. Here a teacher, aide, or other adult works individually with a child. A short passage written on the student's instructional level is chosen. The passage is divided into three or four paragraphs or short segments. If the student has previously read the material (best), he should be reminded of the major concepts. If the material is new, the major concepts are briefly discussed. A segment of a passage is done at a time, and word errors made by the student are recorded. The segment is read back to the student to see if errors are recognized. Word choices that were errors are analyzed to determine whether they were errors of phonics, structure, or context. Often the word choice is poor, a student reading, for example, *chain* for *chair*. The semantic clues that make *chain* a poor choice are pointed out so the student learns to recognize the type of errors made—phonetic, structural, or contextual—to avoid them in the future.

After reading and analyzing all the segments, the student rereads the entire passage as fluently as possible, aiming for shorter reading time, fewer errors, more self-correction, and greater expression.

## Student sharing

Many teachers advocate co-authoring and reading as a method of improving fluency. This method has many variations. Davis (1989) pairs her first grade class with fifth graders who act as teachers as the two create books together. Kemp (1990), a second grade teacher, works with a fourth grade teacher. The two have their students meet together one day a week for 30 minutes to read and enjoy books. A guideline for older students is to allow wait time before they help with a difficult word. Reading specialist Visser (1991), appreciating the importance of sports, persuaded a high school football team to come to her class to read to her students. Juel, (1991), asked university athletes to wear their football jerseys, come to class, and read aloud to elementary school classes. The program benefitted the students, who saw reading as a positive experience for some of their idols, and it also benefited the athletes, who became enthusiastic about reading.

## Reading Recovery

Reading Recovery is an early intervention program for young children who have difficulty in learning to read. Hundreds of school districts in the United States, plus four other countries (New Zealand, Australia, Canada, and England) have implemented this successful program (Pinnell, Fried, and Estice, 1990; Hill and Hale, 1991). Initially designed by Marie Clay, a New Zealand child psychologist, the program's key is teacher knowledge and skill.

One-to-one intensive tutoring takes place for 30 minutes each day in addition to classroom reading. Throughout the tutoring lesson, a Reading Recovery–certified teacher works along with the child, observing reading/writing behavior, intervening to teach "the kind of effective processes good readers use" (Pinnell, Fried, and Estice). Teachers try to get students to monitor and self-correct their own reading, since the goal for the learner is independence.

Teachers become Reading Recovery specialists by participating in a year-long course—the major component of the program is making effective moment-to-moment decisions while teaching intensively in this one-to-one situation. Required materials are minimal: books, pencils, and paper; most important are the hundreds of "little books," short paperbacks with good stories and a few lines of text on each page.

Follow-up studies for the program are impressive: Clay (1990); Hill and Hale (1991); Iversen and Turner (1993); and Bozon (1994).

> The program is characterized as dynamic and intensive, especially for children who need special care and early intervention, and provides on-going support for teachers.*

* Bozon quoting Dr. Gay Su Pinell.

Reading Recovery programs are growing, and an examination of the program suggests why it works. It includes the following:

- initial and follow-up parental involvement.
- a lot of "meaningful time is spent on task" (30 minutes a day extra reading time).
- many books are available and read.
- expert teachers who work continuously to improve their skills—they are evaluated by peers.
- a lot of student writing and reading under direct teacher guidance.
- assessment that takes place through on-going diagnosis in the 30-minute segment of instruction.
- strategies that help students decode language instantly so that fluency is achieved.

The U.S. National Diffusion Network lists many teacher training sites. See the article by Pinnell (1990) for names and places.

## Learning Styles

Carbo (1986) believes teachers should focus on students' individual learning styles. She differentiates between global and analytic students and characterizes them in this way:

**Analytic students**

1. concentrate and learn when information is presented in small, logical steps.
2. process information sequentially and logically.
3. pay close attention to exact directions.
4. enjoy learning facts such as dates, names, and other specifics.
5. learn phonics easily, understand and apply phonic rules.

**Global students**

1. concentrate and learn when information is presented as a gestalt or whole.
2. respond to emotional appeals.
3. tend to like fantasy and humor.
4. get "wrapped up" in a story and do not concentrate on the facts.
5. process information subjectively and in patterns.

## Basic Principles in Remediation

For the classroom teacher who does not have an aide, tutor, or reading specialist to help, finding the time necessary to assist students in need of remediation is not always easy. Reading Recovery outlines the steps necessary in cases where more drastic intervention is crucial and where several different procedures are involved with specialists. With many students, however, simple intervention procedures are sufficient. Harris's suggestions (1981) outlined the broad general philosophy teachers need to keep in mind when working to improve students' reading skills. These are still valid today.

1. Begin at a low enough level and take small enough steps to ensure initial success.

2. Develop a pleasant rapport with each pupil.

3. Be flexible in choosing both method and materials, paying attention to the child's feelings as well as aptitudes.

4. Use ample review and repetition.

5. Use materials that combine high interest appeal with low difficulty.

6. Use progress charts to record progress toward important objectives.

7. Celebrate the child's successes.

8. Apply in connected reading those skills developed in isolation.

## SUMMARY

Chapter 4 discussed the following additional aids in teaching word recognition skills:

1. procedures to follow when meeting an unknown word to find the right combination.

2. presenting and clarifying vocabulary to students.

3. suggestions on remediating certain difficulties.

4. methods for student self-evaluation.

5. ways to gain reading fluency.

6. a model intervention program in remediation called Reading Recovery.

Students must view word recognition skills as something to manipulate to their advantage when meeting unknown words so that minimum clues, but the right clues, are used as quickly as possible. Procedures to follow when meeting an unknown word were suggested. The ECRI method was outlined, and suggestions made for improving the level of accuracy for some students in using word recognition skills. Student self-evaluation is a very important facet of the process, and to that end, checklists for self-evaluation were provided. Suggestions were offered for helping students learn to decode words more easily and to become more fluent as they read. A model intervention program outlined procedures necessary when serious reading problems exist. A philosophy of those factors that are important in improving classroom remediation procedures was provided.

**Chapter 4:**

**Final Review**

1. Suggest a procedure for students to follow when meeting an unknown word.

2. Briefly describe the ECRI method.

3. List the reasons some students decode words with a low level of accuracy.

4. Describe checklists that may be used for student self-evaluation.

5. Suggest some procedures to use that may enable students to read more fluently.

6. Evaluate why the Reading Recovery program is successful.

# Students with Special Needs

## MEETING SPECIAL NEEDS OF STUDENTS

### Parents and Reading

In the last few decades there has been increasing support for the concept of parent involvement in reading. This can be attributed partly to the voluminous research that shows the important role the preschool years play in building experiences children can relate to as they read. Moreover, the economic climate plus the massive school budget cuts have made "parents as partners in education" more than a catch phrase. Not only are they involved in ameliorating reading problems, but there are even parent programs aimed at preventing them. Studies and projects show how supportive home environments (Adams, 1990; Handel 1992) can make a substantial difference.

In researching this section for this new edition, the author found more than 70 articles focusing on the important role parents play in the developing reading proficiency of their children. In addition to many educational articles in periodicals, magazines such as *Family Circle* (Sept. 1, 1994); *Woman's Day* (Apr. 7, 1994); and *Redbook* (Oct. 1993) all have articles outlining the connection of parental involvement with children's success in reading. Family literacy has become a national movement with an estimated 500 family literacy programs in libraries, adult literacy centers, community agencies, preschools, elementary schools, and the workplace. (Handel, 1992). While programs vary considerably in scope and intensity, all recognize the intergenerational nature of literacy problems. Accordingly, family literacy programs attempt to break the cycle of underachievement by providing literacy experiences that benefit all members of the family—adults as well as children.

A National Center for Family Literacy has been established in Louisville, Kentucky. A national newsletter for parents, explaining whole language and what it tries to do, may be subscribed to.* Posters that celebrate family reading and remind parents of the important role they play are found in bookstores, libraries, and schools nationwide (see Figure 5.1).

Parent programs involving reading are of several types: In one type parents receive direct instruction in reading skills (Topping, 1987), while in others, parents simply cooperate by providing extra instruction in the home.

### Paired Reading

Paired reading is a way for parents to pleasurably, and with a minimum of preparation, help their children become more successful readers (Topping, 1987); (*The Reading Teacher* Aug./Sept. 1994, p. 13). The technique is similar to the one used in classrooms where teachers pair students of different ages together so that the more fluent reader assists the lesser reader when there are decoding difficulties.

---

* Contact National Council of Teachers of English, Urbana, IL, for details.

**FIGURE 5.1** Poster celebrating family reading.

National Family Reading Week May 1-5

# READING TOGETHER

Make it a family                            tradition!

Encourage every family in America to read together!
Join our national year-long reading initiative.

*From INSTRUCTOR,* October 1994. Copyright © 1994 by Scholastic Inc. Reprinted by permission.

The difference between classroom-paired reading and parent-and-child paired reading, according to Topping, is that parent-paired reading is (1) more structured, (2) involves actual parent training, and (3) has follow-up evaluation with criterion-referenced tests to show how well it worked, thereby motivating parents to continue. The following list outlines the steps for the paired reading technique:

1. The child chooses the reading material, irrespective of its level of difficulty. This permits the child to be supported by the parent when the text is difficult, with the parent using simple explanations through discussion and questioning. (Children become skilled at choosing the books for paired reading.)

2. Parent and child read all the words out loud together with the parent adjusting for rate so that the language is still fluent and meaningful.

3. The child should say every word correctly. When an error is made, the parent repeats the word until the child reads the word correctly.

4. When the reading is easier, the child makes some prearranged nonverbal signal, such as a nudge or a squeeze, to indicate to the parent that s/he wishes to read alone.

5. The child continues to read alone until an error is made, then the same correction procedure is applied, and parent and child read together until the child again signals s/he is capable of reading alone without prompting.

6. Much emphasis throughout is on praise. This is done for correct reading, the child's self-corrections, and the signals to read alone.

Based on an Ohio State Reading Recovery Conference (*Reading Teacher*, Aug./ Sept. 1994, p.13), there are some additional paired reading suggestions for parents.

1. Before you begin reading, show interest in the book the child has chosen. Talk about the title and the cover, and find out if the child knows any other books by the author. Flip through the pages and talk together about the pictures. Ask your child what he or she expects might happen during the story, and comment on how interested you are in finding out what happens.

2. As the child reads, have him or her point to each word, sliding a finger from word to word (sliding so that the reading is smooth rather than jerky) as the reading progresses.

3. When the child reads a word incorrectly, move his or her finger back under the word and say the word correctly. Have the child say it, and then reread the sentence. (If this happens repeatedly, the book may be too difficult.)

4. When a child comes to an unknown word, wait five seconds to allow the child to figure it out. If the child fails to say it, proceed as above in #3.

5. Usually you will be able to finish a chapter or book each day. Stop at a logical point and place a mark in the text. The following day, start by talking about what happened in the story thus far.

This kind of parental involvement can help students become more fluent, confident, and contextually oriented readers. With parents as models, children can learn not only accurate oral reading, but also expressiveness, pacing, and attention to punctuation, which are particularly relevant to disadvantaged or some ethnic minorities. When existing parental levels of literacy are low, this experience helps parents, some of whom enroll in adult literacy classes to improve their own reading.

When parents are unavailable, sometimes older siblings take over, but parental praise is always part of the process. Some schools further adapt the method by having the teacher read a story onto an audiotape, and the child takes book and tape home to follow while reading, again with much parental praise.

Training for some parents may be essential. Turner suggests a group meeting with children, supervised by a teacher, coupled with a demonstration of this technique by the teacher so that the technique is mastered and understood. At home, a practice session of only five minutes a day (five times per week) over a six- to eight-week period often brings startling improvement.

## Response Form

Fredericks and Rasinski (1990) suggest a type of response form to forge a link between school and home (see Figure 5.2). The most important contribution parents can make, of course, is to foster an atmosphere in which reading is important. Given the present situation in which time is critical for many parents, some of whom head single-parent households or are a "two-working-parent family," involving these parents in school activities is not always easy. The latest figures from the U.S. Department of Education show that only about half of the parents attend school meetings. Still, teachers and schools, knowing the importance of parental support in the academic success of the students, continue in their efforts to involve them.

**FIGURE 5.2**  Example of a response form.

Child's name: _____   Date: _____

Please indicate your observation of your child's reading growth since the last report. Feel free to comment where appropriate.

A = Strongly agree
B = Agree
C = Disagree
D = Strongly disagree

My child:                                                                                   Comments

  1. Understands more of what he/she reads                    A    B    C    D
  2. Enjoys being read to by family members                   A    B    C    D
  3. Finds time for quiet reading at home                     A    B    C    D
  4. Sometimes guesses at words, but they usually make sense  A    B    C    D
  5. Can provide a summary of stories read                    A    B    C    D
  6. Has a good attitude about reading                        A    B    C    D
  7. Enjoys reading to family members                         A    B    C    D
  8. Would like to get more books                             A    B    C    D
  9. Chooses to write about stories read                      A    B    C    D
 10. Is able to complete homework assignments                 A    B    C    D

Strengths I see: _____

_____

_____

Areas that need improvement: _____

_____

_____

Concerns or questions I have: _____

_____

_____

Reprinted with permission of Anthony D. Fredericks and the International Reading Association.

## Hooked on Phonics

A program that parents may ask the classroom teacher to evaluate is *Hooked on Phonics* because of its controversy and accompanying counterclaims. More than one million sets have been sold since it was published in the late 1980s. Following is a brief overview (see *Congressional Quarterly Researcher* May, 1995 for more comprehensive coverage): *Hooked on Phonics* is produced by Gateway Educational Products, the brainchild of John Shanahan, who became concerned when his 11-year-old son was having difficulty in reading. The program promises a way to learn essential word recognition skills through 30 minutes a day of visual and audio exercises and consists of lightly illustrated texts, colorful posters, and sticker badges that reward students. Jazz drums and electric piano provide the background music. The program repeats common combinations of vowels and consonants in a sequence matched by the flashcards and stories.

*Hooked on Phonics* has many critics, among them, the International Reading Association and the National Education Association. No less than Jeanne Chall, a phonics supporter, states, "The reader could miss all the words and sentences in the books and not receive a signal from the tape that mistakes were made."

Despite the criticisms, Gateway brought in an independent researcher who found the program favorable, but critics pointed out that important data had been withheld. Meanwhile, the Federal Trade Commission (FTC) had been investigating the ads for *Hooked on Phonics,* arguing that Gateway did not have adequate substantiation for its claims and that the ads did not describe the typical consumer experience. In 1994, the FTC negotiated a consent decree in which Gateway agreed to cease making its misleading claims. At the same time a class-action lawsuit was filed against Gateway by Seattle attorney Steve Berman, who claims he represents thousands of unhappy consumers seeking refunds.

The FTC's actions, however, angered some pro-phonics activists, home schoolers, and political conservatives. The president of the National Right to Read Foundation sent an appeal to his followers, who sent more than 3,000 letters to the FTC, many of which were from satisfied *Hooked on Phonics* customers. Also weighing in on behalf of the merits of the program were former FTC Chairman James C. Miller III and a group of conservative House members including the present majority whip.

While the FTC continues its vigilance to see that the ads are truthful, *Hooked on Phonics* continues to sell its product and even expand its educational offerings. The program costs several hundred dollars.

## CULTURALLY DIVERSE STUDENTS

New reading programs will continue to be developed and marketed, given the fact that reading problems will not disappear, and the public, as well as educators, search for solutions.

As stated, the most important contribution parents can make is to foster an atmosphere in which reading is important. When the experiences, attitudes, and behaviors accepted by the family and school are the same, children are able to bond with teachers, allowing further development of those social and academic skills of which reading is an essential part. Lacking these, the school's formal learning process is difficult (Hall and Henderson, 1991). Some culturally diverse students find it difficult to learn because of their differing experiences, attitudes, and behaviors.

### The African-American Dialect Speaker

Each dialect of English should be considered a complete and valid form of communication, although it may differ in minor respects from Standard English (SE). Most children who speak with a dialect exhibit some of the characteristics of their dialect but rarely exhibit all of them. Teachers must be aware that it is difficult, if not impossible, for some young dialect speakers to read and pronounce words exactly as they are spoken in SE. The following explanation will help to clarify why setting such a task for them too early may create reading problems.

Some differences between the African-American dialect and SE follow:

*Phonology*

1. Short /ĕ/ and short /ĭ/ do not have the same degree of contrast as in SE.

    pin        pen
    tin        ten
    since    cents
    I have tin cints.

2. As a past tense marker, *ed* is often eliminated. (African-American dialect speakers, however, do have a past tense that becomes apparent when they use irregular verbs such as *told* and *kept*.)

3. There is a high degree of *r*-lessness and *l*-lessness. The following word groups frequently sound similar.

| toe | tore | toll |
|-----|------|------|
| too | tool |      |
| foe | four |      |

4. Final consonant clusters are frequently shortened, with the final consonant eliminated.

| Cluster  | st   | ft   | nt   | nd   | ld   | zd     | md    |
|----------|------|------|------|------|------|--------|-------|
| Standard | past | left | bent | bend | hold | raised | aimed |
| Dialect  | pas  | lef  | ben  | ben  | hol  | rais   | aim   |

The following three words would sound similar:

| men | meant | mend |
|-----|-------|------|

5. Three-letter consonant clusters such as *str* and *scr* are sometimes difficult to pronounce:

| stream | scream | strap | scrap |
|--------|--------|-------|-------|

6. Final *th* is often pronounced like an /f/, sometimes as /d/:

| Ruth  | roof |
|-------|------|
| death | deaf |
| with  | wid  |

7. Diphthongs such as /oi/ and /ou/ are often shortened:

boil    might be pronounced as /ball/

pour    might be pronounced as /por/

8. Accent and voice pitch
   a. Particular words receive a different accent pattern.

   pó lice for policé

   Jú ly for Julý

   b. Wider pitch (at times a far higher pitch than usual) and a more rising level in the final speech contour.

### *Grammar*

1. Third person singular (present tense) is eliminated.

   He see me.

2. Possessive is indicated by word placement, not the traditional /s/ sound.

   You book.    John cousin.

3. There is not always verb agreement.

   They was going.

4. The verb *be* is not always necessary and does not always convey the same meaning as in SE.

   I going.    He a bad boy.

*He be working* means that the action is habitual. *He working* conveys that the person is working now.

5. Double negatives are common.

> I don't get none.

6. Constructions with *here are* and *it is* do not follow standard rules. The following type of sentence is typical.

> It is a whole lot of people.

7. Irregular verbs are often regularized.

> We throwed a party.

8. Past tense and past participle forms are often reversed.

> went for gone
>
> broke for broken
>
> seen for saw
>
> taken for took

9. Differing sentence syntax.

> The lady, she went home. (double subject)
>
> What you mean by that? (*do* eliminated)

Interestingly, many language forms that we insist on as SE are actually the result of historical incidence. For example, one of the reasons we do not use the double negative today (it was used extensively by English speakers in the past) is because eighteenth-century mathematicians said that since two negatives make a positive in math, the same must hold true for language! (Double negatives are still common among African-American dialect speakers today.)

Another interesting feature in African-American dialect is the lack of final *s* with third person singular verbs. This is an irregular feature of SE. Example: I sing, you sing, he/she/it sing*s*, we sing, you sing (plural), they sing. Their dialect simply regularizes this irregular feature of SE. Interestingly, attitudes toward pronunciation differences are not as negative as they are toward grammar differences.

(A third factor to consider with dialect, vocabulary differences, is not included here due to space limitations.)

## Spanish-Speaking Children

*Code switching.*    *"Mira, mira, los bears estan dancing"* (Look, look, the bears are dancing) is an example of *code switching* and is sometimes used by Spanish speaking students. This frequently happens when students switch or alternate between the grammar and lexical system of Spanish and English (Lara, 1989). The switch may occur at the word, phrase, or clause level and still at other times by students borrowing a word from English and "Spanishizing" it as *watchar* (watch) and *puchar* (push).

Switches are sometimes the result of not knowing a word in the primary language, such as *bears,* while at other times with older students, it may be used for humor or emphasis. Cultural identity is also a factor in some code-switching. Many students are proud that they are members of a distinct cultural group and want listeners to know it.

Note other examples of linguistic interference:

SYNTAX VARIANTS:

**English:**   I see the black dog.

**Spanish:**   I see the dog black. (In Spanish, the adjective comes *after* the noun.)

WORD PAIR COMPARISONS

| | | | |
|---|---|---|---|
| ship—sheep | sleep—slip | chop—shop | share—chair |
| year—ear | it—eat | is—ease | her—hair |
| yellow—jello | chip—cheap | | |

In many respects, however, reading preferences of Spanish-speaking children differ little from those of English-speaking children. It is, however, the language interference and cultural differences that sometimes cause reading problems for them. Moreover, the tune or intonational pattern of Spanish is quite different. Directions in English by the teacher can often sound like scolding to the Spanish speaking child. When Spanish is used, speakers generally stand much closer. Because of this, Spanish children are often puzzled when their English-speaking teachers back away from them. The checklist in Table 5.1 may be used by teachers of Spanish-speaking children to individually evaluate the student's oral language. Note many similarities to the problems of other culturally diverse children.

**TABLE 5.1** Checklist for evaluating the oral language of Spanish-speaking children.

| ORAL LANGUAGE RATING | SPANISH INTERFERENCE | 5 | 4 | 3 | 2 | 1 | 0 |
|---|---|---|---|---|---|---|---|
| School _____ Date _____ | | | | | | | |
| Name _____ | | | | | | | |
| Grade _____ Teacher _____ | | | | | | | |
| **Pronunciation (Sounds):** Distinguishes between vowel sounds, such as *sheep-ship, cut-cat, cut-cot, pool-pull,* and between consonant sounds, such as *sink-zinc, vote-boat, sink-think, yellow-jello, cheap-jeep.* | | | | | | | |
| **Pronunciation (Clusters):** Pronounces initial consonant clusters as in school, speak, study, and final consonant clusters as in *land, fast, old, box, act, desk, pulled, touched.* | | | | | | | |
| **Pronunciation (Suprasegmentals):** Pronounces sentences with appropriate rhythm, stress, pause, and pitch. | | | | | | | |
| **Pronouns:** Uses appropriate pronoun forms in subject position (*I, he, she,* etc.) in object position (*me, him, her,* etc.) and possessives (*my, mine; her, hers,* etc.) | | | | | | | |
| **Negatives:** Uses *not* to express the negative after the forms of be *(Bill is not here.)* and between auxiliary and verb in other sequences *(Bill was not talking. Bill did not talk.)* Uses singular rather than double negative. | | | | | | | |
| **Noun Modifier:** Uses adjectives appropriately, as in *the big dog* as opposed to *the dog big* and *Is the dog big?* as opposed to *Is big the dog?* | | | | | | | |
| **Comparison:** Uses the correct form of comparison such as *bigger, biggest, more beautiful, most beautiful,* rather than *more bigger, beautifuller.* | | | | | | | |
| **Present Tense:** Uses the appropriate present forms of regular verbs, with subject-verb agreement when *he* or *she* is used as subject, as in *He walks,* rather than *He walk.* | | | | | | | |
| **Plurals:** Distinguishes between singular and plural in regular forms, such as *dog-dogs, boot-boots, horse-horses,* and in irregular forms, such as *foot-feet, knife-knives.* | | | | | | | |
| **Past and Perfect Tenses:** Uses the past forms of regular verbs, as in *walk-walked, glue-glued, land-landed,* and of irregular verbs, as in *go-went-gone, dig-dug, cut-cut.* | | | | | | | |
| **Uses of Be:** Uses appropriate forms of *be* as an auxiliary and as a verb. | | | | | | | |
| **Uses of Do:** Uses appropriate forms of *do* in questions, answers, and negative statements. | | | | | | | |
| **Future Tense:** Uses the appropriate future forms of regular verbs, as in *run-will run.* | | | | | | | |
| **Possessive:** Uses appropriate possessive forms, as in *John's wagon.* | | | | | | | |

Source: Michigan Oral Language Series.

In summarizing the language differences of the dialect and Spanish-speaking students, Table 5.2 may serve as a guide for the teacher.

## Proposed Teaching Methods

Over the past decade, many educators have presented their views on teaching reading to the dialect/ESL speaker.* These include:

1. teaching Standard English first.

2. using dialect readers, and then gradually introducing Standard English.

3. neutralizing the dialect differences in early books so there is minimum interference between book language and students' dialect.

4. teaching reading to children totally in their dialect or native language.

While at present, the issue is far from settled, few educators today would opt for any of the above methods. Instead, the present position is that standard materials may be used quite successfully, provided the teacher understands and appreciates dialect differences and does not overcorrect when the dialect initially differs. This *does not* imply that teachers should not use, describe, and teach SE when such instruction would be most beneficial to the students.

Coping with a complex linguistic environment is a serious problem for the young dialect speaker who is beginning to learn to read. The situation can only be exacerbated by a teacher's unrealistic expectation of what is appropriate English. We will look at the actual transcripts of two students, one African-Ameri-

**TABLE 5.2**  Summary chart of major areas of differences between Standard English and dialect-speaking/Spanish-speaking students.

PHONOLOGY

| | |
|---|---|
| 1. | Consonant clusters are sometimes modified or eliminated. |
| 2. | Third person singular and past tense forms are frequently eliminated. |
| 3. | /th/ often has the sound of /d/ or /f/. |
| 4. | /r/ modifies and changes the vowel; /r/ is often eliminated. |
| 5. | Vowel sounds are modified and sometimes do not show contrasts. |
| 6. | Diphthongs often eliminate the glide. |

GRAMMAR DIFFERENCES

| | |
|---|---|
| 1. | Verb and subject agreement are frequently lacking. |
| 2. | The verb *be* is used differently. |
| 3. | Irregular verb forms are frequently regularized. |
| 4. | Past tense and past participle forms are sometimes reversed. |
| 5. | *Do* and *don't* forms are inserted or used differently than in Standard English. |
| 6. | Multiple negation is common. |
| 7. | Possessives take different forms. |
| 8. | The expletives *there are/were* and *it is* are used differently. |
| 9. | Syntax is sometimes changed. |

* The term *ESL* stands for "English as a Second Language." Some educators use the term *LEP* to stand for "Limited English Proficiency."

can and the other Hispanic, to draw some conclusions about teaching reading to the minority student.

***Reading transcripts.*** The words in the boxes are actual reading errors while the words appearing above the text words are dialect renderings of the text.

*John's Oral Reading*

go       sto   wiv

"I think he goes to the store with his

| friend |       can he

mother. Ask her if he can stay home

| today |   | he |  con

this time. Then we can get the club-

| starried | firs | maybe |

house started first thing Monday."

Transcript of reading by a third grader who speaks an African-American dialect.

*Carmen's Oral Reading*

theenk  go     duh     wid heez

I think he goes to the store with his

| friend |      eef

mother. Ask her if he can stay home

| today |     he con ged duh

this time. Then we can get the club

houz | stored | theeng | maybe |

house started first thing Monday."

Transcript of reading by a third grader who is bilingual—speaks both English and Spanish.

The classroom teacher who is *un*aware of the influence of dialect in the reading process might conclude that all of these miscued words are errors and do some unnecessary drilling on known words. When changes in the text are due to dialect, the teacher should not demand SE pronunciation from the young reader. Constant overcorrection on the part of the teacher places the child in a quandary, since s/he knows the word and reads the word, and yet is told that it is incorrect. For example, leaving off the *ed* of *jump* in the sentence, *He jump yesterday,* is correct in the language of the dialect speaker and perfectly understood because in the sentence the word *yesterday* indicates past time. In their dialect/language, the *ed* inflectional ending is superfluous and unnecessary.

Moreover, when children's speech is constantly corrected, they usually refrain from active participation in oral and written activities of the reading program. Because it is here that their speech patterns receive the most criticism, they perceive reading as a hostile experience, turning away from the threat it represents.

In the early oral reading situation, what should teachers do, when they understand the dialect system and appreciate the difficulties with which these young children must learn to cope as beginning readers?

1. During early reading activities the teacher accepts and values the oral and written language of children who are bilingual or speak with a dialect—s/he is selective in the nature of correcting errors.

2. Words or word parts to be learned are first presented orally and in meaningful context, related to actions and objects in real-life situations.

3. While the child reads orally, the teacher does not try to teach SE. The concern is whether or not the student comprehends the text.

4. The teacher refrains from insisting children read the standard form if such a feature is *lacking in the child's oral speech,* as this indicates s/he has not internalized an SE rule. It would be as if we who use standard forms were ordered to read and translate them into nonstandard ones. (Try it, and you will see how difficult it would be.)

5. The teacher helps the class as a whole appreciate the wide variance in the way English is used and that each form is a viable mode of communication (Edwards, Bessley, and Thompson, 1991).

## Reading Tests and the Dialect/ESL Speaker

Reading tests in word recognition often penalize dialect/ESL speakers because their "sounding out" ability to discriminate between words such as *sole* and *sold* and *walk* and *walked* are not the same as the SE speaker. When these words are in the context of a phrase or sentence, they do not cause the same difficulty; differentiation for dialect speakers is easier. When dialect-related items are removed from standardized tests, an entire grade difference in achievement is often noticed in the scores. Test performance is also adversely affected when comprehension is assessed for several reasons: They are limited in the knowledge of certain concepts; they are unfamiliar with vocabulary terms used in test questions and answer choices; and they have a tendency to interpret everything literally (Garcia, 1991).

## The Asian-American Student

The large recent influx of Asian-American students, particularly Vietnamese students, also necessitates some consideration. In spite of an excellent attitude toward school learning, the English phoneme system can be quite difficult for these individuals.

The Vietnamese language differs from English in that it is tonal, and one-syllable words change meaning by the tone-value the speaker gives them. Through shifts in tone, the word *ma* can mean "mother" or "ghost." Furthermore, multi-syllabic words are virtually unknown in Vietnamese. A word such as *hippopotamus* would be extremely difficult for them to say. You might have to settle for *hippo!*

As with other ESL speakers, a chronic problem is with verbs. In Vietnamese, there are no verb tenses as English speakers think of them. The same applies to plurals—there are no plural suffixes on nouns. The *s* endings and internal vowel changes *(man, men, woman, women)* are also unfamiliar.* Fortunately, there is uniformity in the written language since the Vietnamese writing system derives from the Roman alphabet, adopted after World War I.

Based on the difference of the two sound systems, the following may cause difficulty.

1. These sounds exist in English but not Vietnamese.

   /ĭ/ as in sit        /o͝o/ as in b<u>oo</u>k        /ă/ as in c<u>a</u>t        /t̶h̶/ as in th<u>en</u>

   /th/ as in <u>th</u>ank    /ch/ as in <u>ch</u>ur<u>ch</u>    /j/ as in bri<u>dge</u>    /r/ as in <u>r</u>ed

2. There is difficulty in hearing the contrast between sounds as /ē/ in s<u>ea</u>t and /ĭ/ in s<u>i</u>t; /o͞o/ in f<u>oo</u>l and /ŭ/ in f<u>u</u>ll; /ĕ/ in b<u>e</u>d and /ă/ in b<u>a</u>d; /sh/ in <u>sh</u>oes and /ch/ in <u>ch</u>oose. The Vietnamese hears these sounds as similar. On the production of these sounds, they cannot produce them accurately since there is only one sound for each pair in their language.

3. Sounds that occur in both English and Vietnamese but have different articulations also constitute problems. Usually the students will assume they have the same sounds in both languages when they do not. Examples are voiceless stops as /p/t/k/.

4. Final position of nasals /m/n/ and also the /l/ sound are pronounced differently in Vietnamese. Also different are the voiced and voiceless consonants in Vietnamese: /k/ in *dock* or /g/ in *dog* are the same, Vietnamese pronouncing both of them as voiceless.

5. Clusters of consonants are particularly difficult, especially when they occur in the final position. When the final clusters contain voiced consonants, the difficulty becomes insurmountable. They drop the excess consonant, pronouncing only one sound. A word like *minds* will be pronounced as if it had one consonant, *min*.

Note the following word pair comparisons:

WORD PAIR COMPARISONS

| | |
|---|---|
| feet—fit | top—stop |
| lock—rock | think—sink |
| cheap—sheep | watch—wash |
| fly—fry | sky—ski |
| bath—path | |

With all the complexities of dialect/ESL, it is impossible for a text of this nature to deal adequately with this problem. Those who have special needs in this area should contact the Center for Applied Linguistics in Washington, DC.

## Teaching Students with Limited English Proficiency: Beginning to Read

Some students come to class without knowing any English. Faced with this problem, French and Danielson (1990) found two useful strategies in such situations. First, they had students draw, label, and cut out characters for settings and stories. They began with *boy* and *girl,* adding the words *jump, walk, run,* and *hop.*

---

* For more detailed information see *Assessment of Vietnamese Speaking for Limited English Proficient Students with Special Needs,* The California State Dept. of Ed., Personnel Development Unit, Sacramento, CA.

This enabled the instructor to model her cut-out characters as the characters would *jump, walk, run*. Word and phrase cards followed, with the child saying the word, reading the word, and acting out the word with the cut-out character. Eventually other cut-out characters were added (*mouse, pony, dog,* and *cat*) and these characters interacted with their environment. As a result of this activity, the students began to build a vocabulary. Second, the teachers used a computer program, *The Print Shop,* for students to make individual alphabet booklets and thereby began teaching them decoding skills. Each student, aided by the teacher, produced a 26-page alphabet booklet of his/her own. Learning to select commands from the computer screen also helped increase the students' vocabulary for reading.

With ESL students (and also for English-proficient ones) Boyle and Peregory (1990) suggested the use of "literacy scaffolds" to support students in understanding and producing written language at a level superior to their competence without the scaffold. The idea is based on predictable patterns, or a scaffold, making use of repeated phrases, refrains, and rhymes. Typically students write their own poetry based on the pattern and share them in peer editing groups and classroom publications. Two examples of patterns are as follows:

"I used to be . . . but now I am. . . ."

"I am the one that. . . ."

Students write several refrains with the pattern, thereby "composing" poetry superior to what they could write without the prompt or repeated phrase.

The best resource for this activity is the sentence writing examples in *Wishes, Lies and Dreams* by Kenneth Koch (1970). The patterns and examples, written by his dialect-speaking and ESL students, are useful as springboards for engaging in this fun and highly successful activity. Also useful in this area are books with repetitive patterns, sometimes referred to as books with predictable features. Some suggested titles follow:

1. R. Brown (1981), *A Dark, Dark Tale.* NY: Dial.
2. E. Carle (1968), *The Very Hungry Caterpillar.* NY: Philomel.
3. N. Hellen (1988), *The Bus Stop.* NY: Orchard.
4. B. Martin (1983), *Brown Bear; Brown Bear; What Do You See?* NY: Holt.
5. L. Tolstoy (1988), *The Great Big Enormous Turnip.* NY: Watts.
6. N. Trafuri (1988), *Spots, Feathers and Curly Tails.* NY: Greenwillow.
7. A. Wood (1984), *The Napping House.* San Diego, CA: Harcourt Brace.

## Teaching Students with Limited English Proficiency: Upper Elementary Students

As these students leave the early primary grades, the cognitive and linguistic demands they face in reading become increasingly challenging (Sutton, 1989). These readers, as all readers, must bring to the text decoding skills and the conceptual framework needed to understand the text message. Thus, word recognition skills and needed background in the area to be read are critical for the limited English speaker. There is no shortcut in either of these two areas. All the skills and strategies employed in teaching mainstream children must be used, plus further refinement, creative activities that speak to their imagination, and much individualization. Sutton suggests the following key points for the teacher:

1. Know the grapheme/phoneme connection between SE and the primary language. You will be able to anticipate difficulties and avoid them as much as possible.

2. When particular phonemic distinctions do not exist in their native language, students will be unable to profit from certain types of discrete phonics instruction. Also, if they are in the early stages of acquiring English, it will be difficult for them to pronounce words whose sounds do not appear in their native language.

3. As much as possible integrate the phonics instruction with actual reading.

4. Focus on contextualized language. Students know many words they see in their extended environment (e.g., *Burger King, EXIT, cinema*). Build on this ability to recognize words in a context by integrating print into the classroom environment as well. Label items, locations, and activities in the room, on bulletin boards, and on display tables.

5. Write down or photocopy familiar dialogues and stories; have students practice reading them as creative dramatics, choral reading, role plays, and interviews.

6. Have students identify words they would like to know in print. This key word approach to the development of a sight word vocabulary has been quite effective with LEP students.

7. Provide students with a place (notebook or word cards) to keep track of important words. The student can use a combination of clues for meaning: an illustration, their own language definition.

8. Use folktales as their stories and plots are universal and easy to identify with. (See Sutton's article for many other worthwhile suggestions.)

In other words, teaching students with limited English proficiency should consist of "saturation in print," carried out by many different reading, speaking, and writing activities conducted in a warm supportive environment. An excellent resource book, by Spangenberg and Prichard, eds., *Kids Come in All Languages: Reading Instruction for ESL Students* (1994), offers many other worthwhile suggestions.

## Building Background

As important as it is for mainstream students to have background information in many of the materials they read, it becomes critical for LEP and dialect/ESL students. Writers of children's materials often take for granted that all children have certain concepts. This is not necessarily so, as shown by a fifth grade student who questioned a story by replying that "sardines didn't come from the water; they came from a can!"

Maria (1989) believes that many ESL students have such concepts but "cannot call them up" because of cultural factors. She believes that group interactive discussion is the most fruitful in building concepts, with children learning much from one another. Sutton (1989) also suggests that group assignments can be carried out successfully, with each student reading a section, writing one or two sentences about it, and then combining the totality into a report that all read and then present to the class.

The lack of concepts and background do not create as much trouble with stories, since most of these center around problems and solving them, and problem solving is an area of strength for these students.

In his book *Using the Newspaper to Teach ESL Students,* Olivares (1993) offers many practical suggestions in both language skills and in the content areas by building background in topics that students will read about in their classes.

## SUMMARY

Parents are continuing to play a more active role in schools' reading programs. Suggestions were given for some of the activities parents may employ with their children. When the experiences, attitudes, and behaviors accepted by the family and school are the same, children find it easier to succeed in the school's academic program.

For those children who speak with a dialect and children for whom English is a second language, there can be difficulty in learning to read. Proposals in the past that would alter the reading texts for them have been discarded in favor of an approach that places standard materials in the hands of a knowledgeable teacher.

Differences between SE and the dialect/ESL students' English were contrasted. While these differences are small, considering the totality of the English lexicon (a million words), they can cause reading problems unless teachers differentiate between what is an error and what is dialect interference.

Reading tests in word recognition skills penalize the dialect/ESL speaker unless words are written in context. This is important to remember in teaching—to place words pronounced similarly (as *toe, tore,* and *tool* in the African-American dialect) in a phrase or sentence.

Suggestions and ideas for teaching students with limited English proficiency were outlined.

1. Why is parental involvement important in the school reading program?
2. What major phonological and grammatical differences occur between dialect/ESL speakers and SE speakers?
3. What five principles must teachers be aware of when teaching the young dialect/ESL speaker?
4. What are some problems the dialect/ESL speaker experience with tests?
5. What is meant by "saturation in print?" Why is this relevant for the dialect/ESL student?

**Chapter 5:**

**Final Review**

# Computers in the Reading Classroom

## THE CURRENT STATUS

While the merits of computer-assisted instruction (CAI) may continue to be debated among educators, such instruction continues to grow. President Clinton set the year 2000 as the target date for having all schools connected in some way to the Information Superhighway.* Moreover, he, as well as many legislators, consider computer instruction as basic as learning to read and write. Some school districts, such as Vancouver in Washington and Cupertino in California, have been able to invest substantial sums in their computer programs, with training available for teachers and adequate programs for students. Additionally, a small but growing number of teachers are creating their own instructional multimedia lessons, combining audio, video, animation, text, and graphics (Sponder and Hilgenfeld, 1994). In contrast to the president's goals and the expertise of computer-literate teachers, some U. S. schools lack even basic hardware and computer programs (see Figure 6.1).

A research and policy group, The Children's Partnership, has released an analysis of new computer technologies and their impact on American children (*MultiMedia Schools,* Jan./Feb. 1995, p. 10) and concluded that

1. Most American children do not have the skills they will increasingly need for the job market they will face. More than half of new jobs require using some form of computer and/or technological skill.
2. Affluent parents are supplementing the technological education their children receive at school, creating a growing gap between information "haves" and "have-nots."
3. America's school system *represents the best way* to teach *every* child computer and technological skills.

## COMPUTERS AND TEACHER TRAINING

Perhaps American students' lack of basic computer knowledge is related to the fact that teachers are not as well trained in using computers as their international counterparts are. Figure 6.2 shows that compared to European and Japanese

---

* The underlying ideas of the Information Superhighway are teams of people or students working together to solve problems and accomplish tasks that involve huge amounts of data. The data may be stored at a variety of sites. The Information Superhighway allows the team members to be located throughout the country. A student may be a member of several different teams. Teams are created and disbanded as the need arises.

**FIGURE 6.1** Schools vary in student access to computers.

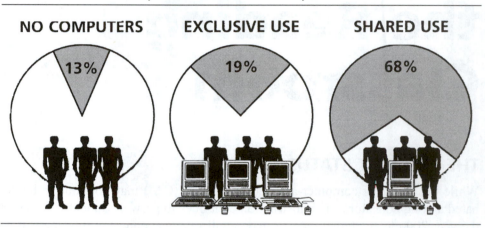

Source: Quality Education Data, Inc. Denver, CO, 1994.

teachers, American educators do not have the necessary staff training in computers. The lack of training is particularly striking in middle schools (Jessie Siegel, 1994). This same concern and criticism has been voiced by teachers and administrators for over a decade (*Learning,* March 1986).

For teachers in schools where there is minimal teacher training in computers, Carol S. Holzberg (1994) offers the following suggestions.

1. Ask questions—lots of questions. Talk to teachers who know more about computers than you do. Ask them to show you how they make use of computers in their classrooms.
2. Give yourself time at the keyboard. Learn some new programs. Touch every key to discover what it can do. If there is a problem and the computer seems uncooperative, simply turn it off and restart it.
3. Once you feel comfortable, try a simple word-processing program. This enables you to create materials on the computer. The benefit is that instead of updating worksheets year after year, they can be produced on the computer, stored on a disk, changed later if needed, and printed. The result is that great-looking documents are produced with much less time and effort.

## COMPUTER PROGRAMS AND THE CONTINUING NEED FOR IMPROVEMENT

Another problem may be associated with some of the computer programs that now proliferate the market. While improvements have been made as the industry has matured, the nature and educational value of some computer programs used in the schools is still somewhat questionable. To some teachers, many are simply electronic workbooks, dull and repetitive, with little educational value. Dr. Roger Schank, an expert in virtual reality, has the following to say about the state of educational software:

> There is this idea that decent educational software is out there. It isn't. The software you are seeing is a bad imitation of books, a good imitation of quizzes, but who wants quizzes as a form of instruction? There hasn't been any money invested in this country in good educational software. You see basically the kind written

**FIGURE 6.2** Percentage of computer-using schools with introductory computer courses available for teachers by country and grade level, 1992.

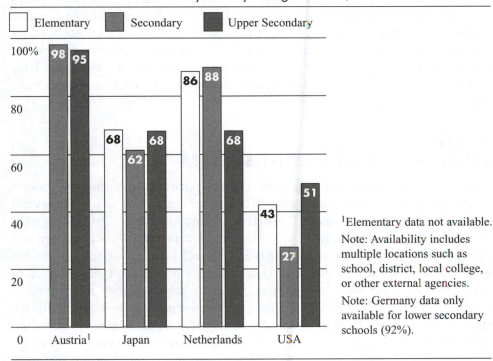

[1]Elementary data not available.

Note: Availability includes multiple locations such as school, district, local college, or other external agencies.

Note: Germany data only available for lower secondary schools (92%).

Source: International IEA Computers in Education Study (Pelgrum & Plomp 1993).

by computer scientists who wouldn't know education . . .and who make things like "Shoot the Verb When It Goes By." These programs are ridiculous.[1]

Tom Snyder (*Reading Teacher,* June/July 1994, p. 17), a technology expert, founder of a software company, and a former teacher, believes we should approach this technology with care. While the computer will increasingly become part of school life, he warns against accepting all the claims made regarding the benefits of its use in the classroom. What buzz words and other computer rhetoric have tended to do, Snyder believes, is to *dee*mphasize the importance of not only the teacher but of art forms such as great stories in print. He believes that computers in education have revitalized what he calls student-centered, "teacher-out-of-the-loop" teaching.

Snyder is especially critical of those who push for interactive learning, where students make all the choices, such as determining the plot elements that will happen next in a story, and jumping around in a text instead of going from beginning to end. He compares those who push for interactive education to individuals who constantly click a television remote control. Snyder wants the great stories in print enjoyed and respected for the art forms they are and not usurped by the overuse of glitzy classroom computer programs.

## THE COST OF PROGRAMS

Newer software such as *Story Club* by Davidson and Associates, although highly recommended, is very expensive (*Electronic Learning,* Jan. 1994, p. 31). The

(1) See Interview/Dr. Roger Schank, *Electronic Learning,* March 1995, p. 7).

program includes extensive explorations of 15 multicultural folktales, using 10 computer videodiscs. It includes audiotape and print materials, and integrates reading, writing, speaking, and listening. It even addresses multiple learning styles. Unfortunately, however, the cost may be prohibitive for most schools. Yet according to Thompson and Montgomery (1994), programs such as these that are expensive and require unrealistic investments of teacher time are changing. They believe that materials rapidly will become financially attainable and much easier to use.

## A TOTAL COMPUTER LEARNING/MANAGEMENT SYSTEM

One of the newest total learning/management systems is published by Josten's Learning Corporation of San Diego.* The program has been in use for several years at the Vancouver School District in Washington. It is a total integrated learning system in which "learning paths" are customized for each student, targeting certain skills in lessons that may last 10 to 20 minutes. Each student has a "menu" and desktop so that his or her "learning paths" are individualized to needs. The program has a built-in management system whereby instructor and student can communicate. The teacher generates reports on outcome with the student gaining immediate feedback. All testing of these skills takes place on the computer. Students can even say words into the computer and receive feedback on pronunciation errors. While some students spend two class periods per week in the computer lab, some classrooms have four computer stations, and students use them in rotation. Part of the time on the computer is also spent writing and publishing in a whole language approach.

## DIFFERENCES IN COMPUTER SOFTWARE

### Type I

Software today can be identified as one of two types. Type I software tends to support more traditional teaching:

- It has been predetermined by the software developers
- There is limited potential interaction between learner and machine.
- It involves a format with few varieties.

Examples would include most drill and practice, tutorial uses, and assessment uses.

### Type II

Type II software tends to emphasize a more cognitive approach:

- It is controlled by the user, rather than the software developer.
- It involves a highly varied (sometimes unlimited) repertoire of acceptable responses between learner and machine.
- It often requires days or weeks of use before all the software's capabilities have been observed.

Type II examples include simulations, problem-solving, graphics, writing aids, and word processing.

* For more information, contact Josten's Learning Corporation of San Diego, CA, at 1-619-587-0087.

For an in-depth questionnaire useful prior to purchasing reading software, see Appendix E. For the names of reading software publishers, also see Appendix E.

## COMPUTER PROGRAMS FOR TEACHING WORD RECOGNITION SKILLS

Most computer programs involving word recognition skills are Type I. Some of these are designed to move in short, repetitive steps in case the student is having difficulty. Other programs switch to longer, faster steps if students easily grasp the materials. The majority of programs require that materials at each level be mastered before proceeding farther. The student is often rewarded with things such as stars, pluses, or a printed or audio recognition with each response.

Most available software programs in word recognition are found in these areas: the alphabet, consonants, blends, and vowels. Programs that teach the consonant and vowel digraphs and the diphthongs are more limited. Programs to teach the basic sight words, context clues, and syllabication rules are also available, but as with the digraphs and diphthongs, are more limited in number. In the area of structural analysis, many programs are available to teach the inflectional endings and contractions. Most prominent are programs with affixes. Programs that teach dictionary skills are also available.

### Example Programs

Examples of some typical software programs for teaching word recognition skills follow:*

*Instant Zoo* (ages 7–10) by Apple Computer. A set of four games plus a word list editor. Two of the games concern reading words. In *Quick Match,* pairs of words appear on the screen. The student decides if they match and presses the correct key. If the student guesses wrong or too slowly, the computer gets a point. In *Scramble,* letters jog in wearing animated tennis shoes and must be unscrambled before they jog to the bottom of the screen. Individual word lists to be used with *Scramble* may be created by the teacher.

*Phonics for Grades* 1–3 by SRA. The program includes nine levels and can be used along with any basal. Tape cassettes with a human voice are the audio component. See Figure 6.3 for an example of the computer graphics in the program.

**FIGURE 6.3**   SRA computer graphics.

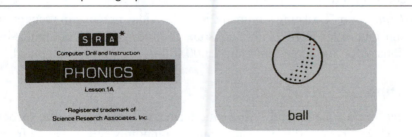

*Swift's Educational Software Directory,* Sterling Swift Publishing Co., 7901 South I-35, Austin, TX 78744.

* For other publisher names and addresses and specific skill titles and cost, see *Swift's Educational Software Directory,* Sterling Swift Publishing Company, 7901 South I H-35, Austin, TX 78744.

*Wordskill for the Microcomputer* by SRA. Levels 1–6 correspond to reading levels for grades 7–12. The program includes four games to improve knowledge of synonyms, definitions, antonyms, and analogies. In the game *KnowIt,* the definition is provided and students type in the correct word from their word list.

All of the following programs were recommended for classroom use by the California Software Clearinghouse (1995).*

### Discrimination of letters, auditorially and visually

*Alphabet Circus* by D. L. M. K–1. Allows user to practice letter identification, letter matching, and alphabetical order.

*Customized Alphabet Drill* by Random House. K–1. Students fill in letters in various sequences.

*Ernie's Quiz* by Apple. K–3. Four games to help students discriminate letters, to use context clues, and to recognize high frequency words.

*Letters and Words* by Learning Well. K–3. Three individual games with animated graphics to help in discriminating letters, develops a sight vocabulary, and using context clues.

### Recognition of high frequency sight words

*Kermit's Electronic Storymaker* by Simon and Schuster. K–2. Children create animal stories using The Muppets as characters. Delightful drills on sight words, also drill on using different kinds of sentence patterns.

*Keygame—Word Works* by Teacher Support. K–6. Children participate in exciting game activities while practicing locating keys in a timed setting. They learn to recognize high frequency words while acquiring keyboarding skills.

*Word Memory—Word Works* by Teacher Support. 1–3. Uses a game format to improve memory sequencing within a time limit. Includes an authoring system and database for several basal reading series. Good graphics to help in recognizing high frequency words.

### Letter sounds

*Building Reading Skills* by Josten's Learning System. K–3. The program features two disks that use graphics and a voice synthesizer to present and review initial consonant letters and sounds. Games for practice and rewards are provided. A third disk presents the short and long vowels.

*Word Spinner* by Learning Company. K–4. Provides practice in recognizing three- and four-letter words with a consonant letter pattern. A computer-based dictionary for 500 three-letter and 1,000 four-letter words is included.

### Structure

*Beamer* by Data Command. 4–6. Game format to teach students to recognize prefixes, suffixes, and roots. The computer randomly selects words from a list of

---

* For further information write to Dr. Ann Lathrop, Bldg. ED-1-17, CA State University, Long Beach, CA 90840-1402. Also see *The Latest and the Best of TESS, The Educational Software Selector,* 1991 ed. EPIE Institute, Hampton Bays, NY, Educational Products Information Exchange, pp. 255–256, and *Swift's Educational Software Directory,* Sterling Swift Publishing Company, 7901 South I-35, Austin, TX 78744.

more than 400. Words reappear until the student correctly identifies the specific word part.

*Classifying—Prefixes and Suffixes* by Random House. 4–6. Teaches recognition of prefixes and suffixes. Also includes root words and compound words. Students add and change prefixes and suffixes. Game format and graphics for reward.

*Micro-Read* by American Educational Computer. 3–6. Students learn to recognize root words and compound words. Prefixes and suffixes are added or changed. Six levels of practice also cover other skills. Branching depends on student achievement.

## Other programs to teach word recognition skills

*ABC With Hickory and Me* by Western Publishing Company, Inc. K–3. The alphabet comes to life through colorful objects in Hickory and Mat's home as children match letters and sounds. Users select different levels of difficulty.

*Monker's Spelling Submarine* by Western Publishing Company, Inc. 1–4. Children join a sea voyage to practice phonics, spelling, and word-building skills. Sea creatures emerge from a coral reef to perform when the correct answer is chosen. The user selects the level of difficulty.

*Sequencing Dictionary Skills* by Random House. 4–6. Students place words in alphabetical order. Incorrect choices generate step-by-step assistance. Creation disk allows teachers to create additional lessons. Good format and ease of use.

*Stickybear Reading* by Weekly Reader. K–3. Designed to reinforce word recognition and comprehension. Students create sentences by combining nouns, verbs, and objects. The Stickybear then acts out the sentence. Appealing graphics and useful repetition for reinforcement.

*Wizard of Words* by Advanced Ideas. 1–6. Five word games reinforce vocabulary and spelling skills. Game characters include a juggler, knight, princess, fire breathing dragon, and two heralds. Eight different learning levels within each game. A management system reports scores and allows teachers to enter new word lists.

*Word Pairs* by Microcomputer Workshop. 5 and up. Offers instruction and practice on homonyms and synonyms by presenting definitions, models, explanations, and appropriate exercises. Users may select either a brief or extensive tutorial and practice.

*Word Quest* by Sunburst. 1–6. Two games utilize alphabetizing skills. In one, students try to find a word that fits between two given words. In another (competition mode), one student picks a mystery word, and another is challenged to guess what the mystery word is by getting clues as to which words it fits between.

See Appendix E for guidelines in purchasing software for students.

Perhaps the most popular of all the recent software programs involving word recognition skills is the *Reader Rabbit* series, *Levels I, II, and III* by The Learning Company.

*Reader Rabbit Level I:* Ages 3–6. The format uses an animated Word Factory to help children build early reading, spelling, and vocabulary skills. Four sequenced games use school reading words to help emerging readers identify more than 200 three-letter words, recognize spelling patterns, and build vocabulary. Highly animated and clear graphics engage the user, and the program is easy for children to use without adult supervision.

*Reader Rabbit Level II:* Ages 6–8. The format used is a fantasy railroad journey built around four sequenced games that build compound words and blends, long and short vowel sounds, word concepts such as homonyms and word opposites, and early dictionary skills.

*Reader Rabbit Level III:* Ages 6–8. The format for this four-game sequence is the newspaper, Wordville's *Daily Skywriter,* covering more than 200 "breaking news" stories. These help to develop and reinforce previously learned skills, while children encounter words in context and build comprehension skills. The children are able to print their own newspapers about happenings in Wordville. The program is also available on CD-ROM.

### Type II software

After some educators criticized software for lacking follow-up reading application, newer software was developed to provide for greater student involvement. Programs such as *Talking Dinosaurs, Talking First Reader,* and *Word Munchers* from MECC and *Explore-A-Story, Explore-A-Classic,* and *Explore-A-Folktale* from William K. Bradford allow students to actively take part in storymaking as they directly interact with stories, adding their own text to them. They also can create their own "big books" with programs such as Pelican Software's *Big Book Maker* (Mageau, 1991).

## SUMMARY

While the merits of computer-assisted instruction are still debated, the use of computers in the classroom continues to grow. This is commendable, but a large investment of time and money is needed in many areas of the country where, unfortunately, the availability of computers for students and adequate computer training for teachers is lacking. The result is that many American children presently are not learning the necessary computer and technological skills they will need in the coming century.

Additional dilemmas include the relative merit of some current programs and the high cost of some programs.

Computer reading programs recommended for classroom use by the California Software Clearinghouse were described. While many of the reading software programs are in the area of word recognition skills, newer programs do integrate more reading and writing. One of the most popular, reasonably priced, and innovative reading programs for primary students is *Reader Rabbit,* which may be purchased in three levels.

**Chapter 6:**

**Final Review**

1. Why is the use of the computer in the classroom a study in contrasts?
2. What is a major problem for teachers in the use of the computer in the classroom? What are some of the other problems?
3. What is a recent innovative and popular computer reading program?
4. What is a learning/management system? How does it operate?

# Answer Keys

## ANSWERS TO QUICK SELF-CHECKS

**1.** p. 5

 1. a. *a, o, u*

  b. *e, i, y*

  c. The *c* generalization works most of the time; the *g* generalization words `
   some of the time.

 2. *S* can encode the sounds of /s/, /z/, and /sh/.

**2.** p. 8

 1. a. *r, l, s,* and *tw*

  b. With *r* and *l* blends the *r* and *l* letter/sounds are second.

  c. With *s* the letter/sounds are first. Also the *s* blends may contain three
   letters.

 2. a. *ld, nd, nt, nk,* and *lk*

  b. As phonograms

**3.** p. 10

 1. a. *ch,* /ch/, /k/, /sh/

   *gh,* /g/, /f/, /-/

  b. *th,* /th/, /t̶h̶/

   *wh,* /w or hw/, /h/

  c. *ph,* /f/

   *sh,* /sh/

 A. *e, i,* and *y*

 B. *r, l, s,* and *tw*

**4.** p. 12

 1. The first letter of each digraph is silent.

 2. They encode one sound.

 3. All follow a short vowel and usually come at the end of a word.

**5.** p. 16

 1. a. *u,* /o͞o/

  b. *a, o, u.* They are sometimes taught as sight words.

  c. It is similar to the sound of /uh/, and is usually heard in unaccented syllable.

 A. *gn, kn, wr,* and *ck*

 B. /ch/, /k/, /sh/

**6.** p. 18

 1. English words do not end in the letter *v* (prove).

 2. A final vowel is needed to complete the final syllable; therefore the first
  vowel remains long (stable).

3. Final *e* gives *c* a soft sound (fence).

4. Final *e* indicates the preceding vowel has a long sound (stake).

5. Final *e* is an historical leftover (else).

**7.** p. 19

1. English words do not end with *i*. *Ai* and *ay* encode a long /ā/ sound.

2. English words do not end with *u*. *Au* and *aw* encode the /ă/ sound.

3. The sounds encoded by these graphemes do not vary.

A. phonograms or rimes

B. /f/

**8.** p. 22

1. *ee*

2. *ei*

3. *ea*

4. *ey*

5. *ie*

6. The *e* digraphs decode mainly as long ē and sometimes as long ā.

**9.** p. 26

1. *ou* /ow/ as in proud, /ŭ/ as in touch, /ō/ as in soul, /o͞o/ as in group; /ow/ and /ŭ/.

2. English words do not end with *i*.

3. *oa*, /ō/

4. /ow/ as in cow, /ō/ as in know

5. /o͞o/ as in moon, /o͝o/ as in book

A. /ē/ and /ā/

B. the letter *v*

**10.** p. 27

1. /o͞o/

2. t*o*, r*u*de, m*oo*n, gr*ou*p

**11.** p. 29

1. At the beginning of words

2. *yes*—as a consonant

3. *cry*—as a vowel

4. *play*—as part of a digraph

5. *royal*—as part of a dipthong

A. Every English syllable must have a vowel.

B. /o͞o/

**12.** p. 33

1. All have the same sound.

2. When the letter *w* precedes *or*, the *or* likewise encodes the /er/ sound.

3. It has a variety of sounds.

4. *Ai* and *ee*. /Âr/ as in pair and /ē-r/ as in peer.

**13.** p. 81

1. did ✓

from ✓    for ✓

about ✓    once ✓

2. Dolch

3. Each word is very carefully introduced followed by lots of review and practice.

4. Through wide and varied reading.

5. Drill with phrase cards, sentence cards, or matching exercises, pointing out pertinent details, creative graphics, configuration; comparing and contrasting words; games.

**14.** p. 86

1. Limited vocabularies; frequently unmotivated; do not use contextual strategies.

2. Semantic and syntactic clues.

3. Explanation, experience, series, restatement, contrast, inference.

4. See pages 84–86.

5. They have had many more experiences and have more developed vocabularies.

**15.** p. 88

1. Sometimes a compound word has the combined meaning of the two root words, but sometimes it does not.

2. Cyberspace, download, cranapple

3. See page 87.

A. *ai, ay, au, aw*

B. *ci, si,* and *ti*

**16.** p. 104

1. Prefixes are usually found before a base word or root, suffixes are placed after. Prefixes usually change the word meaning but not the part of speech. Derivational suffixes may alter both.

2.

| *Absorbed* | *Active* |
|---|---|
| recent | prepay |
| insist | uncertain |
|  | dislike |
|  | impersonal |

3.

| *Inflectional* | *Derivational* |
|---|---|
| singing | foolish |
| jumps | cleverness |
| called | safely |

4. a. Drop final *e* when adding an ending that begins with a vowel.

   b. Double the final consonant when adding a suffix that begins with a vowel if the word

      1) ends in a single consonant.

      2) is preceded by a short vowel.

      3) is a one-syllable word.

   c. Do not drop the letter *y* when adding *ing.*

5. Through wide and varied reading and through classroom discussions that clarify affixed words.

6. As students move through the grades, they encounter more and more affixed words, especially in social studies and science.

7. See pages 99–102.

**17.** p. 108

1. An open syllable ends in a vowel, often long; a closed syllable ends in a consonant and the preceding vowel is often short.

2. Check to see if the word is compound, has affixes, double consonants, or two unlike consonants, or a final *le.* Do not divide blends or digraphs.

3. Syllables are clapped; words may be written in syllables, pronounced in syllables, and then blended together.

4. Some medial vowel sounds in words are no longer pronounced.

5. Our written language relates to a more "formal" English code.

A. A prefix is a group of letters that go in front of a word and that change its meaning. The root carries the main meaning of the word.

B. The sight word list consists of "heavy duty" words such as *at, the, be* that are met frequently in reading. They are words that must be read "at sight" for reading fluency.

**18.** p. 112

1. Alphabetizing skills, understanding guide words, ability to use pronunciation key, understanding phonics respelling, and ability to select proper definition.

2. Through use!

3. See pages 108–112.

A. Younger children have not had as many experiences to draw upon to aid them in using the context. Also, because of maturation factors, they are more limited in their reasoning ability.

B. *l, r, s,* and *tw.*

## ANSWERS TO SECTION REVIEWS AND SELF-CHECKS

### Answers to Chapter 1, Section 1
### Review and Self-Check, p. 13

1. *c, g,* and *s; c, g;* and *a, o,* and *u* condition these letters to have the hard /k/ sound. *I* and *e* condition *c* and *g* to have the soft sound. Word examples are cat, cot, cut (hard c). Cigar, cement, cycle (soft c). Game, gone, gull (hard g). Germ, giant, gym (soft g). The *c* generalization works most of the time. The *g* generalization works about 75 percent of the time.

2. gra*ph,* c*h*aise, *gh*astly, *th*ink, air*sh*ip, *wh*ile

| | | |
|---|---|---|
| *ch* | (3) | *ch*air, s*ch*eme, *ch*andelier |
| *gh* | (3) | *gh*ost, rou*gh,* throu*gh* |
| *ph* | (1) | *ph*one |
| *sh* | (1) | *sh*elf |
| *th* | (2) | *th*ick, *th*em |
| *wh* | (2) | *wh*at, *wh*o |

3.  *gn*     /n/      *gn*ome
    *kn*     /n/      *kn*ow
    *wr*     /r/      *wr*ist
    *ck*     /k/      de*ck*

4.  /k/      de*ck*
    /j/      bri*dge*
    /ck/     sti*ck*

They all follow a short vowel and usually come at the end of a word.

## Answers to Chapter 1, Section 2:
## Review and Self-Check, p. 27

1.  ă act
    ĕ elephant
    ĭ it
    ŏ olive
    ŭ upon

2.  Similar to short *u* as in *u*p or an /uh/ sound. Language is changing: *a*bout, tick*e*t, penc*i*l, sec*o*nd.

3.  *a* encodes /ä/ as in father.
    *o* encodes /o͞o/ as in pr*o*ve.
    *u* encodes /o͝o/ as in p*u*sh.

4.  *u.* Language change. /yū/ and /o͞o/.

    | **/yū/** | **/o͞o/** |
    |----------|-----------|
    | c*u*be   | d*u*ty    |
    | m*u*sic  | l*u*te    |

5.  *ai* and *ay.* English words do not end in *i.*

    | **ai**   | **ay**   |
    |----------|----------|
    | m*ai*d   | tr*ay*   |
    | r*ai*l   | spr*ay*  |

6.  *au* and *aw.* English words do not end in *u.*

    | **au**    | **aw**   |
    |-----------|----------|
    | v*au*lt   | dr*aw*   |
    | *au*tumn  | s*aw*    |

7.  Long /ē/.
    sl*ee*p
    j*ee*p

8.  Long /ē/, short /ĕ/, and long /ā/. Long /ē/ is most common.

    | ***ea* as /ē/** | ***ea* as /ĕ/** | ***ea* as /ā/** |
    |-----------------|-----------------|-----------------|
    | br*ea*the       | h*ea*d          | br*ea*k         |
    | r*ea*p          | spr*ea*d        | st*ea*k         |

9.  Long /ē/ and long /ī/.

    | ***ie* as /ē/** | ***ie* as /ī/** |
    |-----------------|-----------------|
    | bel*ie*f        | p*ie*           |
    | n*ie*ce         | tr*ie*s         |

10. Decodes /ē/ after *c.* Sometimes as /ā/. Also as /ĕ/ and /ĭ/.

11. as /ē/ and as /ā/

    | *ey* as /ē/ | *ey* as /ā/ |
    |---|---|
    | k*ey* | th*ey* |
    | donk*ey* | pr*ey* |

12. *igh,* s*igh*t, r*igh*t

13. Vowel digraphs have two letters with one sound. Vowel diphthongs have two vowel letters with a gliding sound between them.

    *oa* as /ō/, r*oa*d

    *oo* as /o͞o/ and /o͝o/, m*oo*n and l*oo*k

    *ou* as /ow/, /ŭ/ /ō/ and /o͞o/, ar*ou*nd, t*ou*ch, sh*ou*lder, gr*ou*p

    *ow* as /ow/ and /ō/, cr*ow*d and l*ow*

    *oi* as /oy/, *oi*l

    *oy* as /oy/, t*oy*

14. /o͞o/, fr*ui*t, bl*ue,* and st*ew.*

15. As in gr*ou*p, m*oo*n, pr*o*ve, r*u*de, t*o,* s*ui*t, fl*ew,* tr*ue.*

### Answers to Chapter 1, Sections 3, 4, and 5:
### Review and Self-Check, p. 34

1. 

| **Consonant** | **Vowel** | **Digraph** | **Diphthong** |
|---|---|---|---|
| yam | gym | they | employ |
| yellow | dry | play | royal |
| | cycle | key | |

2. All encode the sound of /er/.

   When *w* precedes *or,* it also has the /er/ sound.

3. They are *ea, ai,* and *ee.* When *r* follows *ea,* the sound may be as in *ea*rth /er/; p*ea*r /âr/; or f*ea*r /ē-r/. When *r* follows *ai,* the sound is as in the word *air.* When *r* follows *ee,* the sound is as in the word *peer.*

4. The sounds have changed but the spelling still reflects the sound formerly used: *ch* as in *ch*andelier and *sh* as in *sh*ine.

## ANSWERS TO FINAL REVIEWS

### Answers to Chapter 1, Final Review, p. 36

| Words with Consonant Digraphs | Words with Blends | Words with Vowel Digraphs | Words with Vowel Diphthongs | Vowels With *r*-Control |
|---|---|---|---|---|
| s*ch*eme | wor*ld* | rec*ei*ve | destr*oy* | w*or*ld |
| coa*ch*ing | *br*idge | tr*ea*t | n*ow* | h*air* |
| ba*ck* | *tr*eat | afr*ai*d | ab*ou*t | *ear*n |
| brea*th* | a*fr*aid | coa*ch*ing | t*oi*l | few*er* |
| e*dge*\* | de*str*oy | fl*igh*t | sp*oo*n | s*ur*prise |
| *ch*aise | *fl*ight | brea*th* | few*er* | |
| a*th*lete | su*r*prise | c*oa*st | | |
| sti*tch*\* | *str*eamlined | *ch*aise | | |
| *ph*ysics | *br*eath | str*ea*mlined | | |
| | *st*itch | | | |
| | *sp*oon | | | |

\* Some would not call it a digraph, but a special consonant combination.

## Answers to Chapter 2, Final Review, p. 72

1. a. Discrimination abilities with letters and sounds; maturity; social responsibility; family background; language proficiency; motivation to read.

   b. Word, sentence, begins and ends with, letter, line, top and bottom.

2. a. Students identify the capitals and small letters that encode a particular sound.

   b. Students select words containing the specific sound from words containing related sounds and suggest words with the specific sound.

   c. Students write the capital and lower case letters that represent the specific sound.

   d. Students participate in purposeful activities applying the knowledge of the relationship between the letter and sound.

3. a. 4

   b. 1) No sounds are isolated—words are read as "whole."

   2) Individual phonemes are pronounced and then blended together.

   3) The vowel is pronounced first, followed by the first consonant sound, then the final sound.

   4) The ending phonogram is pronounced first, then the beginning consonant sound.

4. a. In general, with explicit phonics, teachers tell the sound-symbol relationship and have students memorize certain rules. With implicit phonics, students conclude what the sound-symbol relationship is after studying certain known sight words. Linguistic phonics is simply a patterned approach.

   b. The terms have not been standardized, with people claiming synthetic phonics is code-emphasis and analytic phonics is meaning-emphasis. Both can be concerned with meaning, so some of the criticisms do not appear to be supported. "Linguistics" reading is thought of by some as being language experience.

5. a. Text level, word level, discrimination level

   b. Note through formal and informal methods where the decoding process seems to break down.

6. Modeling, rule approach, whole word comparison, family method.

7. See pages 55, 56, 61–64.

8. Teachers sometimes engage in these activities to the exclusion of real reading.

9. To develop independence in word recognition skills.

10. Ongoing observation and diagnosis.

## Answers to Chapter 3, Final Review, p. 119

1. Sight words occur frequently, with percentages cited that range from 50 to 60 percent of running words. Students must know these words on sight in order to read with any degree of proficiency.

2. See pages 76–77.

3. The goal in reading is for students to eventually acquire a large enough storehouse of words so that most all the words they come across are in their sight vocabularies.

4. Sometimes but not always. Meanings of words originally "coined" frequently change.

5. Active prefixes are in the initial position, joined to base words, and alter meaning. Absorbed prefixes are part of the word.

| *Active* | *Absorbed* |
|---|---|
| unsure | contain |
| submarine | preclude |
| preview | exceed |

6.
| *Inflectional* | *Derivational* |
|---|---|
| jumping | courageous |
| smallest | attention |
| women's | merriment |
| draws | |

There are only a few inflectional suffixes, and they are taught in early reading. They do not usually change the part of speech. There are many, many derivational suffixes, and they often alter the part of speech, and sometimes even change the meaning.

Inflectional affixes are much simpler to learn. Derivational affixes are more difficult, frequently changing the part of speech of the root word. Also, there are many more derivational affixes.

7. a. When adding a suffix that begins with a vowel, final *e* is usually dropped.
   b. When a word has one syllable, one short vowel, and one final consonant, double the final consonant before adding the syllable that begins with a vowel.
   c. When a consonant precedes *y*, change *y* to *i* and add the suffix.
   d. Final *y* is not dropped when adding *ing*.

8. Through wide and varied reading and through classroom discussion.

9. Check to see if the word (1) is a compound word or has affixes, (2) has double consonant letters or two unlike consonants, (3) has a final *le*, (4) do not divide blends or digraphs, (5) see if the word makes sense.

10. Caramel, interest, memory (see page 107 for other examples).

11. Syntactic and semantic.
    Through examining books to see how authors supply context clues.
    Through specific exercises.

12. Alphabetizing skills.
    Understanding guide words.
    Ability to use the pronunciation key.
    Understanding phonic/respelling.
    Ability to select the proper definition.
    These skills are best learned through use.

### Answers to Chapter 4, Final Review, p. 131

1. a. Try the context first.
   b. Look at the structure for compound words, roots, and affixes.
   c. Check for syllable or meaning clues of prefixes and roots.

d. Check for phonics clues.

e. Check dictionary if the word is critical to meaning.

2. Teacher shows student a word card and tells her/him the best way to decode it. She offers sentences with the word. So do the students. Students write and say the word and check it against the word card. Teacher shows second word card, one with the target word, the other with a word that differs in one or two letters. Student tells what is the same and what is different about the words. Daily timed practice is required.

3. a. They need to read a little slower.

   b. They only note the outer configuration of words.

   c. They use whole word processing.

4. Use "smiling" faces. Use yes/no questions. Use a chart form.

5. a. Imitative Method (Student listens to a cassette tape of a story, following along in a book, until mastery is complete.)

   b. Student Sharing (Students of different ages read or share together, older students helping younger ones.)

   c. Impress Method (Teacher and student read together, the teacher allowing the student to take the lead when comfortable.)

   d. Repeated Readings (Student reads a selection of about 100 words several times, improving rate and giving the student the feeling of fluency for the first time.)

6. Reading Recovery is an intervention program that concentrates on teaching young children to read in a very intensive daily program with specialists as teachers.

## Answers to Chapter 5, Final Review, p. 147

1. a. Research shows parents can make a significant difference.

   b. School budget cuts.

   c. Importance of preschool years.

2. a. Consonant clusters are sometimes modified or eliminated.

   Third person singular and past tense forms are frequently eliminated.

   /th/ often has the sound of /f/ or /d/.

   /r/ is often eliminated or modified.

   Vowel sounds are modified and sometimes do not show contrasts.

   Diphthongs often eliminate the glide or modify it.

   b. Verb and subject agreement are frequently lacking.

   The verb *be* is used differently.

   Irregular verb forms are frequently regularized.

   Past tense and past participial forms are sometimes reversed.

   *Do* and *don't* forms are sometimes reversed.

   Multiple negation is common.

   Possessives take different forms.

   The expletives *there are/were* and *it is* are used differently.

   Syntax is sometimes changed.

3. a. Value the oral and written language of the child.

b. Present words/word parts orally in meaningful context, related to actions and objects in real-life situations.

c. Concentrate on the child's comprehension of the text.

d. Teach grammar patterns after the child has oral mastery of the pattern.

e. Build an appreciation in the classroom for language variation.

4. Words are difficult to recognize if they are not in context. Also students often lack knowledge of the type of vocabulary used in test questions and answer choices. They also have a tendency to answer everything literally.

5. Using many speaking, reading, and writing activities to foster literacy.

### Answers to Chapter 6, Final Review, p. 156

1. Many schools have adequate computers, software, and provide teacher training in their use. Other schools have no computers at all. Some students receive additional instruction outside of the classroom, resulting in a growing disparity in students' ability to use computers.

2. A major problem is a lack of adequate training for teachers. Other problems include scheduling for time, merits of the available software, and the expense of providing adequate hardware and software for instruction.

3. *Reader Rabbit, Levels I, II, and III* offer innovative methods of not only decoding but also writing and publishing books.

4. These systems not only teach skills and comprehension on an individualized basis but also track student progress, offering immediate feedback to both teachers and students.

# Record Form, Selected Lists, and Scope and Sequence Chart

## RECORD FORM FOR INFORMAL ASSESSMENT OF CODE CONSCIOUSNESS

Name: _____ Assessment dates: #1____ #2____ #3____ #4____

<table>
<tr><td></td><td>Always</td><td>Usually</td><td>Seldom</td></tr>
</table>

1. Identifies boundaries of written words.
2. Matches words.
3. Matches sentences.
4. Builds a word from a model.
5. Supplies a spoken word that begins with the same phoneme as a given printed word.
6. Understands terms including:

   beginning

   end

   same

   different

   first

   last

   line

   top

   bottom

7. Can name letters (circle letters and enter date of observation)

| | | | | |
|---|---|---|---|---|
| _____ Aa | _____ Gg | _____ Ll | _____ Qq | _____ Vv |
| _____ Bb | _____ Hh | _____ Mm | _____ Rr | _____ Ww |
| _____ Cc | _____ Ii | _____ Nn | _____ Ss | _____ Xx |
| _____ Dd | _____ Jj | _____ Oo | _____ Tt | _____ Yy |
| _____ Ee | _____ Kk | _____ Pp | _____ Uu | _____ Zz |
| _____ Ff | | | | |

# INDIVIDUAL PREREADING PHONICS INVENTORY

1. Naming letters. How many of these letters can the child name?

   | o | s | t | a | r | e | n | i | l | u | c | p | d |
   |---|---|---|---|---|---|---|---|---|---|---|---|---|
   | m | b | h | f | y | g | v | w | x | k | z | j | q |

2. Writing letters from dictation. Dictate the letters listed above. Score leniently; either a capital or lowercase letter will do; count reversed letters as correct.

3. Awareness of letter name sounds in spoken words. How many letters can the child name at the beginning of these spoken words? (Do not show the words.) Say, "Say *open;* say it again, *open.* What letter do you hear at the beginning of *open?*" Do the same for these words:

   open, even, iron, apron, useful, beaver, ceiling, deep, effort, genius, jail, Kate, elevator, emerald, enter, peach, army, Esther, teacher, veal, extra, zebra.

4. Syntax matching: awareness of separate words in spoken sentences and the ability to match them with words in print. How many of these words can the child identify in sentences? Put a marker under each sentence; do not point to the separate words while reading them. Say, "This says, *Come here.* Say it. Say it again, *Come here.* Now draw a circle around *Come.*"

   | 1. Come here. | 6. You have two thumbs. |
   |---|---|
   | 2. Don't fall. | 7. These kittens are hungry. |
   | 3. Clap your hands. | 8. This girl has black hair. |
   | 4. Catch the ball. | 9. Can you climb a tree? |
   | 5. Ride my new bike. | 10. You can ride this horse. |

   Words to circle: 1 - Come; 2 - fall; 3 - Clap; 4 - ball; 5 - new; 6 - two; 7 - hungry; 8 - girl; 9 - you; 10 - ride.

# A LIST OF BASIC SIGHT WORDS FOR OLDER READERS

| more | life | American | less |
|---|---|---|---|
| than | being | however | public |
| other | same | Mrs. | almost |
| such | another | thought | enough |
| even | while | part | took |
| most | last | general | get |
| also | might | high | government |
| through | great | united | system |
| should | year | left | set |
| each | since | number | told |
| people | against | course | nothing |
| Mr. | himself | war | and |
| state | few | until | didn't |
| world | during | something | later |
| still | without | fact | knew |
| between | place | though | |

From "A Supplement to the Dolch Word Lists," by Jerry L. Johns, *Reading Improvement* 7 (Winter 1971–1972): 91.

# PHONOGRAM LIST

| | | | | |
|---|---|---|---|---|
| ab | ead | ice | oar | ub |
| ack | eal | ick | oat | ug |
| ad | eam | id | on | ule |
| ag | ean | im | one | ull |
| ail | eat | in | ong | um |
| ain | eed | ind | ook | ump |
| ait | eel | ine | ool | un |
| ake | eep | ing | oom | ung |
| all | eet | ink | oon | unk |
| ame | eg | int | ore | unt |
| an | ell | ip | ort | up |
| and | en | iss | oss | uss |
| ang | end | it | ot | ut |
| ank | ent | ite | ote | ute |
| ap | et | | ound | |
| at | | | | |
| ate | | | | |

# SCOPE AND SEQUENCE CHART[1]

## Consonant strand

| Kindergarten | Readiness | Preprimer | Primer | Book 1 | Grade 2/1 | Grade 2/2 |
|---|---|---|---|---|---|---|
| | | | Final Cons. | Medial Cons. | c /s/ | Initial Digraph |
| | | | | | g /j/ | ph /f/ |
| | | | b /b/ | d /d/ | qu /kw/ | kn /n/ |
| | | | d /d/ | g /g/ | | wr /r/ |
| | | | | g /g/ | b /b/ | Final |
| | | | k, ck /k/ | n /n/ | Cons. | Final Digraph |
| | | | m /m/ | rr /r/ | s /z/ | ck /k/ |
| | | | p /p/ | ss /s/ | x /ks/ | ng /ng/ |
| | | | t /t/ | t /t/ | | gh /f/ |

Some initial consonants are introduced and reinforced in the kindergarten, readiness, and preprimer books. Only one sound of *c, g,* and *s* is introduced.

**Primer**

Double Final Consonant
l /l/
s /s/

Inital Blends
bl, cl, fl, sl
br, cr, fr, dr
sk, sm, st

Initial Digraphs
ch /ch/
sh /sh/
th /th/ /TH/
wh /hw/

Final Digraphs
ch /ch/
sh /sh/
th /th/

**Grade 2/1**

Initial
Blends
sw
scr
spl
spr
str
thr

Final Blends
ft
nd
st
ld, lk
mp

(1) Scott, Foresman Readings "Growing Great Readers," Glenview, IL, 1990.

## Vowel strand

| *Kindergarten* | *Readiness* | *Preprimer* | *Primer* | *Book 1* | *Grade 2/1* | *Grade 2/2* |
|---|---|---|---|---|---|---|
| Short Vowels a /a/ cat e /e/ bed i /i/ pig o /o/ sock u /u/ bus | Short Vowels reinforced | Short Vowels reinforced | | | | |
| | Short Vowel Word Families: -an, -ap -at, -ad -ed, -et -ig, -ot -ug | Short Vowel Word Families -ick -in -ip | Short Vowel Word Families -ed -ent -et -op -ut | Short Vowel Word Families reinforced | Short and Long Vowels reinforced | Short and Long Vowels reinforced |
| | | | | ea (heat) ee (bee) u /u/ mule | ai (train) ay (day) oa (oat) au (taught) | |
| | Long Vowels a /a/ e /e/ o /o/ | Long Vowels reinforced | Long Vowel Word Families -ake, -ame | Long Vowel Word Families -ate -ide, -ike -ines -oke -ule | oi (oil) oy (boy) ou (out) ow (cow) | |
| | | | | | Single Final Vowel e (ewe) o (go) y (by) (baby) | |
| | | | | | r-Controlled Vowels ar (dark) er (her) ir (dirt) or (for) ur (turn) | |

## Structural Analysis Strand in the Scope and Sequence Chart

| Kindergarten | Readiness | Preprimer | Primer | Book I | Grade 2/1 | Grade 2/2 |
|---|---|---|---|---|---|---|
| | | | -s | Final Cons. | Final "Y" | en |
| | | | -es | Doubled | Changed | er (taller) |
| | | | -ed | (run/running) | to "I" | est |
| | | | -ing | | | ful |
| | | | | | | ly |
| | | | | | | Prefixes |
| | | | | | | re |
| | | | | | | un |

| Grade 3/1 | Grade 3/2 | Grade 4 | Grade 5 | Grade 6 | Grade 7 |
|---|---|---|---|---|---|
| er (teacher) | ment | tion | al | ist | ary |
| able | ness | ic | ance | | tive |
| ful | | ish | ent | Prefixes | ian |
| less | Prefixes | | sion | centi | ize |
| ous | over | Prefixes | | ex | |
| | under | im | Prefixes | geo | Prefixes |
| Prefixes | | in | inter | heli | com |
| dis | | out | tele | ir | en |
| mis | | | trans | mal | equ |
| pre | | | | micro | il |

# Example Word Lists

## STRUCTURAL ELEMENTS TAUGHT AT PARTICULAR LEVELS

### Initial Consonants

| b | c | d | f | g | h | j | k | l | m |
|---|---|---|---|---|---|---|---|---|---|
| baby | cab | dark | face | gag | hail | jab | kangaroo | lace | mad |
| bag | cage | date | fact | gale | hall | jack | keep | lad | magic |
| ball | cake | day | fade | game | ham | jade | keg | ladder | magnet |
| band | call | den | fail | gang | hand | jam | kennel | lady | make |
| bang | can | dent | fan | garden | happy | jar | kettle | lake | man |
| bank | cane | desk | farm | gas | hat | jaw | key | lamb | map |
| bat | cap | dig | fat | gate | have | jeep | kick | lamp | mask |
| bed | car | dike | feed | gaze | hay | jello | kid | land | match |
| bee | cat | dill | feet | goat | head | jet | kill | lap | mice |
| belt | cave | dim | fig | gob | heat | jig | kind | last | milk |
| big | coat | disk | file | gold | help | gob | king | lawn | mirror |
| bike | cob | doe | fin | golf | hen | joke | kiss | leaf | mitt |
| bill | coke | dog | find | gone | hike | jolly | kit | leg | mix |
| bird | cold | doll | fish | good | hill | job | kitchen | lemon | money |
| box | cone | door | five | gorilla | hip | judge | kite | lend | mop |
| boy | cub | dot | fix | got | home | jug | kitty | letter | mother |
| bud | cube | down | fond | gull | honey | juice | | like | mud |
| bug | cuff | duck | fox | gum | hop | jumbo | | line | muff |
| bus | cup | dull | funny | gun | hot | jump | | lion | mug |
| buzz | cut | dust | fuzz | gust | hug | jungle | | listen | must |

| n | p | q | r | s | t | b | w | x | |
|---|---|---|---|---|---|---|---|---|---|
| nag | page | quack | rabbit | sack | table | vacation | wade | Xmas | young |
| nail | pail | quail | radio | sad | tack | valentine | wag | X ray | yoyo |
| name | pan | quake | rag | said | taffy | valley | walk | | yule |
| nap | paper | quarrel | rain | sailboat | tail | van | wall | | |
| near | paw | quart | rake | salt | tall | vane | war | **y** | |
| neck | peanut | quarter | rat | sat | teacher | vase | warm | yacht | **z** |
| need | pear | queen | rattle | save | team | vast | was | yank | zeal |
| needle | pen | queer | read | saw | teeth | veil | watch | yap | zebra |
| net | penny | quick | red | seal | ten | vein | water | yard | zero |
| never | pet | quiet | ride | see | tiger | velvet | web | yarn | zest |
| nice | pickle | quirk | ring | sell | time | vent | wedding | yawn | zigzag |
| nickel | picture | quit | road | seven | tire | verb | well | year | zinc |
| night | pie | quite | roar | sew | today | verse | west | yeast | zing |
| nine | pig | quiver | rob | sick | toe | vest | wet | yell | zinnia |
| nod | pill | quiz | robin | sing | top | vet | wind | yellow | zip |
| nose | pizza | | rock | sink | toy | vim | window | yelp | zipper |
| note | pop | | rocket | sister | tug | vine | wing | yes | zone |
| now | puff | | rope | six | tummy | violet | wink | yield | zoo |
| number | puzzle | | rose | sock | turkey | violin | wolf | yogurt | |
| nurse | | | run | sun | turtle | visit | wood | yolk | |
| | | | | | | | | you | |

## Consonant Blends

| bl | cl | fl | gl | pl | br | cr |
|---|---|---|---|---|---|---|
| black | clam | flag | glacier | place | brace | crab |
| blade | clap | flake | glad | plan | braid | crack |
| blank | class | flap | glass | plant | brain | cradle |
| blast | claw | flash | gleam | planet | brash | cream |
| blaze | clay | flat | glee | plaster | brave | crayons |
| block | clean | float | glide | play | bread | crib |
| blond | clock | flock | glitter | please | break | crisp |
| blood | close | floor | glory | plenty | brick | cross |
| bloom | clothes | blower | glove | plot | bride | crow |
| blow | cloud | fluid | glow | plug | bring | crown |
| blouse | clover | flush | glue | plus | brittle | crust |
| blue | clown | | | | brown | cry |
| bluff | | | | | bruise | |

| dr | fr | gr | pr | sc | sk | sl |
|---|---|---|---|---|---|---|
| dragon | fraction | grab | prance | scab | skate | slam |
| drain | frame | grand | pray | scale | skeleton | slap |
| drape | freckle | grape | press | scald | ski | sled |
| drawer | free | graph | pretzel | scalp | skillet | sleep |
| dream | freeze | grass | pride | scan | skin | sleeve |
| dress | fresh | gravy | prince | scar | skinny | slice |
| drink | friend | graze | princess | scare | skip | slime |
| drip | frizz | green | print | scarf | skirt | sling |
| drive | frog | grin | prize | scatter | skull | slip |
| drop | frost | grip | proud | scooter | sky | sliver |
| drown | frozen | grocery | prune | scout | | slot |
| drum | | grow | | | | |

| sm | sn | sp | st | sw | tr | tw |
|---|---|---|---|---|---|---|
| smack | snail | space | stain | swam | tractor | tweed |
| small | snake | spat | stamp | swarm | trade | tweet |
| smart | snap | speak | stand | swat | traffic | tweezers |
| smash | snatch | spear | staple | sway | train | twelve |
| smear | sneak | speed | star | sweat | trap | twenty |
| smell | sneeze | spell | stay | sweep | treat | twice |
| smile | sniff | spend | stem | sweet | tree | twig |
| smock | snooze | spill | still | swerve | tribe | twin |
| smoke | snore | spin | sting | swift | trick | twirl |
| smoky | snow | spoon | stitch | swing | trip | twist |
| smooth | snug | spot | stop | | trot | |
| smuggle | snuggle | | | | truck | |

## Variant Consonant Sounds

| *c* /k/ | *c* /s/ | *g* /g/ | *g* /j/ | *s* /s/ | *s* /z/ |
|---------|---------|---------|---------|---------|---------|
| cabin | cedar | galaxy | gelatin | sack | babies |
| cage | ceiling | gallant | gem | saddle | boys |
| cake | cell | gallon | general | safe | chairs |
| camel | cement | gallop | gentle | sail | cookies |
| camp | census | garage | geography | salt | enemies |
| card | center | garbage | geometry | sample | families |
| cat | century | goat | germ | sand | frogs |
| coconut | cider | golf | giant | satin | girls |
| coffee | cigar | goose | ginger | second | please |
| collar | cinnamon | gorilla | giraffe | seed | rose |
| collie | circus | gown | gym | send | sees |
| cube | city | guard | gyp | settle | shelves |
| cucumber | cycle | guess | gypsy | single | stories |
| cute | cyclone | guide | gyrate | soft | surprise |
| | cypress | guitar | gyro | some | wives |
| | | | | soup | |

## Consonant Digraphs

| *ch* /ch/ | *ch* /k/ | *ch* /sh/ | *gh* /g/ | *ph* /f/ | *sh* /sh/ |
|-----------|----------|-----------|----------|----------|-----------|
| chain | character | chalet | ghastly | phantasy | shade |
| chalk | chasm | champagne | ghetto | phantom | shake |
| champ | chemical | chandelier | ghost | phase | shame |
| change | choral | charade | ghoul | pharmacy | shape |
| chart | chorus | chef | | pheasant | shark |
| chase | chlorine | chenille | *gh* /f/ | phone | sharp |
| check | christen | chivalry | cough | phoneme | shave |
| cheese | chrome | | enough | phonics | shawl |
| chest | chrysalis | | laugh | phonograph | shed |
| chick | scheme | | rough | phony | sheep |
| chief | school | | tough | phosphate | shelf |
| child | | | | photograph | shell |
| chill | | | | phrase | shine |
| chin | | | | physical | ship |
| choose | | | | | shirt |
| church | | | | | |

*Continued.*

| *th* /th/ (voiced) | *th* /th/ (voiceless) | *thr* /thr/ (digraph-blend) | *wh* /wh/ |
|---|---|---|---|
| than | thaw | thrash | whack |
| that | theater | thread | whale |
| the | theft | threat | wharf |
| their | theme | three | wheat |
| them | thick | thresh | wheel |
| themselves | thief | thrift | where |
| then | thimble | thrill | whiff |
| there | thin | throne | whimper |
| these | thing | through | whine |
| they | think | throw | whip |
| this | third | thrust | whirl |
| those | thirsty | | whisk |
| though | thirty | | whisper |
| | thorn | | whiz |
| | thought | | whopper |
| | thousand | | |
| | thumb | | |
| | thunder | | |
| | Thursday | | |

## Consonant Digraphs with First Silent Letters (Also *tch*, *dge*, and *ng*)

| *gn* /n/ | *kn* /n/ | *wr* /r/ | *ck* /k/ | *tch* /ch/ | *dge* /j/ | *ng* /ng/ |
|---|---|---|---|---|---|---|
| align | knack | wrack | back | batch | badge | bang |
| campaign | knapsack | wrangler | brick | catch | bridge | flung |
| design | knead | wrap | crack | crutch | dodge | gang |
| foreign | knee | wrapper | chick | hitch | edge | gong |
| gnarl | kneel | wreath | clock | itch | fudge | hung |
| gnash | knelt | wreck | dock | latch | grudge | long |
| gnat | knew | wrestle | duck | match | ledge | lung |
| gnaw | knife | wring | flick | patch | ridge | prong |
| reign | knight | wrinkle | kick | pitch | sludge | song |
| resign | knit | wrist | lick | splotch | | sing |
| sign | knob | write | lock | stretch | | strung |
| | knock | wrong | look | stitch | | thing |
| | knot | wrote | luck | watch | | wing |
| | know | wrung | peck | witch | | |
| | knuckle | wry | pick | | | |
| | | | quack | | | |
| | | | quick | | | |
| | | | shock | | | |
| | | | slick | | | |
| | | | stack | | | |
| | | | stick | | | |
| | | | tack | | | |
| | | | tick | | | |
| | | | thick | | | |
| | | | trick | | | |
| | | | track | | | |
| | | | truck | | | |

## Short vowels

| ă | ĕ | ĭ | ŏ | ŭ |
|------|------|------|-------|-------|
| act | bed | bib | block | bud |
| add | best | big | box | bus |
| as | den | bit | clock | cub |
| ask | end | dig | cop | cup |
| ax | ever | fig | dot | fun |
| bad | hem | fish | fox | gum |
| bag | jet | hid | got | gun |
| cab | led | hit | hop | jug |
| cat | men | if | lot | jump |
| dad | nest | ill | mop | lunch |
| fast | net | in | odd | mud |
| gap | next | inch | ox | nut |
| hat | pep | its | pot | pup |
| map | pet | kick | rob | rug |
| nap | red | milk | rot | sun |
| pat | sent | nip | shock | truck |
| sand | ten | pin | sock | tug |
| sat | web | sit | spot | under |
| tan | wet | wig | stop | up |
| tap | yes | | top | us |

## Long vowels and silent *e*

| ā | ē | ī | ō | ū | u as o͞o |
|------|---------|------|-------|--------|-----------|
| bake | extreme | bite | bone | abuse | brute |
| base | impede | dime | cone | cube | bugle |
| cave | obese | file | drove | cure | flute |
| date | scene | five | hole | cute | parachute |
| game | scheme | hide | home | fuel | prune |
| gate | serene | hike | hope | fuse | refuge |
| gave | stampede | life | joke | huge | rule |
| lake | supreme | like | poke | mule | salute |
| made | | mile | nose | music | sue |
| race | | pine | note | mute | tube |
| sale | | pipe | robe | refuge | tune |
| take | | ripe | rope | use | |
| tame | | rise | smoke | | |
| tape | | time | tone | | |
| wave | | | | | |

## *y* as a Vowel

| *y* /ī/ | | *y* /ē/* | |
|---------|---------|---------|---------|
| by | sly | busy | penny |
| cry | sty | dirty | pity |
| dye | style | foggy | plenty |
| fly | stylus | foxy | pony |
| fry | styrofoam | funny | puppy |
| my | try | heavy | snowy |
| myself | wry | juicy | spotty |
| rye | | | |

## Vowel Digraphs

| *ai* /ā/ | *ay* /ā/ | *ea* /ē/ | *ea* /ĕ/ | *ee* /ē/ | *ie* /ē/ |
|----------|----------|----------|----------|----------|----------|
| aim | away | beach | ahead | beef | achieve |
| bail | bay | bean | bread | bleed | believe |
| braid | clay | cheat | dead | creek | brief |
| claim | decay | clean | head | creep | chief |
| drain | gray | creak | read | deep | field |
| faint | may | cream | spread | flee | hygiene |
| grain | play | flea | thread | free | piece |
| hail | pray | heat | tread | geese | priest |
| mail | ray | peach | | green | rabies |
| paid | relay | reach | | jeep | relief |
| paint | slay | scream | | peel | shield |
| rain | spray | seat | | queen | shriek |
| sail | stay | steam | | seed | thief |
| snail | stray | team | | sleep | wield |
| train | tray | treat | | | |
| | | wheat | | | |

| *ie* /ī/ | *ei* /ē/ | *ei* /ā/ | *ey* /ē/ | *igh* /ī/ | *oa* /ō/ |
|----------|----------|----------|----------|-----------|----------|
| cried | ceiling | beige | barley | bright | boast |
| die | conceive | eight | donkey | fight | cloak |
| dried | deceive | freight | galley | flight | coal |
| fried | either | neighbor | hockey | fright | coast |
| lied | leisure | reign | honey | high | coat |
| pie | neither | rein | jockey | knight | float |
| pried | protein | skein | journey | might | foam |
| relied | receive | sleigh | kidney | night | goat |
| replied | seize | veil | medley | plight | load |
| spies | | vein | money | right | |
| tie | | weigh | | sigh | |
| tied | | | | sight | |
| tried | | | | slight | |
| | | | | tight | |
| | | | | thigh | |

*In some dialects /ī/

## Diphthongs

| *oi* /oy/ | *oy* /oy/ | *au* /ä/ | *aw* /ä/ | *oo* /o͞o/ | *oo* /o͝o/ |
|---|---|---|---|---|---|
| appoint | ahoy | applause | awning | balloon | book |
| avoid | alloy | auto | brawl | bloom | hood |
| boil | boy | because | crawl | broom | hoof |
| choice | convoy | caught | dawn | cartoon | hook |
| coil | decoy | cause | draw | cool | look |
| coin | destroy | fault | fawn | drool | stood |
| foil | employ | haul | flaw | goose | took |
| join | joy | launch | hawk | moon | |
| moist | joyful | laundry | jaw | pool | |
| noise | loyal | naughty | law | school | |
| oil | oyster | sauce | lawn | scooter | |
| soil | royal | saucer | raw | smooth | |
| spoil | tomboy | taught | saw | spool | |
| voice | toy | vault | yarn | spoon | |
| | | | | tooth | |

| *ow* /ō/* | *ow* /ow/ | *ou* /ow/ | *ew* /o͞o/ | *ue* /yū/ | *ui* /o͞o/ |
|---|---|---|---|---|---|
| below | allow | blouse | blew | cue | fruit |
| blow | brow | bounce | brew | due | juice |
| elbow | clown | cloud | chew | hue | nuisance |
| flow | cow | found | crew | rue | suitor |
| follow | cowboy | ground | drew | sue | |
| glow | drown | house | few | | |
| grow | flower | loud | jewel | | |
| know | frown | mouse | mew | | |
| pillow | gown | ouch | new | | |
| rainbow | plow | ounce | newly | | |
| shadow | power | out | screw | | |
| show | shower | pound | slew | | |
| snow | towel | round | stew | | |
| sparrow | tower | shout | strewn | | |
| throw | town | sound | threw | | |
| | | | view | | |

## *r*-Controlled Vowels

| *ar* /ar/ | *or* /or/ | *er* /er/ | *ir* /er/ | *ur* /er/ |
|---|---|---|---|---|
| alarm | born | clerk | birch | burn |
| arch | corn | fern | bird | burst |
| ark | ford | germ | birth | church |
| arm | horn | herd | chirp | curb |
| armor | morning | jerk | dirt | curve |
| artist | north | nerve | firm | hurl |
| barn | orange | perch | shirk | nurse |
| cart | order | perk | shirt | purse |
| chart | short | refer | skirt | surf |
| dart | sort | serve | squirm | surface |
| mark | sport | stern | squirt | turf |
| part | stork | term | stir | turkey |
| shark | torch | verse | twirl | turtle |
| | torn | worker | whirl | urge |
| | sworn | zipper | | |

* Here, *ow* decodes as a long vowel sound.

The following list of prefixes (active and absorbed) and suffixes have a designated grade level following them. These levels are suggested by Edgar Dale and Joseph O'Rourke in *The Living Word Vocabulary*[1] and are based on considerable research over the years. (Testing was not done at grades three, five, and seven.)

Teachers, however, should use their own discretion in determining whether students in their classroom would profit from learning to decode these words. Note how many words at the fourth, sixth, and eighth grade levels are derived from the use of the following prefixes: *dis, in, un* and the suffixes *tion, less, ly, ment,* and *ness.*

## Active Prefixes

| **dis** | **en** | **for/fore** |
|---|---|---|
| discharge (6) | enclose (4) | forearm (6) |
| discolor (6) | encourage (4) | forefathers (6) |
| discomfort (6) | encouragement (4) | foregone (6) |
| disconnect (4) | endanger (6) | foreground (6) |
| discontent (6) | endear (8) | foreknowledge (6) |
| discontinue (6) | enforce (6) | foreleg (6) |
| discourage (8) | enjoy (4) | foreman (4) |
| discouragement (8) | enjoyable (4) | forenoon (4) |
| discourtesy (6) | enjoyment (4) | forepaw (4) |
| disentangle (8) | enlarge (4) | foresaw (6) |
| disfavor (6) | enlargement (4) | foresee (6) |
| disharmony (8) | enlist (4) | foreseen (6) |
| dishonor (6) | enlistment (4) | foresight (6) |
| disinherit (6) | enrage (6) | foretell (6) |
| disinterest (6) | enrich (6) | forethought (6) |
| dislocate (6) | enroll (6) | foretold (6) |
| dislodge (8) | enrollment (6) | forever (4) |
| disloyal (4) | ensure (4) | forevermore (4) |
| disloyalty (6) | entangle (6) | forewarn (6) |
| dismount (4) | entrust (6) | forgave (6) |
| disobedience (6) | | forward (8) |
| disobey (4) | | |
| disorder (4) | | |
| disorderly (8) | | |
| disorganize (6) | | |
| displace (8) | | |
| displeasure (6) | | |
| disqualify (4) | | |
| disregard (6) | | |
| disrespect (6) | | |
| disrespectful (6) | | |
| dissatisfaction (6) | | |
| dissatisfy (4) | | |
| dissimilar (6) | | |
| distrustful (6) | | |

(1) From *The Living Word Vocabulary* by Edgar Dale and Joseph O'Rourke. © 1976 by Field Enterprises Educational Corporation.

| **im** (means *not,* also *in*) | **in** (means *not,* also *in*) | | **inter** |
|---|---|---|---|
| immature (6) | inability (6) | indirectly (8) | intermarriage (8) |
| immeasurable (6) | inaccurate (6) | indisputable (8) | intermediate (8) |
| immigrant (6) | inactive (8) | indistinct (8) | intermixture (8) |
| immigration (6) | inadequate (8) | indoors (4) | international (8) |
| immodest (8) | inappropriate (8) | inedible (3) | internationalize (6) |
| immortal (8) | incapable (6) | ineffective (6) | intersection (6) |
| immortality (8) | inclose (4) | inefficient (8) | interview (6) |
| immovable (6) | inclosure (6) | inestimable (8) | interweave (8) |
| immunize (8) | income (6) | inevitable (8) | |
| impassable (4) | incoming (8) | inexact (6) | |
| impatience (6) | incomparable (6) | inexpensive (6) | |
| impatiently (6) | incompetent (8) | inexpressible (8) | |
| imperfect (6) | incomplete (4) | infield (8) | |
| imperfection (6) | inconsiderate (6) | inflammable (6) | |
| impersonal (8) | inconvenience (8) | inflammation (8) | |
| impolite (4) | incredible (6) | ingratitude (8) | |
| import (6) | incurable (6) | inhospitable (8) | |
| impossible (4) | indebted (6) | inhuman (6) | |
| impress (6) | indebtedness (8) | inhumane (8) | |
| impressive (6) | indecent (6) | inscribe (6) | |
| imprint (8) | indecision (6) | inscription (8) | |
| imprison (4) | indefinite (8) | insecure (4) | |
| imprisonment (6) | independence (4) | insensitive (8) | |
| improbable (8) | independent (6) | inseparable (6) | |
| improper (6) | indestructible (8) | insoluble (8) | |
| impure (6) | indigestible (6) | insufficient (8) | |
| impurity (6) | indirect (8) | intake (4) | |

**mis**

misapply (8)
misbehave (4)
misbehavior (8)
misconduct (6)
miscount (4)
misdeal (4)
misfit (6)
misfortune (4)
misjudge (4)
mislay (4)
mislead (6)
misleading (6)
mismanage (6)
misplace (4)
misprint (4)
mispronounce (6)
misquote (8)
misread (4)
misrule (6)
misspell (4)
misspent (6)
mistrust (6)
misunderstand (4)
misuse (6)

**non**

noncombatant (8)
nonconductor (8)
nonprofit (8)
nonresident (4)
nonsense (4)
nonstop (4)

**re (meaning *again*)**

rebirth (6)
reborn (8)
rebound (6)
rebroadcast (4)
rebuilt (4)
recall (4)
recapture (6)
recombine (6)
recondition (8)
recycle (6)
rediscover (6)
refill (4)
reforest (6)
refresh (4)
regain (4)
removable (6)
rename (4)
renewal (8)
reopen (4)
reorganize (4)
repaid (4)
repayment (6)
replace (4)
reprint (4)
reproduce (8)
retake (4)

**un**

unable (6)
unacquainted (4)
unaffected (8)
unafraid (4)
unaided (6)
unarmed (4)
unattached (4)
unattainable (8)
unattended (8)
unattractive (6)
unavoidable (8)
unbalanced (4)
unbeaten (8)
unborn (4)
unbreakable (4)
unbroken (4)
unbuckle (4)
unbutton (4)
uncertain (4)
unchanged (4)
unchecked (6)
uncivilized (6)
unclasp (4)
unclothed (4)

uncomfortable (6)
unconcern (6)
uncontrollable (6)
undiscovered (6)
undisturbed (4)
unearth (8)
uneasily (6)
unemployed (6)
unequal (4)
uneven (4)
unexpectedly (6)
unfold (4)
unfortunate (6)
unfurl (8)
unguarded (8)
unhappily (6)
unkindness (4)
unlikely (4)
unlively (6)
unmerciful (8)
unnatural (4)
unoccupied (8)
unopened (4)

unorganized (6)
unpopular (4)
unreality (6)
unsaddle (4)
unscramble (6)
unscrew (6)
unselfish (4)
unsettled (6)
unskilled (4)
unsuccessful (6)
unsuitable (6)
untangle (6)
untiring (6)
untouchable (4)
untried (6)
untrue (4)
untwist (4)
unwashed (4)
unwelcome (4)
unwilling (4)
unwind (6)
unwisely (4)
unworthy (8)

## Absorbed prefixes

### com

combine (4)
comfort (4)
comment (6)
commit (8)
common (6)
compass (8)
compete (8)
compose (6)
composition (6)
compound (6)
compromise (8)

### con

conceal (6)
concern (6)
conclude (6)
condense (8)
conflict (8)
confuse (4)
connection (6)
consist (6)
construct (4)
contact (6)
contest (4)
contract (6)
contraption (8)
contrast (8)

### de

debate (6)
decay (4)
decent (8)
decide (4)
decision (4)
declare (6)
decline (8)
defeat (6)
define (6)

defrost (4)
delay (4)
deliver (4)
demand (6)
depend (4)
deposit (4)
detail (8)
detract (8)

### ex

examine (4)
example (4)
excellent (4)
except (4)
excess (8)
excite (4)
exclaim (6)
exclude (8)
excuse (4)

execute (4)
exhaust (6)
exile (8)
exit (4)
explain (4)
explode (4)
expose (6)
express (6)
extend (8)

### pre*

precipitation (6)
predict (6)
prefer (6)
premium (6)
preparation (4)
prepare (4)
present (4)
pretend (4)
prevent (4)
previous (6)

### pro

procedure (8)
proceed (4)
process (6)
produce (6)
production (6)
program (4)
prolong (8)
promote (4)
propose (4)
protest (6)

*The prefix *pre* is also an active prefix in words as *predetermine, prejudge.*

## Derivational suffixes

### able

acceptable (8)
accountable (6)
admirable (6)
allowable (4)
believable (4)
charitable (8)
comfortable (4)
dependable (4)
desirable (6)
fashionable (4)
favorable (8)
flammable (6)
honorable (6)
justifiable (6)
manageable (6)

movable (4)
navigable (8)
notable (8)
observable (6)
portable (4)
presentable (6)
punishable (6)
reasonable (6)
respectable (6)
sizable (8)
traceable (6)
treasonable (8)
usable (4)
valuable (4)
washable (4)

### ance

acceptance (8)
acquaintance (8)
admittance (8)
allowance (6)
appearance (4)
appliance (4)
assistance (4)
ordinance (8)
performance (4)
remembrance (8)
repentance (8)
resistance (8)
tolerance (8)

### ess

authoress (8)
duchess (8)
enchantress (8)
huntress (6)
lioness (6)
poetess (6)
princess (4)
stewardess (6)
tigress (6)

## ful

beautiful (4)
blissful (8)
careful (4)
cheerful (4)
colorful (8)
cupful (4)
doubtful (6)
faithful (6)
forgetful (4)
graceful (6)
handful (4)
harmful (4)
joyful (4)
lawful (4)
masterful (6)
meaningful (6)
merciful (6)
mournful (6)
playful (4)
shameful (8)
sinful (6)
sorrowful (4)
spoonful (4)
thankful (6)
thoughtful (4)
trustful (4)
truthful (4)
wonderful (4)

## ify

clarify (6)
classify (6)
crucify (6)
glorify (6)
horrify (6)
identify (6)
intensify (8)
justify (6)
magnify (6)
mystify (8)
notify (6)
pacify (8)
terrify (4)

## ion

abbreviation (4)
accusation (8)
addition (4)
admiration (6)
admission (6)
adoption (4)
affection (6)
amputation (8)
application (8)
attention (6)
attraction (6)
construction (6)
division (4)
elevation (6)
expression (4)
formation (6)
introduction (4)
irritation (6)

navigation (8)
nomination (6)
persuasion (8)
presentation (8)
production (6)
protection (4)
radiation (4)
reflection (4)
sensation (6)
starvation (4)
supervision (4)
taxation (6)
temptation (6)
tension (6)
vaccination (6)
vegetation (8)
vibration (6)
violation (8)

## ish

banish (8)
bookish (8)
boyish (4)
brownish (4)
childish (4)
devilish (6)
foolish (4)
girlish (4)
grayish (6)
reddish (8)

## ism

alcoholism (4)
Americanism (4)
barbarism (8)
cannibalism (6)
Catholicism (6)
colonialism (6)
communism (6)
criticism (6)
idealism (8)
liberalism (8)
patriotism (6)
terrorism (8)
vandalism (6)

## ist

abolitionist (8)
accompanist (6)
biologist (6)
botanist (8)
chemist (6)
columnist (6)
duelist (8)
finalist (8)
humorist (8)
opportunist (8)
organist (4)
panelist (8)
terrorist (6)
tourist (6)
violinist (4)
vocalist (6)
zoologist (8)

**ity**

ability (4)

activity (8)

actuality (8)

authority (6)

cavity (6)

community (6)

curiosity (8)

deformity (8)

elasticity (8)

humanity (8)

legality (8)

locality (6)

majority (6)

maturity (8)

minority (8)

nobility (8)

opportunity (6)

personality (4)

possibility (6)

prosperity (8)

rapidity (4)

regularity (6)

scarcity (6)

security (6)

sincerity (8)

stability (8)

stupidity (6)

utility (6)

vitality (8)

**ive**

attractive (4)

defensive (8)

locomotive (4)

possessive (6)

preventive (6)

productive (6)

sensitive (8)

**ize**

apologize (4)

legalize (6)

materialize (8)

modernize (4)

organize (6)

specialize (6)

sterilize (4)

terrorize (8)

vaporize (4)

| less | ly | ment |
|------|-----|------|
| aimless (6) | actually (6) | achievement (6) |
| bottomless (4) | awfully (4) | advertisement (4) |
| boundless (8) | carefully (4) | agreement (4) |
| brainless (4) | certainly (4) | ailment (4) |
| breathless (4) | cheaply (4) | amendment (6) |
| ceaseless (8) | correctly (4) | amusement (4) |
| cheerless (4) | currently (8) | announcement (4) |
| childless (4) | directly (8) | apartment (4) |
| defenseless (6) | doubly (6) | appointment (4) |
| doubtless (6) | earthly (6) | argument (6) |
| fatherless (4) | easily (4) | arrangement (4) |
| faultless (8) | especially (6) | assignment (4) |
| formless (4) | feelingly (6) | detachment (8) |
| friendless (4) | frequently (4) | development (6) |
| guiltless (6) | friendly (4) | employment (6) |
| helpless (4) | furiously (6) | enchantment (6) |
| hopeless (4) | hourly (6) | engagement (4) |
| landless (4) | knowingly (6) | environment (6) |
| largeless (4) | mannerly (4) | government (6) |
| listless (8) | mostly (4) | judgment (6) |
| matchless (8) | naturally (6) | pavement (4) |
| meaningless (6) | nearly (4) | payment (6) |
| merciless (6) | orderly (8) | punishment (4) |
| motionless (6) | ordinarily (6) | refreshment (4) |
| needless (8) | patiently (4) | replacement (4) |
| noiseless (4) | personally (4) | resentment (8) |
| painless (4) | positively (6) | retirement (4) |
| pointless (6) | probably (6) | sentiment (8) |
| regardless (6) | saintly (6) | settlement (4) |
| shameless (8) | scarcely (4) | shipment (4) |
| shapeless (4) | seemingly (8) | statement (4) |
| sleepless (4) | severely (6) | temperament (8) |
| spiritless (8) | shapely (4) | treatment (4) |
| spotless (6) | sincerely (6) | |
| stainless (6) | slightly (6) | |
| thoughtless (4) | sparingly (6) | |
| timeless (6) | stubbornly (6) | |
| treeless (4) | supposedly (8) | |
| valueless (6) | swiftly (4) | |
| voiceless (6) | variously (6) | |
| witless (6) | vertically (8) | |
| | vocally (6) | |

## ness

alertness (6)

attractiveness (4)

bashfulness (4)

bitterness (4)

blindness (4)

briskness (6)

closeness (6)

coarseness (6)

darkness (4)

dimness (4)

drowsiness (6)

drunkenness (4)

dullness (6)

duskiness (6)

emptiness (6)

exactness (6)

fatness (4)

feebleness (6)

filthiness (6)

fitness (8)

flabbiness (6)

foolishness (4)

freshness (4)

greatness (4)

greediness (6)

greenness (4)

keenness (6)

kindness (6)

largeness (4)

lawlessness (6)

loneliness (4)

nearness (4)

nervousness (4)

nobleness (6)

pleasantness (6)

prettiness (4)

rashness (4)

readiness (4)

restlessness (6)

roominess (6)

rottenness (4)

seriousness (6)

shyness (4)

smoothness (6)

steadiness (8)

stiffness (4)

stillness (4)

strangeness (4)

suddenness (4)

sweetness (4)

swiftness (4)

tardiness (4)

tenderness (4)

thankfulness (4)

thickness (4)

thoughtfulness (4)

usefulness (4)

watchfulness (6)

weakness (4)

weariness (6)

whiteness (4)

willingness (6)

## ogy

archeology (8)

astrology (8)

biology (8)

criminology (8)

ecology (8)

geology (6)

mineralogy (6)

## ous

courageous (4)

dangerous (4)

glorious (6)

humorous (4)

joyous (6)

luminous (8)

marvelous (4)

miraculous (6)

mountainous (6)

mysterious (6)

nervous (6)

numerous (6)

odorous (8)

poisonous (6)

prosperous (8)

studious (8)

treasonous (8)

## Practice Words for Syllabication

| 2 syllables | 3 syllables | 4 syllables |
|---|---|---|
| captive | belittle | declaration |
| carbon | capital | deliberate |
| carefree | correctly | embarrassment |
| cortex | corridor | encouragement |
| extent | exposure | exceedingly |
| extreme | extension | impersonal |
| formal | external | introduction |
| fungus | fantastic | magnesium |
| furnace | foundation | majority |
| junction | important | mathematics |
| mailman | imposter | mechanical |
| picket | impression | necessary |
| picture | janitor | pacifier |
| proverb | magnetic | predetermined |
| provoke | mastermind | recognition |
| return | matador | relationship |
| royal | mechanic | revolution |
| rubber | medicine | sensational |
| twilight | medium | spectacular |
| upstream | opportune | supervisor |
| waistline | preamble | totality |
| waitress | prospector | unsuspected |
| welfare | resident | violinist |
| | stimulus | |

# Tests

## TEACHER'S TEST OF DECODING SKILLS
### Part I

1. Define a consonant digraph. (1) List and organize them into (a) digraphs with *h*, (b) digraphs with an initial silent letter, (c) three-letter digraphs. (2) Indicate the sound/sounds each encodes. (3) Give a word/example of each and underline the digraph in the word.

   **Definition:**

   | Digraphs | Sound/Sounds | Word Example/Examples |
   |---|---|---|
   | (a) | | |
   | (b) | | |
   | (c) | | |

2. Some single consonant letters in our alphabet encode more than one sound. What are these letters? What sounds do they encode? What vowels condition these sounds? Give word examples of each.

   | Letter | Sound/Sounds | Vowels That Condition | Word Example/Examples |
   |---|---|---|---|
   | | | | |

3. The letter *y* functions as both a consonant and vowel. Explain and give word examples.

4. Define a consonant blend. Give two examples of each kind of blend, underlining the blend. What is/are the main difference/differences between them?

   **Definition:**

   | Blends | Examples |
   |---|---|
   | | |

5. At the end of some words *ck* is used as the /k/ sound. At the end of other words *ke* is used as the /k/ sound. Explain.

6. Give word examples of the five short sounds of the vowels.

7. Some vowels encode a third in addition to the short and long sounds. What are these vowels? What sounds do they encode? Give word examples.

8. List four "regular" vowel digraphs that follow the rule used by many primary teachers: "When two vowels go a-walking, etc." Give word examples.

   **Vowel Digraph**          **Word Examples**

9. The /$\overline{oo}$/ sound as in the word *spoon* can be encoded in many ways. List the six additional letters or letter combinations that encode this sound. Give word examples.

   | Sound | Letter Combination | Word Examples |
   |-------|--------------------|--------------| 
   | /$\overline{oo}$/ | oo | spoon |

10. Give word examples to show the effect of a final *e* on words. You should have five different examples to indicate five reasons why final *e* appears.

11. Long *e* may be encoded many ways. List the letters that combine to encode this sound. Give word examples.

    **Sound**          **Letter Combinations**          **Word Examples**

12. Define a diphthong. What sounds do these diphthongs encode? Give word examples.

    **Definition:**

    | Diphthongs | Sounds | Word Examples |
    |-----------|--------|--------------| 
    | oo | | |
    | ou | | |
    | ow | | |
    | oi | | |
    | oy | | |

13. Long *i* may *usually* be encoded three ways in addition to the letter *i*. Give the letter combinations with word examples.

    /i/                **Letter Combinations**                **Word Examples**

14. What do *ir, er, ur,* and *wor* have in common?

15. What is the schwa sound? Where is it found? How is it written? Give example words.

16. What happens to words such as *jog* and *brim* when adding endings that begin with a vowel? Why is this?

17. Add the endings *ing* and *ed* to the nonsense words below.

    blath

    gute

    pem

    shane

    colnep

    theg

    cay

18. What suggestions would you make to students when they come to an unknown word?

# Part II

1. Circle the vowel digraphs
2. Underline the blends
3. Place a square bracket around the consonant digraphs
4. Place a checkmark before a word with a diphthong

    | character | afraid | relative | coarse |
    | --- | --- | --- | --- |
    | shook | flight | back | chaise |
    | receive | known | surprise | athlete |
    | treasure | toil | illustration | whether |

# Part III

1. (a) Define the term sight words and give some examples.
   (b) What is the importance of these words?

2. What is the difference between an absorbed and a regular prefix?

3. What is the difference between an inflectional and a derivational suffix?

4. What is the difference between a semantic and a syntactic context clue?

5. What syllabication principles would you suggest to students to incorporate when they meet an unfamiliar word?

# ANSWERS TO THE TEACHER'S TEST OF DECODING SKILLS
## Part I

1. Definition: two consonant letters together encoding one sound
   (a) *ch* /ch/ /k/ /sh/     *ch*amp *ch*aracter *ch*ef
       *gh* /g/ /f/ /-/     *gh*ost thou*gh* bou*gh*
       *ph* /f/     *ph*armacy
       *sh* /sh/     *sh*ape
       *th* /th/ /th/     *th*icket *th*em
       *wh* /w/ /h/     *wh*en *wh*ole
   (b) *gn* /n/     *gn*ome
       *kn* /n/     *kn*ife
       *wr* /r/     *wr*inkle
       *ck* /k/     che*ck*
   (c) *dge* /j/     bri*dge*
       *tch* /ch/     ca*tch*

2. 

| Letter | Sound/Sounds | Vowels That Condition | Word Example/Examples |
|---|---|---|---|
| *c* | /k/ /s/ | When *a, o, u* follow *c*, *c* encodes /k/. When *i, e, y* follow *c*, *c* encodes /s/. | camera, cycle |

| Letter | Sound/Sounds | Vowels That Condition | Word Example/Examples |
|---|---|---|---|
| *g* | /g/ /j/ | When *a, o, u* follow *g*, *g* usually encodes /g/. When *i, e, y* follow *g*, *g* usually encodes /j/. | game, gem |
| *s* | /s/ /z/ /sh/ | none | same, rose, sugar |

3. *y* may be a consonant at the beginning of a word—*yellow.*

   *y* may be a vowel in the middle of words—/ĭ/ gym, /ī/ cycle.

   *y* may be a vowel at the end of words—/ē/ pretty, /ī/ apply.

   *y* may be part of a vowel digraph as ay /ā/ stay and ey /ē/ money.

   *y* may be part of the diphthong oy /oy/ toy.

4. A consonant blend occurs when two or three adjacent letters encode consonant sounds that cluster together and are pronounced very rapidly.

   a. *r* *cr*eam, *pr*ize      b. *l* *bl*ame, *fl*ight      c. *s* *sn*ail, *str*eam      d. *tw* *tw*irl, *tw*ist

5. *ck* is used after a short vowel. *ke* is used after a long vowel.

6. Answers will vary; b*a*t, b*e*t, b*i*t, b*o*p, b*u*t are some examples.

7. *ä* /ä/ father

   *o* /ōō/ to

   *u* /u/ bush

8. *ai*  maid      *ay*  tray      *oa*  oats      *ee*  sleep

9. *ou*  soup      *u*  rude      *ui*  fruit

   *o*  prove      *ue*  clue      *ew*  flew

10. *chance, change.* Final *e* indicates the preceding *c* and *g* have the respective sounds of /s/ and /j/.

    *pipe.* Final *e* indicates the preceding vowel is long. This differentiates pipe from pip.

    *have.* Final *e* is used after *v* because English words do not end in *v.*

    *able.* Final *e* completes a needed second syllable; otherwise the word would be unpronounceable as *abl.*

    *awe.* Historical reasons.

11. *ee*  sheep      *ie*  brief      *ey*  monkey

    *ea*  treat      *ei*  conceive      *y*  candy

12. A diphthong is a gliding sound from one vowel to another.

    *oo* /ōō/ /ŏŏ/      spool, shook

    *ou* /ow/ /ŭ/      crouch, touch

    *ow* /ow/ /ō/      crowd, snow

    *oi* /oy/      moist

    *oy* /o/      employ

13. *y*  cry      *ie*  pie      *igh*  right

14. They all encode /er/; *or* encodes /er/ when *w* precedes it.

15. The schwa is the vowel sound in unstressed syllables with a sound similar to short *uh,* written as ə.

16. The final consonant is doubled to show the preceding vowel is short. This differentiates between words as *stripper* and *striper.*

17.

| | | |
|---|---|---|
| blath | blathing | blathed |
| gute | guting | guted |
| pem | pemming | pemmed |
| shane | shaning | shaned |
| colnep | colnepping | colnepped |
| theg | thegging | thegged |
| cay | caying | cayed |

18. First see if the sentence context can help.

Check for structural parts such as roots and affixes.

Check for syllable and phonics clues.

## Part II

| | | | |
|---|---|---|---|
| [ch] aracter | afr (ai) d | relative | c (oa) rse |
| ✔ [sh] ook | fl (igh) t | ba [ck] | ch (ai) se |
| rec (ei) ve | [kn] own | sur<u>pr</u>ise | a [th] lete |
| <u>tr</u> (ea) sure | ✔ toil | illu<u>str</u>ation | [wh] e [th] er |

## Part III

1. (a) They are "heavy duty" words such as *at, the, be, of* that appear frequently.

   (b) They must be recognized immediately, as it is difficult to read any extended passage without meeting a large number of them.

2. A regular prefix changes the word's meaning as in *preview* (to see before). In an absorbed prefix the *pre* or other like-seeming prefix is part of the word *(presume).*

3. Inflectional suffixes number only eight and are taught early in the reading program. They do not change the part of speech. Derivational suffixes are very numerous and are of four kinds: noun, verb, adjective, and adverb. These do change the part of speech, their main function.

4. A semantic clue is a meaning clue; a syntactic clue is a grammar clue.

5. See if a word is compound or has affixes.

   See if the word has double consonant letters or two unlike consonants.

   Do not divide blends or digraphs.

   If the word ends in *le,* place the preceding consonant before it.

   Always check to see if the word makes sense!

# AN EXAMPLE TEST FOR THE DIAGNOSIS OF STUDENT WORD RECOGNITION SKILLS (TEACHER FORM)

Useful for skill grouping and to check student progress.

For students who should have mastered most of the decoding skills.

Words are taken from Dolch's 1,000-word list.

1. *Alphabet*

   The student recites and recognizes all the letters when out of order.

   B I C F P M K L T E D S A J H W Q V N O Y K X G U Z

   o l y v p i a z k t m n r u h c w f q e x d g b s j

2. *Consonant Sounds*

   The student says a word beginning with each letter sound. (Use flash cards with letters, holding one up at a time.)

   | | | | | | |
   |---|---|---|---|---|---|
   | 1. m | 4. f | 7. s | 10. l | 13. z | 16. k |
   | 2. b | 5. w | 8. v | 11. j | 14. n | 17. y |
   | 3. p | 6. t | 9. d | 12. r | 15. h | 18. g |

   The student writes the first letter of each word after hearing each word.

   | | | |
   |---|---|---|
   | 1. *p*encil | 7. *v*ery | 13. *h*appy |
   | 2. *b*aby | 8. *s*ing | 14. *z*ipper |
   | 3. *m*oney | 9. *d*ark | 15. *n*ever |
   | 4. *w*agon | 10. *r*ain | 16. *y*ellow |
   | 5. *f*oot | 11. *l*ady | 17. *k*ing |
   | 6. *t*eeth | 12. *j*ump | 18. *g*ame |

3. *Blending Consonants and Vowels*

   The student writes the first two letters of each word or nonsense word after hearing each word.

   *Real Words*

   | | | |
   |---|---|---|
   | 1. penny | 3. find | 5. ram |
   | 2. dust | 4. taste | 6. lot |

   *Nonsense Words*

   | | | |
   |---|---|---|
   | 7. rel | 9. sote | 11. wum |
   | 8. wab | 10. kife | 12. bame |

4. *Context Clues*

   The student uses context clues by supplying the missing words.

   Jane and Bill were playing in front of a house. A woman came up and asked, "Is your mother at

   _____?" "Yes," said Jane, _____ is at home." "Good," said the woman, "then I will ring

   the _____." So she _____ the bell, but no one came. She rang the _____ again, but

   still no _____ came.

   She rang again and again and _____, but no one came. Then she said to Bill, "Didn't your sister tell

   me _____ was at _____?"

   "Oh, yes," _____ said. "She did."

   "Then why doesn't she answer the _____ when I ring?"

   "Because," said Bill, "Jane isn't my sister. Her mother *is* at home, but my mother is out shopping."

5. *Consonant Blends*

The student writes the first two letters of each word or nonsense word after hearing each word.

*Real Words*

| | | |
|---|---|---|
| 1. black | 4. smell | 7. slip |
| 2. scooter | 5. grab | 8. spade |
| 3. present | 6. snap | 9. fruit |

*Nonsense Words*

| | | |
|---|---|---|
| 10. bram | 13. swit | 16. trep |
| 11. clep | 14. crute | 17. glod |
| 12. flim | 15. plim | 18. stel |

6. *Consonant Blends (Ending)*

The student writes the last two letters of each word after hearing each word.

| | | |
|---|---|---|
| 1. bend | 3. talk | 5. held |
| 2. lint | 4. almost | 6. comb |

7. *Consonant Digraphs*

The student writes the first two letters of each word.

| | | |
|---|---|---|
| 1. shape | 3. thumb | 5. photo |
| 2. chime | 4. whistle | 6. those |

8. *Variants "c" and "g"*

The student writes the first two letters of each word after hearing each word.

| | | |
|---|---|---|
| 1. city | 5. cake | 9. gum |
| 2. circus | 6. cent | 10. giant |
| 3. card | 7. game | 11. good |
| 4. colt | 8. gym | 12. gentle |

9. *Long and Short Vowels*

The student writes the vowel letter sound of each word after hearing each word.

| | | |
|---|---|---|
| 1. hit | 5. bet | 9. make |
| 2. bat | 6. run | 10. sleep |
| 3. rice | 7. go | 11. use |
| 4. bite | 8. cot | 12. home |

10. *Vowel Diphthongs*

The student reads the following words with vowel diphthongs.

*Real Words*

| | | |
|---|---|---|
| 1. book | 3. moon | 5. mouse |
| 2. coil | 4. toy | 6. grow |

*Nonsense Words*

| | | |
|---|---|---|
| 7. moit | 9. taul | 11. doot |
| 8. faw | 10. voy | 12. haut |

11. *"r" Controlled*

The student reads the following real and nonsense words.

*Real Words*

| | | |
|---|---|---|
| 1. tar | 3. for | 5. stir |
| 2. over | 4. fur | 6. word |

*Nonsense Words*

| | | |
|---|---|---|
| 7. mer | 9. worb | 11. gar |
| 8. tir | 10. murt | 12. torm |

12. *Word Division*

a. The student reads the following words and records the number of syllables in each word.

*Real Words*

| | | |
|---|---|---|
| 1. home | 3. elephant | 5. accident |
| 2. captain | 4. doctor | 6. strong |

*Nonsense Words*

| | | |
|---|---|---|
| 7. timb | 9. tabman | 11. stom |
| 8. bisby | 10. melgan | 12. aritent |

b. *Word Division with Older Students, Grades 5 and above*

The student reads the following nonsense words.

(Prefixes)

| | | |
|---|---|---|
| 1. propan | 5. comjump | 9. uncry |
| 2. dispay | 6. conbent | 10. delike |
| 3. reraw | 7. pregate | 11. exwell |
| 4. enread | 8. instand | 12. perdent |

(Suffixes)

| | | |
|---|---|---|
| 1. sleepance | 5. dorous | 9. cupment |
| 2. skinive | 6. cornable | 10. dreamest |
| 3. turnant | 7. daytion | 11. plantly |
| 4. leatness | 8. waterful | 12. strivence |

(Prefixes and Suffixes)

| | | |
|---|---|---|
| 1. rebushful | 5. inrailest | 9. prestandive |
| 2. retrayment | 6. dispiller | 10. conworktion |
| 3. enlandance | 7. exmilkous | 11. comstipment |
| 4. prowooding | 8. unpostent | 12. disoutless |

# Resources for the Teacher

## BOOKS

Adams, Nancy. *Word Sponges: Enriching Ways to Soak Up Spare Moments.* Dale Seymour Publishers, P.O. Box 10888, Palo Alto, CA 94303, 1981.

Contains ways of using a few moments to build vocabulary and interest in words.

Anderson, Bett, and Joels, Rosie Webb. *Teaching Reading to Students with Limited English Proficiencies.* Charles C. Thomas, 2600 South First St., Springfield, IL 62794-9265, 1986.

*Big Book of Games for Whole Language,* primary and intermediate books. Instructional Fair, Inc., Grand Rapids, MI.

Games and activities at the primary and intermediate levels. Many pages can simply be removed and copied.

Bolton, Faye and Snowball, Diane. *Springboard Ideas for Spelling.* Intac Inc., 1110 Fidler Lane, Silver Spring, MD 20910.

Bradley, Sue K. *Kid's Literature.* Educational Service Inc., P.O. Box 219, Stevensville, MI 49127, 1987.

Presents classic and contemporary titles and ways to share them.

Cunningham, Patricia. *Phonics They Use.* HarperCollins, 10 E. 53rd St., New York, NY 10022, 1991.

Davidson, Marily; Isherwood, Rita; and Tucker, Ernie. *Moving on with Big Books.* Ashton Scholastic, P.O. Box 579, Gosford 2250, New Zealand, 1989.

Donaldson, Judy P. *Transcultural Picture Word List: Teaching English to Children from Any of Twenty-One Language Backgrounds.* LP Learning Pub., Inc., P.O. Box 1326, Holmes Beach, FL 33509, 1980.

In addition to many picture words, the text includes syntax variations, Dolch Word Lists in the 21 languages, and Word Pairs. The last helps the teacher understand the phonological interference with English and the native language.

Evans, Joy, and Moore, Jo Ellen. *How to Make Books with Children.* Evan-Moore Corp., 18 Lower Ragsdale Dr., Monterey, CA 93940-5746, 1985.

Flurkey, Alan D., and Meyer, Richard J., eds. *Under the Whole Language Umbrella.* National Council of Teachers of English, 1111 W. Kenyon Road, Urbana, IL 61801-1096, 1994.

Presents a series of essays on the merits of the whole language approach with some practical ideas for implementation.

Ginott, Haim. *Teacher and Child.* The Hearst Corp., 105 Madison Ave. New York, NY 10016, 1972.

A must read for beginning teachers. Includes how to handle classroom social and disciplinary encounters and difficulties.

Glazer, Susan Mandel, and Brown, Carol Smullen. *Portfolios and Beyond: Collaborative Assessment in Reading and Writing.* Christopher-Gordon Pub., Inc., Norwood, MA, 1993.

Suggests alternatives to the standard methods of assessment and presents ways for students to monitor their own growth and needs.

Howell, Will C. *The Bill Martin Collection.* Simon & Schuster, 1230 Avenue of the Americas, New York, NY 10020, 1991.

Contains wonderful creative writing ideas.

Johnson, Simon O., and Johnson, Verna Jackson. *Motivating Minority Students: Strategies That Work.* Charles C. Thomas, 2600 South First St., Springfield, IL 62794-9265, 1988.

Minderman, Lynne. *Loving Literature: Good Books for Young Readers.* Scholastic Inc., 730 Broadway, New York, NY 10003, 1989.

Muncy, Patricia Tyler. *Hooked on Books.* Prentice Hall, 1995.

Ready-to-use techniques and materials to spark students' interest and involve parents in promoting reading.

Neill, S. B., and Neill, G. W. (1990) *The Annual Guide to Highest-Rated Educational Software Preschool–grade 12.* R. R. Bowker Co., New York, 1991.

Only the best!

Osborn, Susan. *Free and Almost Free Things for Teachers.* Perigree Books from Putnam Publishing Co., 200 Madison Ave., New York, NY 10016, 1990.

*Phonics for Whole Language.* Instructional Fair, Inc., Grand Rapids, MI.

Contains games and activities for each letter of the alphabet.

Platts, Mary E. *Spice* and *Rescue.* Educational Service Inc., P.O. Box 219, Stevensville, MI 49127.

Both of these books are considered classics in activities for word recognition skills.

Powell, Debbie, and Hornsby, David. *Learning Phonics and Spelling in a Whole Language Classroom.* Scholastic Professional Books, 555 Broadway, New York, NY 10012-3999, 1993.

Practical strategies for incorporating phonics and spelling in the whole language classroom.

Roberts, N., and Carter, M. *Integrating Computers into the Elementary and Middle School.* Prentice Hall, 15 Columbus Circle, New York, NY 10023, 1988.

Points out how to integrate computers into the curriculum; also lists recommended software.

Savage, Teresa. *The Ready-to-Read, Ready-to-Count Handbook.* Newsmarket Press, 18 E. 48th St., New York, NY 10017, 1991.

Spangenberg-Urbschat, Karen, and Pritchard, Robert, eds. *Kids Come in All Languages: Reading Instruction for ESL Students.* International Reading Assn., Newark, DE, 1994.

Reviews and synthesizes all the research that pertains to the education of ESL students. Provides specific suggestions to teachers and administrators for organizing instruction. Presents examples of practical ways teachers can develop and implement authentic meaning-centered instructional activities.

Trelese, Jim. *The New Read-Aloud Handbook.* Penguin Books, 375 Hudson St., New York, NY 10014, 1989.

## COMMERCIAL MATERIALS FOR TEACHING WORD RECOGNITION SKILLS

**Fun Phonics.**   A four-part series using music and amusing rhyming songs to help students learn basic phonics. Each consonant has its own song or chant. Repetitive echo technique used. Includes cassette and books. Teacher's Press, P.O. Box 14391, Austin, TX 78762.

**Kid Phonics.**   This CD-ROM builds literacy skills through music, rhyme, annotated graphics, and activities. Students move to word building to construct words from sounds, sentences from words, and even dictionary pages with pictures and sentences. Davidson & Associates, Inc., 1984 Pioneer Ave. Torrence, CA 90503.

**Novel Units.**   Literature-based teacher guides include vocabulary words, comprehension questions, and activities for each novel. Over 300 titles. Novel Units, Box 1461, Dept. R., Palatine, IL 60078.

**Phonic Readers for Writers.**   Materials are in story form and can be taken home. Parents participate in the child's learning experiences as children share their stories. Random House, Dept. of School and Library Books, 201 E. 50th St., New York, NY, 10022.

**Phonics: A Sound Approach.**   For grades 4–adult. Word recognition skills are taught through lists, speaking, and writing. Includes student book with 29 lessons and a teacher's guide. Curriculum Associates, 5 Esquire Rd., N. Billerica, MA 01862–0901.

**Primary Phonics Storybooks.**   Chapter 1 teachers especially like these books for children who have difficulty learning to read. Educators Publishing Service, 31 Smith Place, Cambridge, MA, 02138–1000.

**School Scrabble.**   Used to teach spelling, vocabulary, and the dictionary for grades 4–12. Each kit contains a motivational video for teachers and students, six modified boards, teacher's guide, Scrabble news, and tapes for student skills. Scrabble Kit Office, c/o Hasbro Promotions, P.O. Box 5659, Pawtucket, RI, 02861.

**S.R.A. Phonics.**   An integrated program, readiness level, complete with six student books featuring the alphabet, consonants, and vowel sounds. S.R.A., P.O. Box 543, Blacklick, OH 43004–0543.

**Steck-Vaughn Phonics.**   Integrates phonics with quality literature, mostly poetry, to create writing proficiency. Uses phonics analysis, context clues, and dictionary skills. Includes a detailed Scope and Sequence Chart. Steck-Vaughn Co., P.O. Box 26015, Austin, TX 78755.

**Supersonic Phonics.**   A comprehensive software phonics program with branching activities based on student performance. Includes a management system. Curriculum Associates, 5 Esquire Rd., P.O. Box 2001, Billerica, MA 08162–0901.

**Touchphonics.** A concrete manipulative and multisensory program. Its special feature is the use of 200 color-coded letters and letter combinations called "touch-units," on four 17" by 13" trays. Students can use visual, auditory, and tactile modalities to help them understand the structure of words. Touchphonic Reading Systems, 4900 Birch St., Newport Beach, CA 92660.

**Zoo Phonics.** Includes merged animal/letter sound flash cards and musical tapes. Also includes activity worksheets. Zaner Bloser, 2300 W. 5th St., Columbus, OH 43216.

# PUBLISHERS AND DISTRIBUTORS OF MATERIALS AND ACTIVITIES FOR TEACHING WORD RECOGNITION SKILLS

Milton Bradley
443 Shaker Rd.
E. Longmeadow, MA 01028

Childcraft Education Corporation
52 Hook Rd.
Bayonne, NJ 07002

Creative Learning Assn. Inc.
R.R. 4, Box 330
Charleston, IL 61920

Creative Publications
3977 E. Bayshore Rd.
Palo Alto, CA 94303

Curriculum Associates
5 Esquire Rd.
N. Billerica, MA 01862-0901

Denoyer-Geppert
5235 Ravenswood Ave.
Chicago, IL 60640

Developmental Learning Materials
7440 Natchez Ave.
Niles, IL 60648

Developmental Reading Distributors
5879 Wyldewood Lakes Ct.
Fort Myers, FL 33919

Early Learning Assn. Inc.
25118 35th Ave. S.
Kent, WA 98032

Educational Enrichment Materials
201 E. 50th St.
New York, NY 10022

Educational Teaching Aids
199 Carpenter Ave.
Wheeling, IL 60090

Follett Press
1000 W. Washington Blvd.
Chicago, IL 60607

Garrard Publishers
1607 N. Market St.
Champaign, IL 61820

Good Apple
Box 299
Carthage, IL 62321

Houghton Mifflin
1 Beacon St.
Boston, MA 02108

Ideal School Supply Company
110000 S. Lavergne Ave.
Oak Lawn, IL 60453

Instructo Corporation
180 Cedar Hollow Rd.
Paoli, PA 19301

Kenworthy Educational Service
P.O. Box 3031
Buffalo, NY 14205

McGraw-Hill
Early Learning
Paoli, PA 19301

Media Materials, Inc.
1821 Portal St.
Baltimore, MD 21224

Modern Curriculum Press
13900 Prospect Rd.
Cleveland, OH 44136

Montessori Educational Games
15 Central Dr.
Farmingdale, NY 11735

Multi Media Education
P.O. Box 35396
Detroit, MI 48235

NCS/Educational Systems
4401 West 76th St.
Minneapolis, MN 55435

New Dimensions in Education
61 Mattatuck Heights Rd. No. 7
Waterbury, CT 06705-3832

Parker Brothers Games
50 Dunham Rd.
Beverly, MA 01915

Perfection Form Co.
1000 N. 2nd Ave.
Logan, IA 51546

Phonovisual Products
12216 Parklawn Dr.
Rockville, MD 20852

Playskool
3720 N. Kedzie Ave.
Chicago, IL 60618

Reading Joy, Inc.
2210 Wellington Ct.
Naperville, IL 60532

Remedial Education Press
Kingsbury Center
2138 Bancroft Place, N.W.
Washington, DC 20008

Scott, Foresman and Company
1900 E. Lake Ave.
Glenview, IL 60025

Frank Shaffer Publications
23740 Hawthorne Blvd.
Torrance, CA 90505

Teachers Exchange of San Francisco
28 Dawnview
San Francisco, CA 94131

Teaching Resources Corp.
Div. of *New York Times*
50 Pond Park Rd.
Hingham, MA 02043

Trend Enterprises, Inc.
St. Paul, MN 55165

Troll Associates
100 Corporate Dr.
Mahwah, NJ 07430

Jane Ward Co., Inc.
1642 S. Beech St.
Lakewood, CO 80228

WWF 'N Proof Pubs.
1490 South Blvd.
Ann Arbor, MI 48104

## PICTURE BOOK BIBLIOGRAPHY FOR READINESS AND BEGINNING READING

The following picture books have a total word count of about 100 words or less: The word number is in parentheses.[1]

Bel Geddes, Barbara. *So Do I* (75). NY: Grosset and Dunlap, 1972.

Bright, Robert. *My Red Umbrella* (68). NY: Morrow Junior Books, 1985.

Carle, Eric. *The Very Hungry Caterpillar* (107). NY: Putnam, 1981.

De Paola, Tomie, and Lobel, Arnold. *The Comic Adventures of Old Mother Hubbard and Her Dog* (91). NY: Harcourt Brace Jovanovich, 1981.

Ginsburg, Mirra. *The Chick and the Duckling* (32). NY: Aladdin, 1988.

Hutchins, Pat. *The Surprise Party* (103). NY: Macmillan, 1986.

Kraus, Robert. *Milton, the Early Riser* (81). NY: E. P. Dutton, 1972.

_____. *Whose Mouse Are You?* NY: Aladdin, 1972.

_____. *Where Are You Going, Little Mouse?* (70) NY: Greenwillow Books, 1986.

_____. *Leo, the Late Bloomer* (78). Reissued ed. NY: Crowell Junior Books, 1987.

Lenski, Lois. *The Little Farm* (98). NY: McKay, 1980.

Margolin, Harriet. *Busy Bear's Cupboard* (39). NY: Putnam.

McQueen, John Troy. *A World Full of Monsters* (91). NY: Crowell, 1986.

Raskin, Ellen. *Nothing Even Happens on My Block* (80). NY: Aladdin, 1977.

Rice, Eve. *What Sadie Sang* (105). NY: Greenwillow Books, 1983.

Wells, Rosemary. *Noisy Nora* (103). NY: Dial, 1980.

_____. *Max's Christmas* (95). NY: Dial, 1986.

(1) List is excerpted from *Using Literature in the Elementary Classroom,* edited by Stewig, John Warren, and Sevesta, Sam Leaton. Urbana, IL: NCTE, 1989.

## MANUFACTURERS AND DISTRIBUTORS OF READING COMPUTER SOFTWARE

Advanced Ideas
2920 San Pablo Ave.
Berkeley, CA 94702

American Educational Computer, Inc.
7506 N. Broadway, Suite 505
Oklahoma City, OK 73116-9016

Bertamax Inc.
3420 Stone Way North
Seattle, WA 98103

William K. Bradford, Software Publishers
Acton, MA
800-421-2009 (Phone)

COMPress
338 Commerce Dr.
Fairfield, CT 06430

Conduit
University of Iowa, Oakdale Campus
Iowa City, IA 52242

Cross Educational Software Inc.
504 E. Kentucky Ave.
P.O. Box 1536
Ruston, LA 71270

Data Command, Inc.
162 E. Court
P.O. Box 548
Kankakee, IL 60901

Davidson & Associates
3135 Kashiwa St.
Torrance, CA 90505

D.C. Heath
125 Spring St.
Lexington, MA 02173

Educational Activities
P.O. Box 392
Freeport, NY 11520

Gamco Industries
Box 1911
Big Spring, TX 79721

Hartley Courseware
133 Bridge St.
P.O. Box 419
Dimondale, MI 48821

Hi Tech of Santa Cruz
202 Pelton Ave.
Santa Cruz, CA 95060

Holt, Rinehart, and Winston, Inc.
383 Madison Ave.
New York, NY 10017

Houghton Mifflin Co.
Educational Software Division
1 Wayside Rd.
Burlington, MA 01803-4680

InterLearn
P.O. Box 342
Cardiff By The Sea, CA 92007

Jostens Learning Systems, Inc.
P.O. Box 2377
2860 Old Rochester Dr.
Springfield, IL 62705-2377

Krell Software Corp.
Flowerfield Bldg. No. 7
Saint James, NY 11780

Learning Company
Fremont, CA
800-852-2255

Learning Technologies, Inc.
13633 Gamma Rd.
Dallas, TX 75244

Learning Well
200 South Service Rd.
Roslyn Heights, NY 11577

Midwest Software
22500 Orchard Lake Rd., Suite 1
Farmington, MI 48024

Milliken Pub. Co.
1100 Research Blvd.
St. Louis, MO 63132-0579

Optimum Resource, Inc.
10 Station Place
Norfolk, CT 06058

Paperback Software International
2830 Ninth St.
Berkeley, CA 94710

Pelican Software
Fairfield, CT
800-232-2244

Queue Inc.
338 Commerce Dr.
Fairfield, CT 06430

Research Design Assoc., Inc.
10 Boulevard Ave.
Greenlawn, NY 11740

Scholastic Software
730 Broadway
New York, NY 10003

Spinnaker Software Corp.
201 Broadway
Cambridge, MA 02139-1901

Sunburst
39 Washington Ave.
Pleasantville, NY 10570

Teacher Support Software, Inc.
1035 NW 57th St.
Gainesville, FL 32605

Teacher's Pet Software
P.O. Box 791
Livermore, CA 94550

Wordstar International, Inc.
201 Alameda del Prado
Novato, CA 94949

World Book, Inc.
Software Dept.
Mercandise Mart Plaza, 5th Floor
Mail Station 13
Chicago, IL 60654

# QUESTIONS TO ASK ABOUT COMPUTER-BASED READING PROGRAMS*

1. *Cost.* Is there:
   - program copy protection?
   - charge for back-up copies?
   - expense for supplemental or resource materials?
   - a single program disk or are multiple disks required?
   - provision for refunds or returns?
   - provision for program upgrading as new versions appear?

2. *Computer brands and special equipment.* Does the program need:
   - a color monitor?
   - two disk drives?
   - a student data disk?
   - a printer?
   - a speech synthesizer—which one?
   - anything else?

3. *Where might the program fit in my curriculum?*
   - What grade level?
   - What types of students?
   - What types of teaching styles?
   - What types of reading and language arts materials are compatible?
   - How long do the activities take?

4. *What is read on/off screen?* Do students:
   - read passages?
   - read sentences?
   - read individual words or phrases?
   - recognize letters?
   - read program or activity direction?
   - read or recognize anything else?

5. *Program content.* Do activities include these types:
   - instructional?
   - practice?
   - vocabulary?
   - comprehension?
   - study skills?
   - grammar?
   - syllable or alphabet?
   - game?
   - test?

   - other?
   - multiple activities on one disk?

6. *Video presentations.* Does the program:
   - present information with appropriate speed and legibility?
   - present print appropriately spaced and sized?
   - use graphics (with color) — what types, when, and why?
   - use animation—when and why?
   - have color that interferes with legibility of print?

7. *Audio (and speech) presentation.* Does the program:
   - use speech (synthesized space-age voice or digitalized human voice) — when and why?
   - use nonspeech sound — when and why?
   - allow us to control volume or eliminate the audio?

8. *Reading and language arts goals.* Does the program have stated objectives and goals:
   - for teachers (achievement, motivational, behavioral, management)?
   - for students?
   - for concerned others (parents, administrators, supervisors)?
   - that meet state, provincial, or local educational requirements?
   - that meet objectives and goals of tests I'm required to give?

9. *Prerequisite skills.* Of the following skills, what kinds are needed?
   - computer literacy?
   - keyboard?
   - spelling?
   - entry-level reading?
   - background knowledge?
   - other?

10. *Reinforcement in the program.*
    - What behaviors are reinforced — why, when, how?
    - What control do I have over the reinforcement?

11. *Program operation.*
    - Can the students use the program with little or no help from me?
    - Can I or the students:
      — change an activity's contents?
      — change activity formats?

*Reprinted with permission of the International Reading Association from Blanchard, Jay, "Questions to Ask about Computer-Based Reading Programs, *The Reading Teacher,* November 1985, pp. 250–252.

— receive on-screen prompts or help?

— make mistakes or press keys accidentally without ruining the activity?

— correct our entries?

— work on unfinished sections of an activity without repeating completed sections?

— reread previous screens easily without restarting the activity?

— use the activities without changing to another program disk in the middle?

— use the activities if the program disk is removed from the disk drive?

- Can the program give pretests or posttests?

- Can the activity be used with either groups or individuals?

12. *Program reviews and field-testing.* What's available?

- Critical reviews?

- Descriptive reviews?

- Reports of field testing?

13. *Supplemental or resource material.* Are supplemental materials available for examining:

- the contents of the activities before using them with the computer?

- background information about the activity's content?

- information about instructional strategies used?

- other educational resources?

14. *Scoring and recordkeeping.* Does the program:

- score and record student performance or other information —how?

- permit students as well as teachers to see records?

- allow the recall of information about students— what information, why?

Finally, ask the question, "What does this program offer my students that I cannot otherwise give them?"

# A MODEL SHEET FOR EVALUATING READING MATERIALS

TITLE:

PUBLISHER:

| COST: | Yes | So-So | No |
|---|---|---|---|
| 1. Gives instructions for use that are clear and understandable. | _____ | _____ | _____ |
| 2. Is interesting and acceptable to students at designated age groups. | _____ | _____ | _____ |
| 3. Presents concepts or skills thoroughly and accurately. | _____ | _____ | _____ |
| 4. Uses language suitable for students who will be using the material. | _____ | _____ | _____ |
| 5. Provides for students to apply what they learned to other related areas. | _____ | _____ | _____ |
| 6. Presents follow-up activities for reinforcement. | _____ | _____ | _____ |
| 7. Provides for self-correction. | _____ | _____ | _____ |
| 8. Challenges students. | _____ | | |
| 9. Is easily presented to students. | _____ | | |
| 10. Provides the activity individually, or in a group. | _____ | | |

Strengths: _____

_____

Weaknesses: _____

_____

# GLOSSARY

**affixes**  Refers to either prefixes or suffixes or to both. For example, the affixes in <u>un</u>manage<u>able</u> are <u>un</u>, the prefix, and <u>able</u>, the suffix. See the meanings of *prefix* and *suffix* in this glossary.

**analytic phonics**  A system of teaching sound/symbol relationships whereby a student deduces the phonics principle involved. The teacher does not give the relationship but lets the children reason it out. This is sometimes referred to as *implicit phonics.*

**basic sight words**  A list of high-frequency words, such as *the, up,* and *about,* that constitute from 50 to 66 percent of all running vocabulary. Children must recognize these words at sight in order to read fluently.

**blend**  Two or three consonant letters with their related sounds that cluster together and are pronounced very rapidly such as the *tr* in *tr*ap and the *str* in *str*eet.

**breve**  A diacritic mark (˘) as in the word *mằt* that indicates the vowel has a short sound. A short vowel by definition means simply that the vowel is pronounced with much less breath (hence shorter) than the long vowels, which take "longer" breath to say.

**CAI**  Computer assisted instruction.

**consonant digraph**  Two consonant letters together that encode a single sound. Some digraphs encode more than one single sound, such as /ch/ in <u>ch</u>amp/<u>sch</u>ool/<u>ch</u>ef.

**context**  The words, phrases, and sentences surrounding a word, giving clues to its meaning and part of speech.

**cursive**  A type of handwriting where letters are joined together and where the script differs from the early form of writing known as manuscript. Cursive writing is usually taught at some point in the second grade.

**decode**  This refers to the ability of children to recognize letters and their related sounds as meaningful words. Some educators also believe that it means to pronounce the words correctly.

**diphthong**  Two vowels together that produce a "gliding" sound when pronounced. The most common diphthongs are *oi, oy, ou,* and *ow.* When *ou* and *ow* "say" *ow* as in <u>ab*ou*t</u> and <u>h*ow*</u>, they are diphthongs; when *ou* and *ow* "say" *ō* as in *s*ō*ul* and *t*ō*w,* they act as single vowels.

**embed**  To deliberately place selected words into a sentence for instructional purposes.

**encode**  To write the word, phrase, or sentence using the orthographic patterns of English.

**explicit phonics**  This refers to the direct phonics instruction by the teacher where s/he tells children, for example, that the sound of *d* is the first sound of the word *duck* and that it is written with the letter *d.* The teacher continues to directly teach the sound/symbol relationships.

**language experience**  This can mean two very different things. Language experience can refer to the type of instruction whereby children either dictate to the teacher or write sentences themselves. Subsequently, the teacher, based on these sentences, teaches the children alphabetic principles such as sound/symbol relationships, capitals and periods. On the other hand, language experience is used by some to mean a patterned approach to teaching reading with sentences such as *Dan ran to the tan van,* as with "linguistic" phonics below.

**lexicographer**  A person who assists in the development of a dictionary and who makes decisions about which words to include and how they should be defined.

**lexicon**  Refers to the words in the language. For example, "The English language has a *lexicon* of over 1,000,000 words."

**"linguistics" phonics**  A patterned approach to teaching phonics that shows minimal differences between pairs of words such as *Dan ran to the tan van.* These terms are still the subject of much debate among educators.

**lowercase**  When teaching handwriting, letters that are *not* capitalized are referred to as *lowercase.*

**macron**  A diacritical mark (¯) as in the word *māte* to indicate that the vowel is long.

**manuscript**  A type of handwriting first taught to children that resembles a form of printing. See the word *cursive* above.

**morpheme**  The minimal number of letters or sounds that show meaning. For example, the word *manager* has two morphemes, *manage,* and *er* (one who does); the word *unbelievable* has three morphemes, *un, believe,* and *able;* and the word *crocodile* has only one.

**orthography**   The spelling patterns of the language that enable us to have a standard writing system.

**phoneme**   The smallest units of speech that distinguish one word from another. For example, the word *barn* has four distinct speech sounds, or four phonemes *(b, a, r,* and *n)* while the word *sight* has five letters, but only three phonemes, *s, i,* and *t.*

**phonemic awareness**   The ability to recognize that a spoken word consists of a sequence of sounds and that the sounds are related in some way to an alphabetic principle.

**phonogram**   A cluster of vowel and consonant blends such as *ent* and *ild* to which beginning sounds are added, forming words such as *sent* and *wild.*

**phonology**   The study of speech sounds.

**prefix**   A syllable before the root word that usually changes the meaning, such as <u>pre</u>arrange.

**r-controlled vowels** (sometimes referred to as *r-conditioned vowels*)   The letter r following a vowel (in the *same* syllable) modifies the vowel sound, as in *her* and *stare.*

**root**   A base, such as *astro,* meaning star, to which prefixes and/or suffixes are added; for example, *astronaut.* Sometimes the root is simply a word such as *courage,* to which a suffix may be added; for example, *courageous,* or *courageously* (two suffixes). Most important, roots carry the main meaning of the word.

**schwa**   A reduced vowel sound, shorter than the short sound with the sound of "uh" as in apr*o*n.

Many of our vowels in unaccented syllables have been reduced to the schwa sound. The schwa is written as an upside down "e" as in aprən.

**scope and sequence chart**   A publisher's chart that shows the grade level at which particular reading skills are taught.

**semantics**   This refers to the meaning of the word, phrase, or sentence.

**software**   Programs essential to the computer's operation that have programmed the skills, lessons, and sometimes assessment for the student.

**stem**   Another term for a base word or word part to which affixes may be added. For young children, this term is sometimes used instead of *root.*

**structural analysis**   Understanding word parts as compound words, affixes, roots, and syllabication.

**suffixes**   *Derivational:* There are many of these suffixes such as *ment (argument)* and *ism (capitalism).* They often change the part of speech of the root word and sometimes the word's meaning. *Inflectional:* There are only eight simple inflectional suffixes, such as *ing* and *ed.* These do not change the part of speech. They are learned in the early stages of reading.

**syntactic**   This refers to the grammar involved. For example, while *cautious* is an adjective, it differs syntactically from *cautiously,* which is an adverb.

**synthetic phonics**   Another term used for explicit phonics, in which teachers directly teach the sound/symbol relationships.

**vowel digraphs**   Two vowel letters together that encode one vowel sound, as in c*oa*t (ō). Sometimes the vowel digraph encodes several single sounds as *ie* in f*ie*ld (ē) and in t*ie* (ī).

# REFERENCES

Adams, Marilyn Jager. *Beginning to Read: Thinking and Learning about Print.* Cambridge, MA: The MIT Press, 1990.

———. "Beginning to Read: A Critique by Literacy Professionals and a Response by Marilyn Jager Adams." *The Reading Teacher* 44, no. 6 (February 1991): 390–95.

———. " Resolving the 'Great Debate'." *American Educator* 19, no. 2 (Summer 1995): 7, 10–19.

Agnew, Ann T. "Using Children's Dictated Stories to Assess Code Consciousness." *The Reading Teacher* 35, no. 4 (January 1982): 450–53.

Ahmann, Linda. "Some Tips on Teaching Vowel-Sound Discrimination." *Academic Therapy* 17, no. 5 (May 1982): 570–71.

Alexander, Clara Franklin. "Black English Dialect and the Classroom Teacher." *The Reading Teacher* 33, no. 5 (February 1980): 571–76.

Anderson, Richard C.; Hiebert, Elfreida H.; Scott, Judith A.; and Wilkinson, Ian A. G. *Becoming a Nation of Readers: The Report of the Commission on Reading.* Washington, DC: National Institute of Education, 1985.

Anderson, William W., and Fordham, Ann E. "Beware the Magic Phonics Program!" *Childhood Education* 68, no. 1 (Fall 1991): 8–9.

Angeletti, Sara. "Spelling Dictionaries." *Learning* 21, no. 7 (March 1993): 36.

Armbruster, Bonnie B., and Nagy, William E. "Vocabulary in Content Area Lessons." *The Reading Teacher* 45, no. 7 (March 1991): 550–51.

Ashton-Warner, Sylvia. *Teacher.* Simon & Schuster, 1963.

Atwell, Nancie. "Nancie Atwell Talks about Teachers and Whole Language." *Instructor* 102, no. 4 (Nov./Dec. 1992): 48–49.

Azar, Teri Oberstein. "Teaching the Short Vowel Sounds Using Visual Imagery." *The Reading Teacher* 38, no. 9 (May 1985): 926–28.

Bacharach, Nancy, and Alexander, Patricia. "Basal Reading Manuals: What Do Teachers Think of Them and How Do They Use Them?" *Reading Psychology* 7 no. 3 (Spring 1986): 163–72.

Ball, Eileen W., and Blachman, Benita A. "Does Phoneme Awareness Training in Kindergarten Make a Difference in Early Word Recognition and Developmental Spelling?" *Reading Research Quarterly* 26, no. 1 (Winter 1991): 49–59.

Balmuth, Miriam. *The Root of Phonics: A Historical Introduction.* New York: McGraw-Hill, 1982.

Bajtelsmit, Lynn, and Naab, Helen. "Partners as Writers?" *The Reading Teacher* 48, no. 1 (Sept. 1994): 92–93.

Beck, I., and McKeown, M. "Conditions of Vocabulary Acquisition." In *Handbook of Reading Research,* Vol. 11, edited by R. Barr, M. Kamil, P. Mosenthal, and P. D. Pearson. New York: Longman, 1988, 789–814.

Beck, Isabel L. and Juel, Connie. "The Role of Decoding in Learning To Read." *American Educator* 19, no. 2 (Summer 1995): 8, 21–25; 39–42.

Belsie, Laurent. "Reading, Writing—and Computers: High-Tech Teaching Tool Moves Children Beyond Traditional Basic Skills to Keyboard 'Literacy.'" *The Christian Science Monitor* 84, no. 20 (Dec. 23, 1991): 12.

Blachowicz, Camille L. A. "C(2)QU: Modeling Context Use in the Classroom." *The Reading Teacher* 47, no.3 (Nov. 1993): 268–269.

———. "Vocabulary Instruction: What Goes On in the Classroom?" *The Reading Teacher* 41, no. 2 (November 1987): 132–137.

Blachowicz, Camille L. A., and Lee, John J. "Vocabulary Development in the Whole Literacy Classroom." *The Reading Teacher* 45, no. 3 (November 1991): 188–94.

Blanchard, Jay. "Questions to Ask about Computer-based Reading Programs." *The Reading Teacher* 39, no. 2 (November 1985): 250–56.

Blanton, William E., and Moorman, Gary B. *Reading Research and Instruction* 28 (Spring 1990): 35–55.

Boyle, Owen F., and Peregory, Suzanne F. "Literacy Scaffolds: Strategies for First and Second-

Language Readers and Writers." *The Reading Teacher* 44, no. 3 (November 1990): 194–97.

Bozon, Meg. "What is Reading Recovery?" *Instructor* 104, no. 1 (July/Aug. 1994): 15–16.

Bracey, W. "Basals and Literature as Partner," *Phi Delta Kappan* 74, no. 4 (Dec. 1992): 344–46.

Burmeister, Lou E. *Words—from Print to Meaning*. Reading, MA: Addison-Wesley, 1975.

Carbo, Marie. "Advanced Book Recordings: Turning It Around for Poor Readers." *Early Years* 15, no. 5 (January 1985): 46–48.

————. "An Evaluation of Jeanne Chall's Response to 'Debunking the Great Phonics Myth'." *Phi Delta Kappan* 71, no. 4 (October 1989): 152–58.

Carbo, Marie; Dunn, Rita; and Dunn, Kenneth. *Teaching Students to Read Through Their Individual Learning Styles*. Englewood Cliffs, NJ: Prentice Hall, 1986, p. 61.

Carey, Laura. "On Alienation and the ESL Student." *Phi Delta Kappan* 71, no. 1 (September 1989): 74–75.

Casale, Ula Price. "Motor Imaging: A Reading-Vocabulary Strategy." *Journal of Reading* 28, no. 7 (April 1985): 619–21.

Chall, Jeanne. *Learning to Read: The Great Debate*. New York: McGraw-Hill, 1967.

————. *Learning to Read: The Great Debate*. 2nd ed. New York: McGraw-Hill, 1983.

————. "Learning to Read: The Great Debate 20 Years Later—A Response to 'Debunking the Great Phonics Myth'." *Phi Delta Kappan* 70, no. 7 (March 1989): 521–25.

————. "The Uses of Educational Research: Comments on Carbo." *Phi Delta Kappan* 71, no. 2 (October 1989): 158–61.

Chall, Jeanne, and Goodman, Kenneth. "Point/Counterpoint Whole Language vs. Direct Instruction Models." *The Reading Teacher* 10, no. 3 (December 1992/Jan. 1993): 8–10.

Chomsky, Carol. "After Decoding: What?" *Language Arts* 53, no. 3 (March 1976): 288–96.

Clark, Charles. "Learning to Read." *CQ Researcher* 5, no. 19 (May 19, 1995): 443–61.

Clay, M. M. "Reading Recovery in the United States: Its Successes and Challenges." Address to the American Educational Research Assn., Boston, 1990.

Coley, Joan D. "Self-Evaluation Techniques for Young Children." *Reading World* 22, no. 3 (March 1983): 197–202.

Collins, Cathy. "Content Mastery Strategies Aid Classroom Discussion." *The Reading Teacher* 40, no. 8 (April 1987): 816–817.

Corcoran, Frances. "Children's Dictionaries." Reference Books Bulletin, *Booklist* (June 15, 1991): 1,988–1,992.

Cowley, Joy. "Joy of Big Books." *Instructor* 101, no. 3 (October 1991): 19.

CQ Researcher *(Congressional Quarterly)*. "Hooked on Phonics Racks Up Sales . . ." (May 19, 1995): 452–453.

Cudd, Evelyn T., and Roberts, Leslie L. "A Scaffolding Technique to Develop Sentence Sense and Vocabulary." *The Reading Teacher* 47, no. 4 (Dec./Jan. 1993–94): 346–48.

Cunningham, James W. "An Automatic Pilot for Decoding." *The Reading Teacher* 32, no. 4 (January 1979): 420–24.

Cunningham, Patricia M. "Teaching Were, With, What and Other 'Four-Letter' Words." *The Reading Teacher* 34, no. 3 (November 1980): 160–63.

————. "A Teacher's Guide to Material Shopping." *The Reading Teacher* 35, no. 2 (November 1981): 181–84.

————. *Phonics They Use*. New York: HarperCollins, 1991.

Cunningham, Patricia M., and Allington, Richard L. "Words, Letters, Sounds and Big Books." *Learning* 20, no. 2 (September 1991): 91–92.

Cunningham, Patricia M., and Cunningham, James W. "Making Words: Enhancing the Invented Spelling-Decoding Connection." *The Reading Teacher* 46, no. 2 (Oct. 1992): 106–115.

Cunningham, Patricia M.; Cunningham, James W.; and Rystrom, Richard C. "A New Syllabication Strategy and Reading Achievement." *Reading World* 34, no. 3 (March 1981): 208–13.

Dale, Edgar, and O'Rourke, Joseph. *Techniques of Teaching Vocabulary*. Palo Alto, CA: Field Educational Publishers, Inc., 1971, 183.

Dale, Edgar, and O'Rourke, Joseph. *The Living Word Vocabulary.* Elgin, IL: Dome Press, Inc., 1979.

Dale, Edgar; O'Rourke, Joseph; and Barbe, Walter B. *Vocabulary Building: A Process Approach.* Columbus, OH: Zaner-Bloser, 1986.

Davis, Deborah J. "1st and 5th Graders Coauthor Books." *The Reading Teacher* 42, no. 8 (April 1989): 652.

DeGroff, Lina. "Is There a Place for Computers in Whole Language Classrooms?" *The Reading Teacher* 43, no. 8 (April 1990): 568–72.

Devall, Yvonna. "Evaluating Microcomputer Software for Reading Instruction." *Journal of Reading* 26, no. 6 (March 1983): 553.

Dole, Robert. "When Fads and Bureaucracy Rule, Reading Skills Suffer." *San Jose Mercury News,* Dec. 24, 1995.

Dreyer, Lois G.; Futtersak, Karen R.; and Boehm, Ann E. "Sight Words for the Computer Age: An Essential Word List." *The Reading Teacher* 38, no. 12 (October 1985); 12–15.

Durkin, Dolores. "Dolores Durkin Speaks on Instruction." *The Reading Teacher* 43, no. 7 (March 1990): 474–476.

Durrell, Donald D., and Murphy, Helen A. "A Pre-reading Phonics Inventory." *The Reading Teacher* 31, no. 4 (January 1978): 385–89.

Edwards, Bessley, and Thompson. "Teachers in Transition: Accommodating Reading Curriculum to Cultural Diversity." *The Reading Teacher* 44, no. 6 (February 1991): 436–37.

Ehri, Linnea C. "A Critique of Five Studies Related to Letter-Name Knowledge and Learning to Read." In *Reading Research Revisited,* edited by Lance M. Gentile, Michael L. Kamil, and Jay S. Blanchard. Columbus, OH: Charles E. Merrill, 1983.

Eldredge, Lloyd J., and Butterfield, Dennie D. "Alternatives to Traditional Reading Instruction." *The Reading Teacher* 39, no. 9 (October 1986): 32–37.

Eldredge, Lloyd J.; Quinn, Bill; and Butterfield, Dennie D. "Causal Relationships Between Phonics, Reading Comprehension, and Vocabulary Achievement in the Second Grade." *Journal of Educational Research* 83, no. 4 (March/April 1990): 201–05.

Farr, R.; Tulley, M. A.; and Powell, D. "The Evaluation and Selection of Basal Readers." *Elementary School Journal* 87, no. 3 (January 1987): 267–81.

Field, James C., and Jardine, David W. "Bad Examples as Interpretive Opportunities." *Language Arts* 71, no. 4 (April 1994): 245–262.

Fielding, Elizabeth Nolan. "Learning to Spell vs. Using the Spellcheck." *Reading Today* 12, no. 5 (Apr./May 1995): 27

Flesch, Rudolph. *Why Johnny Can't Read,* Cutchogue, NY: Buccaneer Books, reprinted 1993.

Foss, Kit. "Finger Spelling." *Reading Today* 12, no. 3 (Dec. 1994/Jan. 1995): 28.

Fox, Deborah. "The Debate Goes On: Systematic Phonics vs. Whole Language." *Journal of Reading* 29, no. 7 (April 1986): 678–80.

Fox, Paula. *The One-Eyed Cat,* New York: Bradbury Press, 1984.

Fredericks, Anthony D., and Rasinski, Timothy V. "Involving Parents in the Assessment Process." *The Reading Teacher* 44, no. 4 (December 1990): 346.

Freebody, Peter, and Byrne, Brian. "Word-Reading Strategies in Elementary School Children: Relations to Comprehension, Reading Time, and Phonemic Awareness." *Reading Research Quarterly* 28, no. 4 (Fall 1988): 441–51.

French, Michael P., and Danielson, Kathy Everts. "Vocabulary." *The Reading Teacher* 43, no. 8 (April 1990): 612–16.

Freppon, Penny A., and Dahl, Karin L. "Learning about Phonics in a Whole Language Classroom." *Language Arts* 68, no. 3 (March 1991): 190–94.

Frese, Mary. "Thrill of the Drill." *Instructor* 101, no. 3 (October 1991): 34.

Frey, Sandra J. "The Long and Short of It." *The Reading Teacher* 35, no. 5 (August 1982): 54.

Fuller, Jan. "Let's Use Phonics and Whole Language." *The Reading Teacher* 12, no. 2 (Oct./Nov. 1994): 31.

Garcia, Georgia Earnest. "Factors Influencing the English Reading Test Performance of Spanish-Speaking Hispanic Children." *Reading Research Quarterly* 26, no. 4 (March 1991): 371–72.

Gates, Louis, and Heath, Lowry. "A Face Lift for the Silent e." *The Reading Teacher* 17, no. 1 (October 1983): 102–03.

Gentile, Lance. *Using Sports for Reading and Writing Activities: Middle and High School Years.* Phoenix, AZ: Oryx Press, 1983, p. 11.

Gersten, Russell, and Gersten, Keating. "Long-Term Benefits from Direct Instruction." *Educational Leadership* 44, no. 2 (March 1987): 289–91.

Gibson, Fred. "A New Factor in the Phonics Debate: Some Students Are Phonetic Learners and Some Are Not." *Phi Delta Kappan* 72, no. 5 (January 1991): 402–03.

Gillis, M. K. "Combining Phonics: Approaches for Problem Readers." *Academic Therapy* 17, no. 4 (March 1982): 389–94.

"Give and Take," (Interview with Dr. Roger Schank) *Electronic Learning* 14, no. 6 (March 1995): p.13.

Glasser, William. *Schools Without Failure.* New York: Harper & Row, 1975.

Glazer, Susan Mendel. "Do I Have to Give Up Phonics to be a Whole Language Teacher?" *Reading Today* 12, no. 4 (Feb./Mar. 1995): 3.

Glazer, Susan Mendel, and Brown, Carol Smullen. *Portfolios and Beyond.* Norwood, MA: Christopher-Gordon Pub. Inc., 1993.

Goff, Patrick. National Right to Read Foundation's Right to Read Report. Sept. 1993.

Goodman, Kenneth S. "I didn't found whole language. . . ." *The Reading Teacher* 46, no. 3 (Nov. 1992): 196–98.

Goodman, Kenneth S. *What's Whole in Whole Language. Heinemann Publishers,* 1986. Portsmouth, N H:

Goodman, Kenneth S.; Goodman, Yetta M.; and Hood, Wendy J. *The Whole Language Evaluation Book.* Portsmouth, NH: Heineman Educational Books, 1989.

Goodman, Kenneth S.; Shannon, Patrick; Freeman, Yvonne; and Murphy, Sharon. *Report Card on Basal Readers.* Katonah, NY: Richard C. Owen Publishers, Inc., 1988.

Groff, Patrick. "Teaching Reading by Syllables." *The Reading Teacher* 34, no. 6 (March 1981): 686–91.

_____. "A Test of the Utility of Phonics Rules." *Reading Psychology* 4 (July/Dec. 1983): 217–25.

_____. "Resolving the Letter Name Controversy." *The Reading Teacher* 37, no. 4 (January 1984): 384–88.

_____. "The Maturing of Phonics Instruction." *Education Digest* 52 (January 1987): 40–41.

*A Guide to Curriculum Planning in Reading.* Madison, WI: Wisconsin Dept. of Public Instruction, 1985.

Hahn, Mary Downing. *Time for Andrew.* New York: Clarion Books, 1994.

Hall, Susan Hlesciak, and Henderson, Anne. "Uniting Schools and Families." *The Educaton Digest* 56, no. 8 (April 1991): 47–53.

Hanna, Paul R.; Hodges, Richard E.; and Hanna, Jean S. *Spelling Structure and Strategies.* Boston, MA: Houghton-Mifflin, 1971, pp. 79–83.

Hannum, Wallace. "Reconsidering Computer Literacy: Is it a Basic Skill?" *The High School Journal* 74, no. 3 (February-March 1991): 152–59.

Hansen, Jane. *When Writers Read.* Portsmouth, NH: Heinemann, 1987.

Harris, Albert J. "What is New in Remedial Reading." *The Reading Teacher* 34, no. 6 (January 1981): 405–10.

Harris, Albert J., and Jacobson, Milton D. *Basic Elementary Reading Vocabularies.* New York: Macmillan, 1972.

Harris, Albert J., and Sipay, Edward R. *How to Increase Reading Ability.* New York: David McKay, 1975.

Heath Reading Series. "Look Out" *Cats Sleep Anywhere.* Lexington, MA: D. C. Heath & Co., 1996.

Hewison, Jenny. "The Long-Term Effectiveness of Parental Involvement in Reading: A Follow-Up to the Haringey Reading Project." *British Journal of Educational Psychology* 58, no. 5 (June 1988): 184–90.

Hiebert, Elfrieda H. "A Comparison of Young Children's Self-Selected Reading Words and Basal Reading Words." *Reading Improvement* 20, no. 1 (Spring 1983): 41–45.

Higdon, Patsy. "Sticker Books Sight Words." *The Reading Teacher* 41, no. 3 (December 1987): 369.

Hill, Lola Bailey, and Brown, Mary G. "Reading Recovery: Questions Classroom Teachers Ask." *The Reading Teacher* 44, no. 7 (March 1991): 80–84.

Hill, Lola Bailey, and Hale, Mary Groenewoud. "Reading Recovery: Questions Classroom Teachers Ask." *The Reading Teacher* 44, no. 7 (March 1991): 480–83.

Holland, Kathy W., and Hall, Lee Ellis. "Reading Achievement in the First Grade Classroom: A Comparison of Basal and Whole Language Approaches." *Reading Improvement* 26, no. 6 (Winter 1989): 323–29.

Hollingsworth, Paul M.; Reutzel, D. Ray; and Weeks, Elaine. *Reading Research and Instruction* no. 29 (Spring 1991): 14–16.

Honig, Bill. *How Should We Teach Our Children to Read: The Role of Skills in a Comprehensive Reading Program, a Balanced Approach.* San Francisco, CA: Far West Lab, 1996.

"In the Classroom." *The Reading Teacher* 46, no. 8 (May 1993): 716.

"The Invented Spelling Bugaboo" *Instructor* May/June 1995: 53.

Isaak, T., and Joseph J., "Software and the Teaching of Reading." *The Reading Teacher* 43, no. 3 (December 1989): 254–55.

Iversen, Sandra, and Turner, William E. "Phonological Processing Skills and the Reading Recovery Program." *Journal of Educational Psychology* 85, no. 1 (March 1993): 112–127.

Jacobs, Joan. "Why Juan and Jenny Can't R-E-A-D" *San Jose Mercury* (Aug 17, 1995): 7B

Jacobs, Vicki; Baldwin, E. Luke; and Chall, Jeanne. *The Reading Crisis: Why Poor Children Fall Behind.* Cambridge, MA: Harvard University Press, 1990.

Janicke, Eugene M. "Massive Oral Decoding." *Academic Therapy* 17, no. 2 (November 1981): 157–60.

Jenkins, Joseph R.; Matlock, Barbara; and Slocum, Timothy A. "Two Approaches to Vocabulary Instruction: The Teaching of Individual Word Meanings and Practice in Deriving Word Meaning from Context." *Reading Research Quarterly* 24, no. 4 (Spring 1989): 215–35.

Jenkins, Yolanda L. "Touching the Mind: Technology and Assessment." *Computing Teacher* 21, no. 6 (March 1994): 6–8.

Johns, Jerry L. "The Revised Dolch List: Data and Rationale." *Reading World* 18, no. 1 (October 1978): 24–26.

Johnson, Dale D., and Baumann, James F. "Word Identification." In *Handbook of Reading Research,* edited by P. David Pearson. New York: Longman, 1984.

Johnson, Dale D., and Pearson, David P. *Teaching Reading Vocabulary.* New York: Holt, Rinehart & Winston, 1978.

Johnston, Mary Minor, senior author. *Total Reading.* Los Angeles, CA.

Jones, Linda T. *Strategies for Involving Parents in Their Children's Education.* Bloomington, IN: Phi Delta Kappa Educational Foundation, 1991.

"Joy of Big Books." *Instructor* 101, no. 3 (October 1991): 19–20.

Juel, Connie. "Learning to Read and Write: A Longitudinal Study of 54 Children from First Through Fourth Grade." *Journal of Educational Psychology* 80 (Spring 1988): 437–47.

———. "Cross-Age Tutoring Between Student Athletes and At-Risk Children." *The Reading Teacher* 45, no. 3 (November 1991): 178–83.

Kameenui, Edw. J. "Response to Deegan: Keep the Curtain Inside the Tub." *The Reading Teacher* 48, no. 6 (May 1995): 700–702.

Kasner, Joan. ". . .neglect of phonics." *Reading Today* 12, no. 1 (Aug./Sept. 1994): 31.

Kemp, Joyce. "Reading Buddies." *The Reading Teacher* 44, no. 4 (December 1990): 356.

Kim, Yeu Hong, and Goetz, Ernest. "Context Effect on Word Recognition and Reading Comprehension of Poor and Good Readers . . ." *Reading Research Quarterly* (Apr/May 1994): 179–186.

Koch, Kenneth. *Wishes, Lies and Dreams: Teaching Children to Write Poetry.* New York: Chelsea House, 1970.

Kraske, Robert. *The Story of the Dictionary.* New York: Harcourt Brace Jovanovich, 1975.

Krieger, Veronica K. "Differences in Poor Readers' Abilities to Identify High-Frequency Words in

Isolation and Context." *Reading Research Quarterly* 20, no. 4 (May 1981): 263–69.

Lara, Susan G. Martin. "Reading Placement for Code Switchers." *The Reading Teacher* 42, no. 4 (January 1989): 278–82.

*Latest and Best of TESS, The Educational Software Selector.* Hampton Parkways, NY: EPIE Institute, The Educational Products Information Exchange, 1991.

Lauritzen, Carol. "A Modification of Repeated Readings for Group Instruction." *The Reading Teacher* 35, no. 4 (January 1982): 456–58.

Layton, Kent, and Irwin, Martha E. "Enriching Your Reading Program with Databases." *The Reading Teacher* 42, no. 9 (May 1989): 724.

Levine, Art. "The Great Debate Revisited." *Atlantic Monthly* 27, no. 6 (Dec. 1994): 38–44.

Lewkowicz, Nancy K. "The Bag Game: An Activity to Heighten Phonemic Awareness." *The Reading Teacher* 47, no. 6 (March 1994): 508.

Loban, Walter, *Language Development: K-12.* Urbana, IL: National Council of Teachers of English, 1976.

Mageau, Therese. "Teaching with Technology." *Instructor* 10, no. 6 (August 1991): 6.

———. "Teaching with Technology." *Instructor* 10, no. 7 (September 1991): 82.

Manning, Maryann and Gary. "Reading: Word or Meaning-Centered." *Teaching PreK–8* 25, no. 2 (Oct. 1994): 98–99.

———. "The Texts Students Read." *Teaching K–8* 25, no. 4 (Jan. 1995): 102–103.

———. "Whole Language: They Say, You Say." *Teaching K–8* (May 1995): 50–54.

Maria, Katherine. "Developing Disadvantaged Children's Background Knowledge Interactively." *The Reading Teacher* 42, no. 4 (January 1989): 296–99.

———. "The Computer in the Reading Clinic." *The Reading Teacher* 36, no. 6 (February 1983): 504–07.

Mathis, Judi. "Software Reviews." *The Computing Teacher* 19, no. 1 (August/ September 1991): 44.

McCallum, Richard D. "Don't Throw the Basals Out with the Bath Water." *The Reading Teacher* 42, no. 3 (December 1988): 204–07.

McGee, Lea M., and Richgels, Donald J. "K is Kristen's: Learning the Alphabet from a Child's Perspective." *The Reading Teacher* 43, no. 3 (December 1989): 216–25.

McKenna, M.C.; Stahl, S.A.; and Reinkin, D. "A Critical Commentary on Research, Politics, and Whole Language." *Journal of Reading Behavior* vol. 26 no. 2 (1994): 211–233.

McKeown, M. G. "The Acquisition of Word Meaning from Context by Children of High and Low Ability." *Reading Research Quarterly* 10, no. 4 (Summer 1985): 482–96.

Mills, Heidi; O'Keefe, Timothy; and Stephens, Diane. *Looking Closely: Exploring the Role of Phonics in One Whole Language Classroom.* Urbana, IL: National Council of Teachers of English, 1991.

Moats, Louisa Cook. "The Missing Foundation in Teacher Education." *American Educator* 19, no. 2 (Summer 1995): 9, 43–51.

Mobley, Lillian H. "Reading Strategies for Non-English-Speaking Students." *The Reading Teacher* 44, no. 2 (October 1990): 182.

Monson, Robert J., and Pahl, Michele M. "Charting a New Course with Whole Language." *Educational Leadership* 48, no. 6 (March 1991): 51–54.

Moon, Louise, and Scorpio, Carolyn M. "When Word Recognition Is OK—Almost!" *The Reading Teacher* 27, no. 9 (May 1984): 825–27.

Mooney, Margaret. "Guided Reading—The Reader in Control." *Teaching K–8* 25, no. 5 (Feb. 1995): 54–58.

Moses, Joseph. *The Great Rain Robbery.* New York: Houghton Mifflin, 1975.

Nagy, E. *Teaching Vocabulary to Improve Reading Comprehension.* Newark, DE: International Reading Association, 1988.

National Right to Read Foundation. 322 N. St. NW., Suite 174., Washington, DC 20007.

Negin, Gary A. "A Multisensory Supplement to Reading Instruction." *The Clearing House* 64, no. 6 (July/August 1991): 381–82.

"New Findings in the 'Great' Debate." *Phi Delta Kappan* 71, no. 4 (December 1989): 2.

Newman, Judith M., and Church, Susan M. "Myths of Whole Language." *The Reading Teacher* 44, no. 1 (September 1990): 20–26.

"New Study Examines How Technology Affects Children." *Multimedia Schools* 2, no. 1 (Jan./Feb. 1995): 10.

Noden, Harry, and Moss, Barbara. "Portfolio Assessment: Getting Started." *The Reading Teacher* 48, no. 2 (Oct. 1994): 180–182. (book review).

Novelli, Joan. "Strategies for Spelling Success." *Instructor* 102, no. 9 (May/June 1993): 41–42.

Opitz, Michael F., and Cooper, Donna. "Adapting the Spelling Basal for Spelling Workshop." *The Reading Teacher* 47, no. 2 (Oct. 1993): 110–13.

Otto, Jean. "The New Debate in Reading." *The Reading Teacher* 36, no. 1 (October 1982): 14–18.

Palmer, Barbara. "Dolch List Still Useful." *The Reading Teacher* 38, no. 7 (March 1985): 708.

"The Past, Present, and Future of Literacy Education: Comments from a Panel of Distinguished Educators." *The Reading Teacher* 43, no. 4 (January 1990): 307–09.

Pearce, Mary. "Where Should Phonics Fit in Your Reading Toolbox?" *Instructor* 104, no. 8 (May/June 1995) 55–58.

Perry, Leslie Anne, and Sagen, Patricia Smith. "Are Basal Readers Becoming Too Difficult for Some Children?" *Reading Improvement* 26, no. 4 (Summer 1989): 181–85.

Peterson, Marilyn L. "Mexican-American Children: What Do They Prefer and Read?" *Reading World* 22, no. 2 (December 1982): 129–31.

Peterson, Susan, and Phelps, Patricia H. "Visual-Auditory Links: A Structural Analysis Approach to Increase Word Power." *The Reading Teacher* 44, no. 7 (March 1991): 524–25.

Pikulski, John J. "Questions and Answers." *The Reading Teacher* 40, no. 8 (April 1987): 831–32.

Pinnell, Gay Su. "Success for Low Achievers through Reading Recovery." *Educational Leadership* 48, no. 1 (September 1990): 17–21.

Pinnell, Gay Su; Fried, Mary D.; and Estice, Rose Mary. "Reading Recovery: Learning How to Make a Difference." *The Reading Teacher* 43, no. 4 (January 1990): 282–85.

"Primary Place." *Instructor* 10, no. 1 (July/Aug. 1992): 81–82.

Ray, Doris. "Removing Barriers of Social Organization in Schooling So Technology Can Aid Restructuring." *The Computing Teacher* 18, no. 7 (April 1991): 8–12.

*Read: An Individual Pupil Monitoring System.* Boston, MA: Houghton Mifflin Publishers.

Readence, John E., and Baldwin, Scott R. (eds.) *Dialogues in Literacy Research.* Chicago, IL: National Reading Conference, 1989.

Reading Reform Foundation. Box 98785, Tacoma, WA 998498.

Reutzel, Ray D., and Cooter, Robert B. "Whole Language: Comparative Effects on First Grade Reading Achievement." *Journal of Educational Research* 83, no. 5 (May/June 1990): 252–57.

Reutzel, Ray D.; Oda, Linda K.; and Moore, Blaine H. "Developing Print Awareness: The Effect of Three Instructional Approaches on Kindergartners' Print Awareness, Reading Readiness, and Word Reading." *Journal of Reading Behavior* 21, no. 4 (September 1989): 197–217.

Richgels, Donald. "Invented Spelling Ability and Printed Word Learning in Kindergarten." *Reading Research Quarterly* 30, no. 1 (Jan./Feb./March): 96–98.

Roberts, N., and Carter, M. *Integrating Computers into the Elementary and Middle School.* Englewood Cliffs, NJ: Prentice Hall, 1988.

Rosenshine, Barak, and Stevens, Robert. "Classroom Instruction in Reading." In *Handbook of Reading Research,* edited by P. David Pearson. New York: Longman, 1984.

Rosso, Barbara Rak, and Emans, Robert. "Children's Use of Phonics Generalizations." *The Reading Teacher* 34, no. 6 (March 1981): 653–57.

Routman, Regie. "The Use and Abuse of Invented Spellings." *Instructor* 102, no. 9 (May/June 1993): 37–39.

Samuels, Jay S. "Decoding and Automaticity: Helping Poor Readers Become Automatic at Word Recognition." *The Reading Teacher* 41, no. 8 (April 1988): 756–60.

Samuels, Jay S., and Farstrup, Alan E., eds. *What Research Has to Say about Reading Instruction.* Newark, DE: International Reading Association, 1992.

Scott, Diana, and Barker, Jeanne. "The Status of Computer Technology in Florida Middle Schools in the Areas of Reading and Language Arts." *Journal of Reading Education* 15, no. 3 (Spring 1990): 35–39.

Selfe, Cynthia L. "Re-Defining Literacy: The Multi-Layered Grammars of Computers." *The Education Digest* 57, no. 5 (January 1992): 18–24.

Shuck, Annette; Ush, Florence; and Platt, John S. "Parents Encourage Pupils. An Intercity Parent Involvement Reading Project." *The Reading Teacher* 36, no. 6 (February 1983): 524–28.

Siegel, Jessica. "Teach Your Teachers Well." *Electronic Learning* 13, no. 7 (April 1994): 34.

Sippola, Arne E. "What to Teach for Reading Readiness—A Research Review and Materials Inventory." *The Reading Teacher* 39, no. 2 (November 1985): 162–63.

Sittig, Linda Harris. "Involving Parents and Children in Reading for Fun." *The Reading Teacher* 36, no. 2 (November 1982): 166–68.

Snowball, Diane. "A Sensible Approach to Teaching Spelling." *Teaching K–8* 23, no. 8 (May 1993): 49–50.

Snyder, Geraldine V. "Learner's Verification of Reading Games." *The Reading Teacher* 34, no. 6 (March 1981): 686–91.

Snyder, Tom. "Technology Expert Urges Skepticism." *Reading Today* 11, no. 6 (June/ July 1994): 17.

Spiegel, Dixie Lee. "Six Alternatives to the Directed Reading Activity." *The Reading Teacher* 34, no. 8 (May 1981): 916.

———. "Reinforcement in Phonics Materials." *The Reading Teacher* 43, no. 4 (January 1990): 328–30.

———. "Decoding and Comprehension Games and Manipulatives." *The Reading Teacher* 44, no. 3 (November 1990): 258–59.

———. "Vocabulary Development." *The Reading Teacher* 44, no. 7 (March 1991): 506–07.

Sponder, Barry, and Hilgenfeld, Robert. "Cognitive Guidelines for Teachers Developing Computer-Assisted Instruction." *Electronic Learning* 22, no. 3 (Nov. 1994): 30–31.

St. John-Brooks, Caroline. "Real Books Plus Phonics Make Confident Readers." *Times Educational Supplement,* September 28, 1990, p. 14.

Stahl, Steven A. "Saying the `P' Word: Nine Guidelines for Exemplary Phonics Instruction." *The Reading Teacher* 45, no. 8 (April 1992): 618–24.

Stahl, Steven A., and Kapinus, Barbara A. "Possible Sentences: Predicting Word Meanings to Teach Content Area Vocabulary." *The Reading Teacher* 45, no. 1 (September 1991): 36–43.

Stahl, Stephen A.; McKenna, Michael C.; and Pagnucco, Joan R. "The Effects of Whole Language: An Update and Reappraisal," *Educational Psychologist* (Fall 1994): 175.

Stahl, Steven A.; Osborn, Jean; and Lehr, Fran. *Beginning to Read: Thinking and Learning about Print—A Summary.* Newark, DE: International Reading Association, 1990.

Sutton, Christine. "Helping the Nonnative English Speaker with Reading." *The Reading Teacher* 42, no. 9 (May 1989): 684–88.

Swaby, Barbara. "How Parents Can Foster Comprehension Growth in Children." *The Reading Teacher* 34, no. 2 (December 1980): 280–83.

———. "Using Repeated Readings to Develop Fluency and Accuracy." *The Reading Teacher* 36, no. 3 (December 1982): 317–18.

Taylor, Barbara M.; and Frye, Barbara J. "Pretesting: Minimize Time Spent on Skill Work for Intermediate Readers." *The Reading Teacher* 42, no. 2 (November 1986): 100–04.

*Technology in the Curriculum, Language Arts Resource Guide.* Sacramento, CA: California State Department of Education, 1986.

Thomas, Donald. "Meaningful Student Interaction Matters More Than Technology." *Teacher Magazine* 2, no. 8 (May/June 1991): 56–57.

Thompson, Verlinda, and Montgomery, Lee. "Promises, Problems, and Possibilities: Reading and Writing with Technology." *The Computing Teacher* 22, no. 3 (Nov. 1994): 6–8.

Tiedt, Pamela L., and Tiedt, Iris M. *Multicultural Teaching: A Handbook of Activities, Information and Resources.* Needham Heights, MA: Allyn and Bacon, 1990.

Tobin, Aileen W., and Pikulski, John J. "A Longitudinal Study of the Reading Achievement of

Early and Nonearly Readers through Sixth Grade." In *Dialogues in Literacy Research,* edited by John E. Readence and R. Scott Baldwin. Chicago, IL: International Reading Association, 1988, pp. 49–58.

Topping, Keith, "Paired Reading: A Powerful Technique for Parent Use." *The Reading Teacher* 40, no. 7 (March 1987): 608–14.

Trachtenburg, Phyllis. "Using Children's Literature to Enhance Phonics Instruction." *The Reading Teacher* 43, no. 9 (May 1990): 648–53.

Trotter, Andrew. "Technology in Classrooms: That's Edutainment." *The Executive Educator* 13, no. 4 (June 1991): 20–24.

Turner, Richard L. "The 'Great Debate'—Can Both Carbo and Chall be Right?" *Phi Delta Kappan* 71, no. 4 (December 1989): 276–83.

Urbschat-Spasngeberg, Karen, and Prichard, Robert, eds. *Kids Come in All Languages: Reading Instruction for ESL Students.* Newark. DE: International Reading Assn. 1994.

Variable, Mary Ellen. "Analysis of Writing Samples of Students Taught by Teachers Using Whole Language and Traditional Approaches." *Journal of Educational Research* 83, no. 5 (May/June 1990): 245.

Visser, Cindy. "Football and Reading Do Mix!" *The Reading Teacher* 44, no. 9 (May 1991): 710.

Von Harrison, Grant, and Branvold, Dwight. "Personalized Reading Materials for Beginning Readers: An Experiment in Cross-Age Tutoring." *The Computing Teacher* 18, no. 3 (November 1990): 26–27.

Walde, Anne C., and Baker, Keith. "When Parents Don't Care." *The Education Digest* 56, no. 8 (April 1991): 41–43.

Walmsley, Sean A., and Adams, Ellen L. "Realities of Whole Language." *Language Arts* 70, no. 4 (April 1993): 272–80.

Ward, Angela. "Whole Language: Is it Still Politically Correct?" *Reading Today* 12, no. 5 (Apr./May 1995): 31.

"We Can Become a Nation of Readers." *Instructor* 95, no. 4 (November/December): 1985.

Wedman, Judy. "Reading Software: What's Out There." *Language Arts* 60, no. 4 (April 1983): 516–17.

————. "Software: What's in It for Reading." *Journal of Reading* 26, no. 7 (April 1983): 642.

"What Teachers Had to Say about Using Computers in Today's Schools." *Learning* 15, no. 3 (March 1986): 48–52.

White, Bailey. PBS broadcast, January 1992.

White, Thomas G.; Sowell, Joanne; and Yanagihara, Alice. "Teaching Elementary Students to Use Word-Part Clues." *The Reading Teacher* 44, no. 2 (January 1989): 302–07.

"What Works in Reading." *Learning* (Apr./May 1995): 69.

"The Whole Language Debate. . ." *Reading Today* ll, no. 3 (Dec. 1993/Jan. 1994):.

"Whole Language—Starting Out and Staying Strong." *Instructor* 102, no. 1 (July/Aug. 1992): 81.

Wiesendanger, Katherine D., and Bader, Lois A. "Teaching Easily Confused Words: Timing Makes the Difference." *The Reading Teacher* 41, no. 3 (December 1987): 328–32.

William, Richard P., and Hoover, Dean. "Matching Computer Software to Learning Theory in the Reading Classroom." *The Reading Teacher* 64, no. 5 (May/June 1991): 334–35.

Williams, Joanna P. "The Case for Explicit Decoding Instruction." In *Reading Education: Foundations for a Literate America,* edited by Jean Osborn, Paul T. Wilson, and Richard C. Anderson. Lexington, MA: Lexington Books, 1985, pp. 206–13.

Wood, Karen D., and Robinson, Nora. "Vocabulary, Language and Prediction: A Prereading Strategy." *The Reading Teacher* 36, no. 4 (January 1983): 392–95.

Wood, Regina A. "Our Golden Road to Illiteracy." *National Review* 65, no. 20 (Oct. 18, 1993): 56–57.

Yopp, Hallie Kay. "Developing Phonemic Awareness in Young Children." *The Reading Teacher* 45, no. 9 (May 1992): 698–702.

# Index